Kosovo, Intervention an Statebuilding

A timely and engaging assessment of the intervention in Kosovo, ten years on, and many of the still unresolved consequences that followed in train. This important collection of essays is neither a sentimental celebration nor a polemical denunciation of the Kosovo project. The result is a careful illumination of crab-like normative development in contemporary international relations, as well as the very real challenges that stand before internationally directed statebuilding efforts.

(Dr William Bain, Senior Lecturer in International Political Theory,
Department of International Politics, Aberystwyth University)

This book examines international engagement with Kosovo since NATO's intervention in 1999, and looks at the three distinct phases of Kosovo's development: intervention, statebuilding and independence.

Kosovo remains a case study of central importance in international relations, illustrative of key political trends in the post-Cold War era. During each phase, international policy towards Kosovo has challenged prevailing international norms and pushed the boundaries of conventional wisdom. In each of the three phases 'Kosovo' has been cited as constituting a precedent, and this book explores the impact and the often troubling consequences and implications of these precedents. This book explicitly engages with this debate, which transcends Kosovo itself, and provides a critical analysis of the catalysts and consequences of contemporary international engagement with this seminal case study.

Each chapter focuses on a particular aspect of the international engagement with Kosovo and situates events there in an international context, highlighting the extent to which international policy towards Kosovo has challenged existing norms and practices. Kosovo has been cited in certain texts as a positive template to be emulated, but the contributors to this book also identify the often controversial and contentious nature of these new norms.

This book will be of much interest to students of humanitarian intervention and statebuilding, war and conflict studies, security studies and IR in general.

Aidan Hehir is a Senior Lecturer in International Relations at the Department of Politics and International Relations, University of Westminster.

Series: Routledge studies in intervention and statebuilding
Series editor: David Chandler

Kosovo, Intervention and Statebuilding

The international community and the transition to independence

Edited by Aidan Hehir

 Routledge
Taylor & Francis Group

LONDON AND NEW YORK

First published 2010
by Routledge
2 Park Square, Milton Park, Abingdon, Oxon OX14 4RN

Simultaneously published in the USA and Canada
by Routledge
711 Third Ave, New York, NY 10017

Routledge is an imprint of the Taylor & Francis Group, an informa business

First issued in paperback 2012

Typeset in Times by Wearset Ltd, Boldon, Tyne and Wear

British Library Cataloguing in Publication Data
A catalogue record for this book is available from the British Library

Library of Congress Cataloging-in-Publication Data
Kosovo, intervention and statebuilding: the international community and the transition to independence/edited by Aidan Hehir.
p. cm.
1. Kosovo (Republic)–Politics and government–1980–2008. 2. Kosovo (Republic)–Politics and government–2008- 3. Humanitarian intervention–Kosovo (Republic) 4. Nation-building–Kosovo (Republic) I. Hehir, Aidan, 1977-
DR2086.H44 2010
949.71–dc22   2009035324

ISBN13: 978-0-415-56167-9 (hbk)
ISBN13: 978-0-203-86179-0 (ebk)
ISBN13: 978-0-415-62220-2 (pbk)

As always, for Sarah, Esmé, Elsie and Iris
and Melosa Tahiri – may you live a long and peaceful life…

Contents

Illustrations

Figures

Tables

Contributors

Alex J. Bellamy, Department of Political Science & International Studies, University of Queensland, Brisbane, QLD, Australia.

Giovanna Bono, Institute for European Studies, Free University of Brussels, Brussels, Belgium.

Rick Fawn, School of International Relations, University of St Andrews, St Andrews, UK.

James Gow, Department of War Studies, King's College London, London, UK.

Aidan Hehir, Department of Politics and International Relations, University of Westminster, London, UK.

James Ker-Lindsay, European Institute, London School of Economics, London, UK.

Anthony F. Lang, Jr, School of International Relations, University of St Andrews, St Andrews, UK.

Alynna J. Lyon, Department of Political Science, University of New Hampshire, Durham, New Hampshire, USA.

Mary Fran T. Malone, Department of Political Science, University of New Hampshire, Durham, New Hampshire, USA.

Oliver P. Richmond, School of International Relations, University of St Andrews, St Andrews, UK.

Barry J. Ryan, School of Politics International Relations and the Environment, Keele University, Keele, UK.

Acknowledgements

I would like to thank Andrew Humphrys and Rebecca Brennan at Routledge. Thanks also to David Chandler and James Gow for their helpful advice. I would like to thank each of the (unusually punctual) contributors to this book.

Thanks to my colleagues at the Department of Politics and International Relations at the University of Westminster, especially Paulina Tambakaki, Tom Moore, Lizzy Griffin, Gio, Dan Greenwood and Suzy Robson.

Thanks to my family, Mary, George, Nial, Rita, Aran, Ashling, Niamh, Paul, Jay, Hazel, Sue, Lucy, Emily and Lola Bee. No thanks to you Chris.... I always forget Antigua and Barbuda...

Thanks also to Ferit Jashari, Xhafer Tahiri, Korab Sejdiu, Dawn Carter, Chris and Kyra, Compulsion, Carlos Sorín, Rochester Film Salon, Culla Holme, Francis Stuart, Michael Azerrad, Lester Ballard, Mark Arm, Dennes Boon, Kim Gordon, Roger Miller, Greg Ginn, Toby Vail, Mark Lanegan and Donita Sparks.

The publisher would like to thank Taylor & Francis (Taylor & Francis Ltd, www.informaworld.com) for granting permission to reproduce the following articles from the *Journal of Intervention and Statebuilding*.

Bellamy, Alex J., 'Kosovo and the Advent of Sovereignty as Responsibility', *Journal of Intervention and Statebuilding*, 3/2, 2009, pp. 163–184.

Lang, Anthony F. Jr, 'Conflicting Rule: Global Constitutionalism and the Kosovo Intervention', *Journal of Intervention and Statebuilding*, 3/2, 2009, pp. 185–204.

Fawn, Rick and Richmond, Oliver P., 'De facto States in the Balkans', *Journal of Intervention and Statebuilding*, 3/2, 2009, pp. 205–238.

Gow, James, 'Kosovo: The Final Frontier?', *Journal of Intervention and Statebuilding*, 3/2, 2009, pp. 239–257.

Abbreviations

BiH	Bosnia and Herzegovina
CIVPOL	Civilian Police
ESDP	European Security and Defence Policy
EU	European Union
EUCY	European Union's Conference on Yugoslavia
EULEX	European Union Rule of Law Mission in Kosovo
FRY	Federal Republic of Yugoslavia
ICB	International Commission on the Balkans
ICG	International Crisis Group
ICISS	International Commission on Intervention and State Sovereignty
ICO	International Civilian Office
ICR	International Civilian Representative
IDPs	internally displaced persons
IFIs	international financial institutions
I-FOR	Implementation Force
IL	International Law
IMP	International Military Presence
IR	International Relations
ISG	International Steering Group
KFOR	Kosovo Force
KLA	Kosovo Liberation Army
KPC	Kosovo Protection Corps
KPS	Kosovo Police Service
KSF	Kosovo Security Force
LDK	Democratic League of Kosovo
NAM	Non-Aligned Movement
OHR	Office of the High Representative
OIC	Organisation for Islamic Conference
OSCE	Organization for Security and Cooperation in Europe
P5	Permanent Five Members of the UN Security Council
PfP	Partnership for Peace
PIPA	Program on International Policy Attitudes
PISG	Provisional Institution of Self-Governance

R2P	Responsibility to Protect
RS	Republika Srpska
SAA	Stabilisation and Association Agreement
SC	Security Council
SFRY	Socialist Federal Republic of Yugoslavia
SRSG	Special Representative of the Secretary General
SSR	Security sector reforms
UN	United Nations
UNDP	UN Development Program
UNHCR	United Nations high Commission for Refugees
UNMIK	UN Interim Administration Mission in Kosovo
UNPROFOR	United Nations Protection Force

1 Introduction

Kosovo and the international community

Aidan Hehir

Introduction

Kosovo is of profound importance to contemporary international relations. Since 1999, this inauspicious corner of Europe has been at the centre of some of the most controversial episodes in the post-Cold War era. As Marc Weller notes, many observers 'have begun to see in the international response to the Kosovo crisis a new paradigm of international relations, a blue print for a new world order, in either a positive or a negative sense' (2009: 259). International engagement with Kosovo since 1999 has gone through three distinct phases: intervention, statebuilding and, most recently, independence. During each phase international policy towards Kosovo has challenged prevailing norms, and 'Kosovo' has been cited as an exemplar for a new broader trend in international relations. The authors in this book explore the impact, and the often troubling consequences and implications, of the international response to the crisis in Kosovo.

This introductory chapter provides a historical overview of the period 1989–2009, setting up the background context and key issues for the book.[1] There is, however, no accepted objective history of this period; as Tim Judah notes: 'In Kosovo history is war by other means ... history is not really about the past, but about the future. In other words, he who holds the past holds the future' (2000: 2). Nonetheless, it is possible, and certainly necessary, to identify the key junctures during this twenty-year crisis, spanning the revocation of Kosovo's autonomous status on 24 February 1989 by the Serbian parliament in Belgrade to the declaration of independence on 17 February 2008 by the Kosovo Assembly in Pristina.

Before engaging with this history, I discuss a particularly prevalent feature of the recent analysis of and international policy towards Kosovo, and the Balkans more generally; namely, the idea that 'ancient ethnic hatreds' are pervasive throughout the region. This shibboleth has been trotted out time and again over the past twenty years and has had a definite effect on international policy towards Kosovo, though often in divergent ways. Finally, this introduction provides an overview of Chapters 2–9.

The Balkans: ancient ethnic hatreds or international interference?

At the 1878 Berlin Conference, the German Chancellor Otto Von Bismarck reportedly declared: 'The whole of the Balkans are not worth the bones of a single Pomeranian Grenadier.' Twenty years later he predicted that the next European war would be caused by 'some damned foolish thing in the Balkans'. Bismarck's prediction proved prescient when, on 28 June 1914, Gavrilo Princip assassinated Archduke Franz Ferdinand in Sarajevo. Bismarck's view of the Balkans, epitomized by these two quotes, is indicative of a general disposition whereby the Balkans are considered to constitute a peripheral region plagued by mutually antagonistic ethnic groups whose incestuous conflicts have a troubling habit of spreading and embroiling the Great Powers. International involvement in Balkan affairs has invariably been a function less of a concern with endogenous factors, but more with the implications of Balkan affairs on international politics. The Balkans has been an interface between competing empires for centuries, a shifting fault-line which has hosted some of the most important events in European and world history. While the Balkan's historical role as stage, rather than actor, has ensured that it has received international attention, the people of the Balkans have often been sidelined by the larger international conflicts and convulsions played out on their territory.

Much of the violence in the Balkans in the 1990s was attributed to 'ancient ethnic hatreds', whereby the different ethnic groups were considered to be irreconcilably blinded by past grievances (Kaplan 1993). During the implosion of the Socialist Federal Republic of Yugoslavia (SFRY), former US Ambassador to Yugoslavia George Kennan claimed that the people of the Balkans were driven by 'deeper traits of character inherited, presumably, from a distant tribal past', and he argued that no state or coalition would be able to 'subdue its excited peoples and to hold them in order until they can calm down and begin to look at their problems in a more orderly way' (Todorova 1997: 185). Western inaction in the face of the disintegration of the SFRY was routinely excused on the grounds that external wise counsel was ineffective in the face of these historically embedded ferocious hatreds. In September 1992, US Secretary of State Lawrence Eagleburger stated:

> I have said this 38,000 times.... This tragedy is not something that can be settled from outside and it's about damn well time that everybody understood that. Until the Bosnians, Serbs and Croats decide to stop killing each other, there is nothing the outside world can do about it.
>
> (Holbrooke 1998: 23)

Robert Kaplan's 1993 book, *Balkan Ghosts*, is said to have greatly influenced President Clinton, who, after reading its accounts of endemic internecine warfare, decided against embroiling himself in the Balkans. According to Alex J. Bellamy, 'Learning from Kaplan', Clinton stated in 1993, 'it is no accident that WWI started in this area. There are ancient ethnic hatreds that have consumed people and led to the horrible abuses' (2002: 50).

In his memoirs, *To End a War*, US Diplomat Richard Holbrooke argued that the ancient hatreds theory 'trivialised and oversimplified the forces that tore Yugoslavia apart in the early 1990s.... Those who invoked it were, for the most part, trying to excuse their own reluctance or inability to deal with the problems in the region' (1998: 23). He attributed the reluctance of George Bush Senior's administration to intervene in Yugoslavia to the acceptance of this erroneous theory, describing it as 'our greatest mistake of the entire Yugoslav crisis' which 'made an unjust outcome inevitable and wasted the opportunity to save over 100,000 lives' (ibid.: 27). Yet when Holbrooke's own diplomatic initiatives in Kosovo in the late 1990s failed, he too reverted to the ancient ethnic hatreds motif – accommodation between Kosovo's Serb and Albanian communities was impossible because

> The hatred between Serbs and Albanians in Kosovo was far, far greater than any of the so-called ethnic hatreds of Bosnia.... This was the real thing in Kosovo between Albanians and the Serbs. Different cultures, different languages, and different histories, but a common obsession with the same sacred soil.
>
> (PBS 2000)

This reliance on the 'ancient ethnic hatreds' excuse was again evident in the wake of the March 2004 riots in Kosovo, which claimed the lives of 19 people and resulted in the widespread destruction of hundreds of Serbian religious sites. In December 2003, amidst much optimism, UNMIK had committed itself to overseeing the achievement of eight standards before resolving the issue of Kosovo's final status (UNMIK 2003). This attempt to circumvent the status issue in the hope that a focus on achieving political, economic and social standards would allow time for opposing perspectives on status to mellow proved counterproductive, as noted by a subsequent UN report.[2] The citizens of Kosovo, quite understandably, resented the ongoing fudge of the status issue, and vented their anger at UNMIK, KFOR and the minority Serb population. The riot was, however, portrayed as a typical instance of Balkan inter-ethnic animosity rather than a function of poorly conceived international policy. Whilst surveying the damage caused by the rioting in late March 2004, the then head of UNMIK, Harri Holkeri, declared, 'The concept of multiethnic Kosovo that the international community has been persistently attempting to implement in recent years is no longer tenable' (Hehir 2006a: 200). Likewise, an editorial in the *Guardian* blamed 'the deep and intense hatred between 2 million ethnic Albanians and fewer than 100,000 Serbs for the resumption of violence and lack of progress in the province' (*Guardian* 2004: 27).

The idea of the Balkans being rife with 'ancient ethnic hatreds' has served as a malleable basis for various international actors. The policy of inaction pursued by George Bush Senior was justified on the basis that the ethnic hatreds were irreconcilable and thus external intervention would be futile. Conversely NATO's intervention in 1999 was justified on the basis that without external help the warring factions would never stop until one ethnic group had been either 'cleansed' or killed, and the conflagration could spread across the region.[3] UNMIK's failure to create a 'multi-ethnic' Kosovo was deemed to be a function of the immutable ethnic hatreds which hindered the implementation of UNMIK's enlightened policies. The maintenance of international oversight even after Kosovo's declaration of independence in February 2008 has also been justified as a function of the need to oversee relations between sworn enemies. Of course, recent history in the Balkans, and especially Kosovo, *has* been extremely bloody, and ethnic conflict has undeniably occurred. Since 1990, borders across Europe have come down, or diminished in importance, and states have become more multicultural. In the Balkans, by contrast, borders have been strengthened, ethnic, religious and linguistic differences have been accentuated, and pluralism has been replaced by ethnic concentration. Of course, in many cases this has been actively supported by Western states and mediators, most notoriously during Operation Storm in August 1995 when, with tacit Western support, up to 200,000 Serbs were expelled from Eastern Slavonia, Croatia, in what the then European Union Special Envoy to the former Yugoslavia, Carl Bildt, described as 'the most efficient ethnic cleansing we've seen in the Balkans' (Pearl 1999). Whatever explanation one accepts for the accentuation and consolidation of ethnic difference in the Balkans since 1989, it can only be seen as a tragedy, and one which undermines faith in the capacity of the international community to prevent conflict and promote pluralism.

In contrast to the purveyors of the 'ancient ethnic hatreds' theory, Mark Mazower argues that a 'less jaundiced' understanding of Balkan history requires us to situate the Balkans in a broader European context which demonstrates that events there have been driven by 'more sweeping narratives of the development of European identity and civilisation' (2003: 14–15). Events in the Balkans have very often been catalysed by exogenous rather than endogenous forces. In this respect, the Balkans has often been a microcosm of broader systemic clashes and changes. This is particularly apposite with respect to Kosovo. Since 1999 Kosovo has regularly topped the agenda of the UN, the EU, NATO, the OSCE and the World Bank, been the focus of myriad academic books and articles from a diverse range of disciplines, and embroiled all the world's major powers at some point. While most people probably cannot locate Kosovo on a map, it is known worldwide as a case study (or perhaps guinea pig) for some of the major global issues in the post-Cold War era. The following section outlines the nature of the crisis in Kosovo since 1989, and charts the mercurial international response.

The Kosovo crisis and the international response

According to the Independent International Commission on Kosovo (IICK):

> From the 1980's onwards, Kosovo exhibited all the signs of a catastrophe waiting to happen ... the failure to respond adequately at an early stage of

the evolution of the conflict created difficulties in later stages. At each stage of the conflict, the diplomatic options narrowed.

(2000: 62)

Given that Kosovo's explosive potentiality was so widely discussed, it is paradoxical that it never received the attention its reputation should have commanded. Whereas in Macedonia from 1993 to 1999 a coordinated international conflict prevention mission – the UN Preventative Deployment Force – was largely successful, Kosovo was largely ignored. Weller describes the international community's policy towards Kosovo as 'schizophrenic'; time after time statesmen acknowledged Kosovo's explosive potentiality, but the policies they pursued, Weller argues, paradoxically derived from 'a hope that the situation would go away if ignored for a sufficiently long time' (1999: 33). Indicatively, before the second meeting of the European Union's Conference on Yugoslavia (EUCY) in London in August 1992, the Chairman of the Conference, Lord Carrington, wrote to Ibrahim Rugova, the leader of the Democratic League of Kosovo (LDK), the largest Kosovo Albanian party. At the first meeting of the EUCY in 1991 the issue of Kosovo had been described, to the dismay of the Kosovo Albanians, as an 'internal' problem. In his letter to the unrecognised and unofficial, though democratically elected, President of Kosovo, Lord Carrington stated that it might be possible to hold some meetings with his delegation 'if you are planning to be in London at the time of the conference', but he noted 'for practical and other reasons [it would] not be possible to grant your delegation access to the conference'. Nevertheless, Lord Carrington assured Rugova, 'We are making strenuous efforts to ensure that the views of the Kosovar Albanians are heard' (ibid.: 344). The Kosovo Albanian delegation did travel to London, where they observed proceedings through a glass screen in another room. In 1991, after an unofficial referendum organised by the Kosovo Albanians overwhelmingly supported independence, Rugova wrote to Carrington and the Badinter Commission – charged with examining the validity of the various independence claims within Yugoslavia – to appeal for action on Kosovo; neither replied.

Tensions amongst SFRY's constituent republics (Serbia, Croatia, Bosnia, Macedonia, Montenegro and Slovenia) emerged in the early 1980s due to a combination of factors, including the death of Tito in 1980, the global economic crisis and ongoing dissatisfaction with the provisions of the 1974 constitution. A protest by students at the University of Pristina in 1981 escalated from a demand for better facilities to a widespread pro-independence movement. This angered Kosovo's Serbs, who felt that the 1974 constitution had privileged the Kosovo Albanians. The Kosovo Serbs in fact claimed that the Albanian-dominated local Communist Party presided over the oppression of the Serb community. Many Serbs left Kosovo with tales of Albanian-inspired ethnic violence and the widespread rape of Serb women (Mertus 1999). Without Tito to dampen nationalist sentiment, there began a public escalation of nationalistic tension. In 1986 the Memorandum of the Serbian Academy of Sciences and Arts was published, outlining a sensational litany of Albanian-instigated violence against Kosovo's Serbs. The bitter disagreement within Kosovo soon embroiled other republics, and Kosovo became a catalyst for the emergence of nationalism throughout the SFRY (Horton 1992; Pesic 1996: 33–34).

In 1989, Slobodan Milošević, then President of Serbia, repealed Kosovo's autonomy within Serbia. In response, the majority of the members of the Kosovo Assembly convened an illegal meeting and declared independence for Kosovo. While Milošević's revocation of Kosovo's autonomous status, and the implementation of certain discriminatory laws between 1989 and 1991, are widely acknowledged as the beginning of most recent conflict in Kosovo, from 1990 to 1995 Kosovo remained largely peaceful while violence raged elsewhere in the Balkans. The Kosovo Albanians subverted the new legislation by establishing their own schools, hospitals and taxation system, funded to a large extent by money sent from expatriates.

On Christmas Eve 1992, the outgoing Bush administration issued the so-called 'Christmas warning'. US Secretary of State Lawrence Eagleburger sent a cable to the US *chargé d'affaires* in Belgrade with the instruction that it be read to Milošević in person. The message stated, 'In the event of conflict in Kosovo caused by Serbian action, the US will be prepared to employ military force against Serbians in Kosovo and Serbia proper.' This warning was subsequently endorsed by the Clinton administration. As the situation in Kosovo degenerated, especially after 1995, this commitment increasingly became an embarrassment as inaction prevailed (IICK 2000: 344; Bellamy 2002: 50).

The omission of Kosovo from the 1995 Dayton Peace Accords was an enormous blow for the Kosovar Albanians. The Dayton Accords explicitly recognised the territorial integrity of the Federal Republic of Yugoslavia (FRY), including Kosovo; Article 1 reads, 'The Parties shall conduct their relations in accordance with the principles set forth in the United Nations Charter.... In particular, the Parties shall fully respect the sovereign equality of one another.' The Accords eroded support for the LDK, who had assumed that their the pacifist politics would engender international support; in fact, according to Judah, '[Dayton] confirmed to them in the most dramatic and humiliating way, that Rugova's ... idea that they would be rewarded for their 'good behaviour' by Western countries had been just plain wrong' (2000: 124–125). Ironically, the Kosovo Albanians' pacifism had led international observers to focus on the conflicts elsewhere. Whereas the majority of Kosovo Albanians had embraced pacifism, the Bosnian Serbs had achieved international infamy through their violent campaign. Yet Dayton established the legitimacy of Republika Srpska and ignored Kosovo. This in particular, according to Chris Hedges, 'shattered all hopes for peaceful change in Kosovo' (1999: 31). The lesson of Dayton thus appeared to be, 'if you want international attention you must generate a conflict'. This suited the Kosovo Liberation Army (KLA); as Carl Hodge states, 'In effect Dayton told autonomists in Kosovo that the metal in Kosovo was not hot enough to bring about political change. The KLA decided to make it glow' (2000: 26). There followed an escalating cycle of retaliatory violence between the KLA and the

FRY's police and military. The KLA adopted a strategy of provoking Belgrade into launching excessive counterattacks in order to generate domestic support and, more importantly, force the international community to condemn the Milošević regime and ultimately intervene on the side of the Kosovo Albanians (Gow 2003: 256; Kuperman 2006).

By Autumn 1998 Kosovo was at the top of the international agenda, with Security Council Resolution 1199 describing the situation as a threat to peace and stability in the region and empowering the Council to act under Chapter VII of the Charter. By mid-1998, the number of internally displaced persons and refugees fleeing to Albania and Macedonia ensured that Kosovo could no longer be ignored. According to the World Refugee Survey Kosovo ranked in the top five globally for the number of refugees and internally displaced people, with the total figure an estimated 300,000. The number of deaths in the year prior to NATO's intervention is estimated at 500, with some 400,000 people displaced (Wheeler 2002: 269). The death toll is, comparatively, quite low, but it was routinely stated at the time that without international action Milošević would accelerate his oppression of the Kosovo Albanians and ultimately the death toll would rise drastically. The situation was often said to be analogous to that of the early stages of the war in Bosnia, and the eventual carnage in 1995 was proffered as the likely consequences of inaction (Hehir 2006b).

The credibility of the West, and NATO in particular, diminished as the conflict escalated without resolution. The more NATO threatened action and yet failed subsequently to do anything, the more the Milošević regime appears to have concluded that nothing would ever happen (Weller 1999: 398; Bellamy 2002: 124). A settlement was negotiated in October 1998 but failed to hold, in large part because the chief US negotiator – Richard Holbrooke – gave personal assurances that the KLA would comply with the agreement; assurances later described by the IICK as 'ill founded' (2000: 149). The KLA did not honour the agreement, and by the end of the year the cycle of retaliatory violence resumed. Following the Răcak massacre on 15 January 1999, international opinion turned sharply in favour of robust action. At the end of the month, the Contact Group (the US, UK, France, Russia, Germany and Italy) summoned all relevant parties to attend negotiations at Rambouillet, France on 6 February. The following day NATO issued what Weller described as a 'remarkable' statement, which threatened to use force against any party that did not attend and also against any group which was deemed to have caused a breakdown in the forthcoming negotiations. Weller describes the NATO threat as, 'entirely unprecedented in post UN Charter history and somewhat reminiscent of an exercise of Great Power diplomacy in the classical balance of power system of the post Napoleonic Concert of Europe' (1999: 397). Indeed, Holbrooke described Rambouillet as 'a very legitimate attempt to bring the parties together to *force* them to agree' (PBS 2000).

Ultimately, the FRY rejected the agreement proffered at Rambouillet while the Kosovo Albanian delegation, with major reservations, signed. It has subsequently been claimed that NATO powers contrived this very situation so that the FRY would be cast as recalcitrant spoiler, thereby clearing the way for a bombing campaign (Chomsky 1999: 108). The provisions of Appendix B (8) in particular have been cited as consciously unpalatable to Belgrade (Gowan 2000: 8; Hagen 1999: 59). Rambouillet is variously described as 'Albright's charade to get a bombing campaign', 'a textbook example of how not to practice diplomacy' and as having constituted 'an inherently unstable' agreement (Jatras 2000: 24; Layne 2000: 15; Bandow 2000: 33).

The counter-perspective suggests that, while certain mistakes were made, Rambouillet was a genuine attempt to broker an agreement (Bellamy 2002: 147–150). Though he describes Rambouillet as 'more a shambles then a grand design', Weller concludes that Rambouillet was 'a heroic failure', given the earnest attempts made to reconcile the parties, and he dismisses as 'conspiracy theories' the argument that the contentious provisions of Appendix B were responsible for the Serbs' unwillingness to sign (1999: 392, 397). The IICK detailed many of the flaws in both the deal proposed at Rambouillet and the manner in which the negotiations were pursued, particularly in relation to NATO's intransigence on the issue of Appendix B. While they argued that compromising on this aspect of the deal was 'an obvious negotiating opening that might have broken the impasse', they ultimately concluded, 'The minimum goals of the Kosovar Albanians and of Belgrade were irreconcilable' (IICK 2000: 157–161). Either way, the breakdown of the negotiations led directly to the initiation of NATO's air strikes.

NATO began air strikes against the FRY on the 24 March. Support for the strikes was strong amongst NATO member-states, with the exception of Greece. At the Security Council, both China and Russia strongly opposed NATO's actions, with the Russian Foreign Minister claiming the bombing constituted 'a strike against Russia' (Bellamy 2002: 166). Additionally, the West's traditional allies, such as Japan, Indonesia and South Korea, far from being supportive of NATO, were 'mute in their response' (ibid.: 167). Prior to NATO's intervention it was suggested to the UK Foreign Office that NATO could use the Uniting for Peace provision,[4] but this was rejected because officials felt it was highly unlikely that two-thirds of the General Assembly would vote in favour of NATO's actions (Chesterman 2003: 57). Given the potential for an embarrassing failure to win the requisite two-thirds, the Uniting for Peace resolution was, according to Nigel White, 'conveniently forgotten in the case of the Kosovo crisis' (2000: 41).

The international reaction to NATO's intervention was thus mixed. Supporters of NATO point to Russia's failed attempt to have Operation Allied Force condemned by the Security Council and the support afforded to the operation by the Organisation for Islamic Conference (OIC) (Caplan 2000: 24). While the twelve to three SC vote against Russia's draft resolution appears conclusive, Nicholas Wheeler has noted that the result was less emphatic than it appears; five of the twelve states who voted against the resolution were members of NATO, and only three of the remaining seven spoke in support of the intervention (2002: 291). Additionally, White notes, 'lack of condemnation by the Security Council cannot be seen as an authorization to use force' (2000: 33). The OIC's support for the intervention was largely a function of an expression of solidarity with Kosovo's predominantly Muslim population; indeed, fifty of the fifty-seven members of the OIC were among the 133 states in the G77 that voted twice to condemn unilateral humanitarian intervention in the wake of Operation Allied Force.

The termination of Operation Allied Force came on 10 June, with the signing of the Military Technical Agreement. Though heralded in some quarters as a capitulation by Milošević, the provisions of the peace plan were considerably less draconian than those presented at Rambouillet, leading Simon Chesterman to ask: 'why were the terms presented to Serbia at Rambouillet more onerous than those offered after a 78 day bombing campaign?' (2003: 54). Significantly, Appendix B had been removed from the Military Technical Agreement; as the IICK noted, 'The final agreement did contain some gains from the FRY point of view' (2000: 96). Security Council Resolution 1244, which endorsed this agreement, also recognised FRY's territorial integrity and Belgrade's jurisdiction over Kosovo. Of course, all FRY military did have to leave Kosovo, and they have not returned since.

Statebuilding and independence

Security Council resolution 1244 established

> an international civil presence in Kosovo in order to provide an interim administration for Kosovo under which the people of Kosovo can enjoy substantial autonomy within the Federal Republic of Yugoslavia, and which will provide transitional administration while establishing and overseeing the development of provisional democratic self governing institutions to ensure conditions for a peaceful and normal life for all inhabitants of Kosovo.
>
> (Security Council 1999: 3)

The situation in Kosovo facing the UN Interim Administration Mission in Kosovo (UNMIK) was far from propitious. Kosovo's economy and political institutions were in a state of total collapse, and following NATO's intervention widespread 'reverse ethnic cleaning' occurred. This was described by the then chief prosecutor for the International Criminal Tribunal for the former Yugoslavia, Carla Del Pointe, as being 'as serious as what happened there before [NATO's intervention]' (Bardos 2003: 150).

Paragraph 11 of resolution 1244 emphasised the temporary nature of UNMIK's tenure, noting that the powers vested in the administration were undertaken 'pending a final settlement'. Paragraph 11(f) defined UNMIK's role as 'overseeing the transfer of authority from Kosovo's provisional institutions to institutions established under a political settlement'. UNMIK was established to run for twelve months, with further extension subject to annual review.

UNMIK constituted a new departure for the UN in terms of its aims and the extensive operational powers it was afforded (Matheson 2001: 76). In particular, unprecedented power was devolved to the Special Representative of the Secretary General (SRSG) (Hehir 2007: 245–246). UNMIK and the SRSG had clear parallels with the international administration in Bosnia established in 1995 and the Office of the High Representative. Unlike Bosnia, however, UNMIK was placed in an invidious position in terms of the ultimate purpose of its administration due to the need to accommodate Russia's objections to independence within the Security Council. While the administration of Bosnia confronted problems relating to the functioning of the new political institutions and the interaction between the Serb, Croat and Bosnian communities, the status of Bosnia as a state was at least clear. UNMIK was tasked, however, with guiding Kosovo towards an undefined 'final status'. Initially it was feared that any decision about Kosovo's end-state would cause instability, and the preferred option was to, as the IICK put it, 'leave questions about the future in limbo, since a constructive ambiguity about the political future of the province might make it easier for all sides to overcome their reluctance to work together' (2000: 261). Instead of a focus on Kosovo's status UNMIK proposed the idea of 'standards before status', whereby the achievement of certain administrative, social and political goals was made a prerequisite to a decision on status. This policy failed, however, and UNMIK soon began to be seen by the Kosovo Albanian community as an obstacle, rather than a means, to independence (Covey *et al.* 2005: 121; Human Rights Watch 2004: 17). Frustration boiled over in March 2004, when province-wide riots orchestrated by the Kosovar Albanians resulted in nineteen deaths and the deliberate targeting of UN and NATO personnel. A 2005 report by the International Commission on the Balkans (ICB) noted that 'the international community has clearly failed in its attempts to provide security and development to [Kosovo]', and stressed the need for action on the issue of status. According to the ICB, the demand for sovereignty had steady increased, with the result that UNMIK was perceived by the Kosovo Albanians as 'corrupt and indecisive' (International Commission on the Balkans 2005: 19–20).

The earlier idea of overseeing a progression from the achievement of standards to the determination of status was abandoned in light of the March 2004 riots. A new approach was contained in the 'Comprehensive Review of the Situation in Kosovo', presented by Kai Eide to the UN Security Council on 24 October 2005. While the Eide Report argued for the substitution of the 'Standards before Status' policy in favour of progressing to focus specifically on Kosovo's status, it essentially proposed a reorganisation of the international commitment to governance in Kosovo. Eide's Report suggested an extended mandate for international oversight, albeit in a less direct form, with, as the process's final goal, a status for Kosovo that ultimately falls short of full sovereignty. The implementation of the agreed arrangements on Kosovo's future status will require an 'international presence – military and civilian … to manage the implementation of the settlement in a stable and orderly way' (United Nations Security Council 2005: 21). The orderly and stable implementation of a settlement continued to be envisaged, therefore, as possible only under international supervision.

In October 2005 Martti Ahtisaari was appointed as head of the UN Office of the Special Envoy for Kosovo, to start a political process to determine Kosovo's future status. Negotiations began in Vienna between Serbia, representatives from Kosovo and the UN. At the end of the Vienna talks in February 2007, Ahtisaari produced the 'Comprehensive Proposal for the Kosovo Status Settlement'. Ahtisaari's proposal constituted the manifestation of the Eide recommendations, and outlines a reconfigured balance of competencies between the local institutions and the international administration. The proposal increased the powers devolved to the Kosovo institutions, but did not provide for the removal of ultimate international oversight and authority. UNMIK was to be replaced by a tripartite 'international presence'; NATO was retained as the basic guarantor of security, and a new European Security and Defence Policy Mission was to be established with the remit to develop the judicial system. The third element of the international presence was the International Civilian Representative (ICR) – chosen by the International Steering Group comprised of 'key international stakeholders' – which would serve as the European Union Special Representative. The ICR 'will have specific powers to allow him/her to take the actions necessary to oversee and ensure successful implementation of the Settlement' and may 'correct or annul decisions by Kosovo public authorities that he/she determines to be inconsistent with the letter or spirit of the Settlement' (Comprehensive Proposal for the Kosovo Status Settlement 2007). Ultimately it proved impossible to 'square the circle', as the positions of the Serbs and Kosovo Albanians were diametrically opposed on the issue of Kosovo's final status (Weller 2009: 191). The Ahtisaari Plan was rejected by Serbia and Russia, and a further 120 days of negotiations in mid-2008 failed to bridge the differences. On 17 February 2008, the Assembly of Kosovo, in defiance of Belgrade, declared independence. As of November 2009, sixty-three states have recognised Kosovo, though there is no consensus in the EU on the issue, and Russia and China remain firmly opposed. Despite the declaration of independence, the international community remains deeply engaged in Kosovo, however, and the declaration of independence marks the next stage of the statebuilding project rather than its culmination.

Kosovo's declaration of independence has catalysed new interest in Kosovo owing to its implications for self-determination and state recognition, and it remains to be seen what impact the 'Kosovo precedent' will have on international relations. While the President of Kosovo, Dr Fatmir Sejdiu, has rejected the idea of Kosovo constituting a precedent (see p. 198) Russia's recognition of South Ossetia and Abkhazia on 26 August 2008 was legitimised as akin to the Western recognition of Kosovo

Overview of chapters

The contributors in this book explore international polices towards Kosovo, and the impact of these policies on the contemporary evolution of international norms. The diversity of issues dealt with in this volume is testimony to Kosovo's wide-ranging importance.

Alynna J. Lyon and Mary Fran T. Malone rightly note that understanding the factors that convince the general public to support humanitarian interventions is of great importance. To this end they examine US domestic opinion towards NATO's intervention in Kosovo in 1999. Their statistical analysis initially assesses the role of public opinion in the decision to go to war, and they additionally analyse the extent to which the public supported the intervention at key junctures during the military campaign. This is supplemented by further statistical analysis of those factors that influenced public attitudes. Their findings suggest that the American public finds humanitarian rationales for intervention appealing, and that this disposition remains intact in the post-9/11 era.

Today the term 'Responsibility to Protect' is widely used, if not at times misused. Alex J. Bellamy charts the evolution of this pervasive idea and highlights the central importance of NATO's intervention in Kosovo in 1999 in this evolution. Though the fragmentation of opinion over Operation Allied Force has often been portrayed as indicative of a pronounced disagreement as to the relationship between states and their citizens, and the role of the international community in the regulation of this relationship, Bellamy argues that this perspective overlooks the emerging consensus around the concept of sovereignty as responsibility evident during the controversy in 1999. Since the furore surrounding Operation Allied Force, Bellamy claims, it is no longer tenable to claim that sovereignty enables states to abuse their citizens with impunity. NATO's intervention in Kosovo thus constitutes a milestone in the evolution of international norms governing the use of force.

Anthony F. Lang, Jr argues that NATO's intervention constituted the eruption of a previously simmering clash between the rules governing non-intervention and the rules concerning human rights. Lang identifies a 'hole in the international constitutional order'; namely, the lack of an acceptable authoritative institutional mechanism by which such a clash can be resolved. This has resulted, he notes, in an often dogmatic reliance on 'rules' and a necessarily subjective, circular and irresolvable debate about legal doctrine. Lang argues that the legalistic semantics which are pervasive in the debate about Kosovo, and are also characteristic of the debate regarding the invasion of Iraq, provide no effective means by which the obvious disjuncture between law and ethics can be resolved.

Rick Fawn and Oliver P. Richmond argue that the external relations of both Bosnia and Kosovo, post-intervention, have overlooked regional cooperation in deference to an engagement with the 'international community'. 'Ethnic sovereignty', they argue, 'means that the relationships between local states, entities, and internationals are riven by inconsistencies that slow progress on peace'. This lack of regional cooperation caused by excessive international involvement highlights the capacity of even well-intentioned international administration to adversely affect local and regional politics. They advocate a form of shared sovereignty whereby 'The relation of local actors with internationals should ... be conditional upon shared governance – accepting a level of interdependence with neighbouring entities.'

Barry J. Ryan, utilising Carl Schmitt's conception of sovereignty, critiques policing practices in Kosovo since the establishment of UNMIK. He argues that the UNMIK's mission to create a multi-ethnic liberal democracy maintained Kosovo in a state of exception whereby the maintenance of order was given preference over the rule of law. The international community's desire to essentially impose ethnic integration lacked both an understanding of the history of inter-community relations in Kosovo and an appreciation of the level of animosity pervasive in the aftermath of NATO's intervention. The idea of a multi-ethnic police force was, and largely remains, Ryan argues, contrary to local expectations, particularly those of the majority ethnic Albanian community. The contradiction between the means and stated ends of the international administration's governance, he claims, corroded the legitimacy of a multi-ethnic Kosovo police service.

Giovanna Bono assesses competing explanations proffered for what she argues is the UNMIK's failure in the security and justice sectors in Kosovo. While the most common explanation cites the lack of a coherent strategy on the issue of final status, Bono argues that the Western states involved in the Vienna talks had a clear preference for independence due to their bias towards the Kosovo Albanians, and thus this explanation is flawed. Bono argues that the Kosovo Albanians skilfully exploited the West's patronage and manipulated the new security and justice institutions to their own advantage. Russia's and Serbia's continued opposition to independence, even after February 2008, has disrupted the West's vision for Kosovo, however, and precipitated a crisis which, she argues, may push Kosovo towards state failure.

James Gow outlines the different phases of the international administration in Kosovo, situates these developments in the broader international context, and notes the extent to which events in Kosovo since 1999 have been driven by broader machinations, particularly within the Security Council. The administration of Kosovo, he argues, is characterised by 'exceptional action', and ultimately constitutes a missed opportunity. Due to what Gow describes as an 'inexplicable' rush to 'finish the period of Yugoslav dissolution', UNMIK did not guide Kosovo to a fully formed outcome but to 'a transitional state'. This status means that, for all the excitement generated by the declaration of independence in February 2008, Kosovo remains in limbo; though recognised as an independent 'state' by over sixty other states, Kosovo is an entity which has some way to go before it can be said to have the qualities of complete statehood.

James Ker-Lindsay examines the international reaction to Kosovo's declaration of independence, and analyses why Kosovo has failed to achieve wider recognition. He argues that the dominant justification proffered for bypassing the Security Council – namely that Russia's position precluded consensus – has failed to win majority support amongst states for two principle reasons. First, Russia's stance on Kosovo may well have been born from a concern for its own national interest, but nonetheless, its public defence of the principle of sovereign inviolability and opposition to separatism has widespread appeal. Second, Ker-Lindsay argues that while many states are sceptical about Russia's motives, there is a strong constituency in favour of respecting the primacy of the Security Council and indeed the principle behind the veto power of the permanent five members. While many states remain sympathetic to Kosovo, they are keen to avoid creating a precedent whereby states can pick and choose when to recognise UN authority.

Notes

1 The chapters focus primarily on the period 1999–2009, though the crisis in 1999 was a direct function of the upheavals in 1989.
2 The 'Comprehensive Review of the Situation in Kosovo', presented by Kai Eide to the UN Security Council on 24 October 2005, recognised the 'Standards before Status' policy as having contributed to 'a period of political stagnation and widespread frustration' which finally erupted in the March 2004 riots (United Nations Security Council 2005: 2).
3 In a televised speech the day before NATO's air strikes began, President Clinton described the Balkans as 'a powder keg at the heart of Europe that has exploded twice before in this century with catastrophic results'. He noted the 'ancient grievances' prevalent in Kosovo, and warned 'Let a fire burn here in this area and the flames will spread' (Clinton 1999).
4 On 3 November 1950 the General Assembly passed Resolution 377, subsequently known as the 'Uniting for Peace' resolution. This resolution enables the General Assembly to act when the Security Council is unable to unanimously sanction action, or demand a cessation to ongoing military action when there is a threat to international peace and stability. The General Assembly may take up an issue under two conditions: first, when nine members of the Security Council vote to move the issue to the General Assembly (this vote is immune from the P5 veto)' and second, when a majority of UN member states vote to move the issue to the General Assembly. The General Assembly can only take the lead on an issue that is not under consideration at the Security Council, but, provided this condition is met, then technically the General Assembly can sanction a military intervention if two-thirds of its members so agree. See Krasno and Das (2008).

References

Bandow, D. (2000) 'NATO's Hypocritical Humanitarianism', in T. G. Carpenter (ed.) *NATO's Empty Victory*, Washington, DC: Cato Institute.

Bardos, G. (2003) 'International Policy in Southeast Europe: A Diagnosis', in R. Thomas (ed.) *Yugoslavia Unravelled: Sovereignty, Self Determination, Intervention*, Oxford: Lexington Books.

Bellamy, A. J. (2002) *Kosovo and International Society*, New York, NY: Palgrave Macmillan.

Caplan, R. (2000) 'Humanitarian Intervention: Which Way Forward?', *Ethics and International Affairs*, 14: 23–38.

Chesterman, S. (2003) 'Hard Cases Make Bad Law', in A. F. Lang, Jr (ed.) *Just Intervention*, Washington, DC: Georgetown University Press.

Chomsky, N. (1999) *The New Military Humanism: Lessons from Kosovo*, London: Pluto.

Clinton, B. (1999) 'By Acting Now we are Upholding our Values', *Guardian*, 24 March.

Comprehensive Proposal for the Kosovo Status Settlement (2007). Available: www.unosek.org/unosek/en/statusproposal.html (accessed 1 July 2009).

Covey, J., Dziedzic, M. J. and Hawley, L. (2005) *The Quest for Viable Peace*, Washington, DC: United States Institute of Peace Press.

Gow, J. (2003) *The Serbian Project and its Adversaries*, Montreal: McGill-Queens University Press.

Gowan, P. (2000) 'The Euro-Atlantic Origins of NATO's Attack on Yugoslavia', in T. Ali (ed.) *Masters of the Universe?* London: Verso.

Guardian (2004) 'Editorial: The Latest Flames', *Guardian*, 19 March.

Hagen, W. (1999) 'The Balkans Lethal Nationalisms', *Foreign Affairs*, 78/4: 52–64.

Hedges, C. (1999) 'Kosovo's Next Masters', *Foreign Affairs*, 78/3: 24–42.

Hehir, A. (2006a) '"Autonomous Province Building": Identification Theory and the Failure of UNMIK', *International Peacekeeping*, 13/2: 200–213.

Hehir, A. (2006b) 'The Impact of Analogical Reasoning on US Foreign Policy Towards Kosovo', *Journal of Peace Research*, 43/1: 67–81.

Hehir, A. (2007) 'Kosovo's Final Status and the Viability of Ongoing International Administration', *Civil Wars*, 9/3: 243–261.

Hodge, C. (2000) 'Casual War: NATO's Intervention in Kosovo', *Ethics and International Affairs*, 14: 39–54.

Holbrooke, R. (1998) *To End a War*, New York, NY: Random House.

Horton, J. (1992) 'The National Question', in J. Allcock, J. Horton and M. Milivojevic (eds) *Yugoslavia in Transition*, Oxford: Berg.

Human Rights Watch (2004) *Failure to Protect*, 16(D) July. Available: www.hrw.org/en/reports/2004/07/25/failure-protect-0 (accessed 1 July 2009).

IICK (Independent International Commission on Kosovo) (2000) *Kosovo Report*, Oxford: Oxford University Press.

International Commission on the Balkans (2005) *The Balkans in Europe's Future.* Available: www.balkan-commission.org/activities/Report.pdf (accessed 1 July 2009).

Jatras, J. (2000) 'NATO's Myths and Bogus Justifications for Intervention', in T. G. Carpenter (ed.) *NATO's Empty Victory*, Washington, DC: Cato Institute.

Judah, T. (2000) *Kosovo: War and Revenge*, New Haven, CT: Yale University Press.

Kaplan, R. (1993) *Balkan Ghosts*, New York, NY: St Martins.

Krasno, J. and Das, M. (2008) 'The Uniting for Peace Resolution and Other Ways of Circumventing the Authority of the Security Council', in B. Cronin and I. Hurd (eds) *The UN Security Council and the Politics of International Authority*, London: Routledge.

Kuperman, A. (2006) 'Suicidal Rebellions and the Moral Hazard of Humanitarian Intervention', in T. Crawford and A. Kuperman (eds) *Gambling on Humanitarian Intervention*, London: Routledge.

Layne, C. (2000) 'Miscalculations and Blunders Lead to War' in T. G. Carpenter (ed.) *NATO's Empty Victory*, Washington, DC: Cato Institute.

Matheson, M. (2001) 'United Nations Governance of Postconflict Societies', *American Journal of International Law*, 95/76: 76–85.

Mazower, M. (2003) *The Balkans*, London: Phoenix.

Mertus, J. (1999) *Kosovo: How Myths and Truths Started A War*, London: University of California Press.

PBS (Public Broadcasting Service) (2000) 'Interview with Richard Holbrooke', *Frontline*. Available: www.pbs.org/wgbh/pages/frontline/shows/kosovo/interviews/holbrooke.html (accessed 1 July 2009).

Pearl, D. (1999) 'Few Serbs Chased from Croatia Have Made it Back Home', *The Wall Street Journal*, 22 April. Available: http://online.wsj.com/public/resources/documents/pearl042299.htm (accessed 29 June 2009).

Pesic, V. (1996) 'The War for Ethnic States', in N. Popov (ed.) *The Road to War in Serbia*, New York, NY: CEU Press.

Security Council (1999) Security Council Resolution 1244, SR/1244, 10 June.

Todorova, M. (1997) *Imagining the Balkans*, Oxford: Oxford University Press.

United Nations Security Council (2005) 'Letter dated 7 October 2005 from the Secretary General to the President of the Security Council', S/2005/635, 7 October.

UNMIK (2003) 'Standards for Kosovo', UNMIK press release PR/1078, 10 December. Available: www.unmikonline.org/press/2003/pressr/pr1078.pdf (accessed 30 June 2009).

Weller, M. (1999) *The Crisis in Kosovo 1989–1999*, Cambridge: Documents and Analysis Publishing.

Weller, M. (2009) *Contested Statehood: Kosovo's Struggle for Independence*. Oxford: Oxford University Press.

Wheeler, N. (2002) *Saving Strangers: Humanitarian Intervention in International Society*, Oxford: Oxford University Press.

White, N. (2000) 'The Legality of Bombing in the Name of Humanity', *Journal of Conflict and Security Law*, 5/1: 27–43.

2 Responding to Kosovo's call for humanitarian intervention

Public opinion, partisanship and policy objectives

Alynna J. Lyon and Mary Fran T. Malone

Introduction

The modern international political system clearly brackets internal politics, and thus humanitarian crisis, from international concern. The principle of sovereignty plainly holds that countries are not to interfere in the domestic affairs of other nations without a clear invitation to do so. Despite this legal boundary, the international community holds growing ambitions to protect human rights and respond to widespread human suffering. Kosovo presents one such example. In March 1999, NATO, headed by the United States and eighteen other member states, began a massive air campaign against the former Yugoslavia to end the violence between Serbian paramilitary forces from the Federal Republic of Yugoslavia and the ethnic Albanian Kosovo Liberation Army. In this case the government, as well as a significant portion of the population, did not want (or request) the international community to intervene. In addition, the United Nations did not authorize a humanitarian intervention.[1] Yet the President of the United States asserted that the United States had a 'moral imperative' to protect the people of Kosovo from the ethnic cleansing campaign and the wrath of Milošević's nationalistic regime. In addition, a strong majority of Americans supported intervening to end the suffering in Kosovo.

The recent history of multilateral interventions in domestic conflicts presents a mixed picture of success. In the ashes of Kosovo we find an excellent opportunity to evaluate humanitarian intervention, as well as the role public opinion played in both the creation of the NATO campaign and the implementation of the operation. This chapter examines the case of Kosovo in terms of the qualities and quantities of public opinion concerning the intervention. It measures the extent to which the public supported operations in Kosovo at distinct points in the campaign, and the role of public opinion in the creation and implementation of the NATO mission. Finally, this chapter uses statistical analysis to examine the factors that influenced public attitudes towards humanitarian engagement in Kosovo, assessing the importance of elite cues, policy objectives, media coverage, risk assessment and historical milieu.

Humanitarian intervention, public opinion, and the case of Kosovo

Kosovo was initially slow to appear on the American radar, as operations in Bosnia monopolized policymakers' focus. Yet, in the aftermath of the Yugoslav civil war, tensions in the Kosovo region of Serbia escalated. Nationalist sentiments flared as struggles between ethnic Serbs, Croats and Albanians mirrored events in the other former Yugoslav Republics. By late 1998, reports of rebellion, state repression and increasing human displacement brought Kosovo into the world's view. Despite warnings and sanctions from the international community, Slobodan Milošević, the President of Serbia, refused to restrain the escalating violence.

These events in Kosovo generated significant debate within the United States as well as other Western countries. Discussions that began in policy sectors extended to society as both American politicians and the public questioned the morality, utility and methods of engagement. In contrast to many other areas of foreign policy, the situation in Kosovo was highly salient to the public. Indeed, surveys indicated that 43 percent of respondents reported that they followed the situation in Kosovo somewhat closely, and almost 30 percent said they followed it very closely (PIPA 1999). Media coverage of the developments in Kosovo was extensive, and provided significant information to the American public. Furthermore, the content of the media coverage included information on the motivation for involvement, issues of morality and obligation, national interest and tactical concerns.

In addition to higher levels of public awareness, Kosovo is distinct due to politicians' receptivity to public concerns. Indeed, President Clinton was notorious for his consultation of public opinion polls when weighing policy matters, and it is clear that when responding to Milošević's defiance, he deliberately chose tactics that would minimize public backlash fueled by anger over casualties. To this end, the United States led NATO in a massive air campaign against Yugoslavia on 24 March 1999. NATO's campaign, lasting eleven weeks, included 1,000 planes and over 14,000 explosive shells (Fromkin 1999). To minimize the threat of military casualties during the bombing campaign, the aircraft flew above 15,000 feet. A marine colonel claimed at the time that the US

> sent the strongest possible signal that while it is willing to conduct military operations in situations not vital to the country's interests, it is not willing to put in harm's way the means necessary to conduct these operations effectively and conclusively.
>
> (*Wilson Quarterly* 2000: 97)

As Everts notes,

> The decision of the NATO allies to rely on air power alone ... was, among other things, motivated by an assumption or perception that public opinion

would not support a war in which the risk of military casualties on the allied side was anything but minimal.

(Everts 2001a: 1)

President Bill Clinton justified NATO's campaign by asserting that the United States had a moral imperative to protect the ethnic Albanians (Clinton 1999). Prominent political elites disagreed with Clinton's assessment, however. Elites disagreed sharply over the decision to intervene in Kosovo, giving the public mixed messages regarding the efficacy and necessity of American involvement. Furthermore, the policy objectives of the Kosovo intervention were mixed. The Clinton administration framed the mission primarily in humanitarian terms, envisioning it as 'the first of a new kind of international use of force, not aimed at protecting or furthering traditional national interests, but at protecting people and their fundamental rights' (Everts 2001b). At the same time, there was a strategic component to American involvement as well. European allies were concerned about the geopolitical stability of their own backyard, and pressured the US to demonstrate that NATO was not an antiquated Cold War relic; it could be used effectively in the post-Cold War era to promote stability. Thus, the case of Kosovo provides some interesting variation in terms of elite cues and policy objectives.

After Yugoslavia accepted a peace plan on 10 June 1999, and the Yugoslav military withdrew, NATO ceased its air campaign and established the cooperative peacekeeping mission KFOR. On 12 June 1999, NATO implemented a peace plan, allowing KFOR to enter Kosovo. The United Nations soon followed with the establishment of UNMIK. According to the peace accords, both UN and NATO peacekeepers were charged with assisting refugee return, stabilizing Kosovo's multi-ethnic society and normalizing the political environment.

The US played a leading role in the multinational operations in Kosovo, and the American public generally supported intervention. As Table 2.1 indicates, while support for air strikes was tepid in early March, a majority supported the dispatch of ground troops to enforce a peace treaty. Once NATO actually began its air campaign, the American public did exhibit a 'rally around the flag' tendency, with over 70 percent of the public in favor of air strikes. Public support for the air campaign remained high throughout April, and the majority of the public stated that they would support sending ground troops if the air campaign was unsuccessful. The week after Yugoslavia accepted the peace plan, the majority of Americans indicated that they were supportive of the commitment of forces. Almost a year later, in April 2000, support for the operation dipped slightly; still, 60 percent of the American public supported the mission.

Public support for the Kosovo operation indicated that Americans were willing to commit military forces and finances for humanitarian intervention. What factors explain this level of public support? Were Americans swayed by President Clinton's appeal to morality? Did the press coverage matter? Did Americans base their views on previous experiences with humanitarian intervention? To answer these questions, we turn to a review of the literature on public opinion and humanitarian intervention.

Table 2.1 American public opinion of the Kosovo operation from March 1999 to April 2000

Date of poll	Percentage in favor of air strikes against Serbia	Percentage in favor of ground troops to enforce peace treaty*	Percentage supporting ground troops if bombing doesn't work
March 11–14, 1999	29.8	54.5	
March 23, 1999	49.9	61.7	
March 26, 1999	65.5		
April 4–5, 1999	70.1		58.5
April 8, 1999	67.6		59.6
April 25–26, 1999	68.6		58.1
May 14, 1999	60.1		51.9
June 10, 1999		72.8	
April 4, 2000		59.6	

Sources: The source of the 1999 survey statistics is ABC News' *Nightline Kosovo Polls*. The source of the 2000 survey statistics is the CNN/USA Today/Gallup Poll.

Notes
*Question wording slightly different for each survey.
Percentages are taken from two data sources: ABC News. Nightline Kosovo Polls, March–June 1999 [Computer file]. ICPSR version. Horsham, PA: Chilton Research Services [producer], 1999. Ann Arbor, MI: Inter-university Consortium for Political and Social Research [distributor], 1999 and Gallup. CNN/USA Today/Gallup Poll. April, Wave 1, 2000. The above sources were used since they provided ready summary statistics to measure support for the Kosovo mission. These datasets were not used for the later multivariate analysis, however, as they did not contain questions that allowed for the operationalization and measurement of many of the hypotheses of interest.

Factors influencing public attitudes towards humanitarian engagement

While in the 1960s much research portrayed American foreign policy attitudes as apathetic, ill-informed and moody, today scholars regard public opinion as a salient factor in policy formation (Almond 1960; Rosenau 1961). Substantial evidence indicates that the public is capable of forming foreign policy preferences (Hurwitz and Peffley 1987). However, these preferences are highly susceptible to media and elite framing, particularly when public knowledge is low, as is frequently the case in matters of foreign policy (Aldrich *et al.* 2006; Delli Carpini and Keeter 1996; Page and Shapiro 1984, 1992).

Recently, several scholars have highlighted the relationship between public opinion and foreign policy, noting that 'a mounting body of evidence suggests that the foreign policies of American presidents – and democratic leaders more generally – have been influenced by their understanding of the public's foreign policy views' (Aldrich *et al.* 2006; Berinsky 2007; Foyle 2003). Thus, a sympathetic public may push its leaders to intervene in troubled areas. In contrast, an unsupportive population might lessen political support, block monetary commitments and enhance overall 'collective reluctance' (Der Meulen and Soeters 2005). Thus, public opinion can potentially play an important role in the creation and continued success of humanitarian operations.[2] In their explorations of the determinants of public opinion, scholars have identified several factors that appear to influence public attitudes towards intervention, highlighting the importance of risk assessment, elite cues and media coverage in particular. We examine the ability of these variables to predict public support for humanitarian operations in Kosovo. In addition, we present an additional variable that merits closer scrutiny; the historical milieu, or a nation's recent experience with a peacekeeping operation or a humanitarian intervention. We argue that public attitudes towards humanitarian missions might also be a product of evaluations of prior experience with such operations. We hold that the historical context of previous missions may be a significant determinant of attitudes towards current and future operations. We conceptualize this as a historical milieu where 'previous events shape and inform the public and policy elite consciousness' (Lyon and Dolan 2007: 50). Perceptions of previous engagements may act as a prism that shapes and informs public attitudes about humanitarianism. Recent success might create a 'halo' around current and future missions, and a recent disaster may create a 'hangover', leading the public to be wary of future involvement. Historical milieu is important to examine in light of past conflicts in the Balkans.

To examine the impact of historical milieu, and test it alongside other variables featured prominently in the literature, we rely upon public opinion data collected from 13–17 May 1999 by the Program on International Policy Attitudes (PIPA). PIPA designed this survey to gauge American views of the 1999 humanitarian intervention in Kosovo, conducting it six weeks after NATO air strikes began. Thus, this dataset provides for the ready operationalization and measurement of the variables of interest in this study. We turn now to a discussion of the theoretical importance, as well as our measurement, of each of these variables.

Policy objectives

In a seminal piece, Jentleson and Britton (1998) provide compelling evidence that the principal policy objective of an intervention has a significant impact on public support for that intervention. They identify three types of principal policy objectives: foreign policy restraint, internal political changes and humanitarian intervention. Following their argument, if an operation is viewed as vital to the national interest, the public will be more supportive of such a mission. However, the public also views military missions with humanitarian goals quite favorably. Jentleson and Britton found that when humanitarian concerns triggered military interventions, Americans were strikingly supportive, with 75 percent in favor.[3] This stands in marked contrast to those operations targeting internal political change, for which Americans registered the lowest levels of public support (ibid.: 402).

To test this theory, we rely upon two survey items that gauge public perceptions of policy objectives in Kosovo. One survey question measures the perception that humanitarian concerns drove the Kosovo intervention, while the other focuses on the perception of the strategic value of the mission. While we would ideally like to include a measure of internal political change, as highlighted by Jentleson and Britton, unfortunately our dataset did not contain a corresponding survey question. Still, the data do allow for the examination of two crucial policy objectives.

We gauge respondents' assessment of the humanitarian imperative to intervene in Kosovo through the following survey item: *'The Serbs' effort at "ethnic cleansing" through killing many ethnic Albanians and driving hundreds of thousands of them out of Kosovo is a form of genocide. The US has a moral obligation to join in efforts to stop this genocide.'* Respondents were asked to state if they found this statement (1) convincing or (0) not convincing. As Figure 2.1 illustrates, at the bivariate level there is a significant relationship between this measure of humanitarian perception and the dependent variable, support for ground troops.[4] Consistent with Jentleson and Britton's thesis, Americans who thought that the US had a moral obligation to intervene were significantly more likely to support humanitarian efforts.

To examine the impact of respondents' evaluations of the strategic importance of Kosovo operations, we rely upon another survey item: *'Kosovo is far from the US and we have no real interests there. Therefore it is wrong to risk the lives of American soldiers in a NATO operation there.'* Respondents were asked to state if they found this statement (1) convincing or (0) not convincing. As Figure 2.2 illustrates, at the bivariate level, there was a significant relationship between strategic interest and support for troops, yet the magnitude of this relationship was smaller than that found in Figure 2.1. The percentage difference

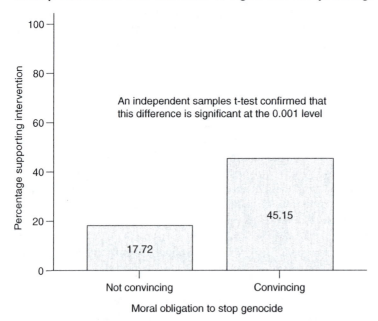

Figure 2.1 Support for humanitarian intervention by policy objectives (source: Program on International Policy Attitudes 1999).

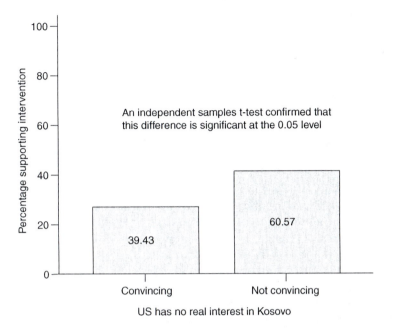

Figure 2.2 Support for humanitarian intervention by strategic policy objectives
(source: Program on International Policy Attitude 1999).

between those who found moral arguments convincing and not convincing was 27 percent, while the percentage difference between respondents who found strategic interests convincing and not convincing was 21 percent. Also, the statistical relationship in Figure 2.1 is much stronger ($P<0.001$) than in Figure 2.2 ($P<0.05$).

Elite cues

Extant literature suggests that policymakers provide cues to the public about goal preference and obligations in the general conduct of foreign policy (Berinsky 2007; Katz 1957; Newman 1986; Powlick and Katz 1998). As Boulding (1959) points out, it is not the 'objective' components of a situation, but the 'image of the situation that is effective'. In the US, the most significant opinion leader in the realm of foreign policy is the president. Given the prominence of the president, it is logical to surmise that either approval of the president and/or identification with his party might influence public attitudes towards intervention. The president's endorsement of a mission might sway members of the public to support a given cause, as they approve of the president and/or his party. In the case of Kosovo, given President Clinton's public statements in favor of NATO intervention, we would expect self-identifying Democrats to be more supportive of humanitarian operations.[5] For instance, on 24 March 1999 he proclaimed:

We act to protect thousands of innocent people in Kosovo from a mounting military offensive. We act to prevent a wider war, to defuse a powder keg at the heart of Europe that has exploded twice before in this century with cata-strophic results. We act to stand united with our allies for peace. By acting now, we are upholding our values, protecting our interests, and upholding the cause of peace.

(Clinton 1999)

At the same time, many Republicans were very vocal in their opposition to the Kosovo operation both before and during the bombing campaign as well as the operations that followed. For example, Senator John McCain remarked on CNN:

They [the administration] have not made the case either to the Congress or to the American people, and the President has to explain why our interests are there, what is going to happen, especially – I believe we must tell the Ameri-can people that any ground troops or peacekeeping force has to be European and not US, and I think also these air strikes have to be very sufficient.

(Kagan 1998)

This lack of elite consensus provides the public with viable political altern-atives; when elites disagree publicly, citizens have access to more viewpoints

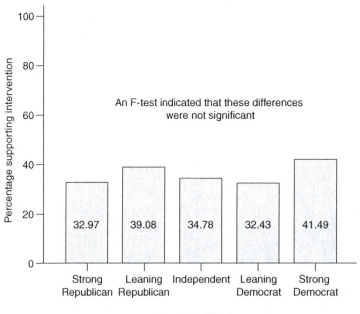

Figure 2.3 Support for humanitarian intervention by partisanship (source: Program on International Policy Attitudes 1999).

and policy options. This can lead to public support for the policy option touted by one group of elites (e.g., the Clinton administration) being less than if elites uniformly praise the benefits of intervention in Kosovo. As Berinsky notes, 'when political elites disagree as to the wisdom of intervention, the public divides as well. But when elites come to a common interpretation of a political reality, the public gives them great latitude to wage war' (Berinsky 2007).

To test the impact of elite cues, ideally we would like to include a measure of approval of President Clinton as well as leading members of the opposition. Such a measure is not available in the PIPA survey; however, there is a suitable proxy – identification with the president's party. If elite cues have an impact on support for intervention in Kosovo, we would expect that greater identification with the president's party would lead to greater support for ground troops. We measure identification with the president's party through the following survey item: *'In politics today, do you think of yourself as: strongly Republican; leaning toward Republican; leaning toward Democrat; strongly Democrat; Independent; other?'* Responses were recoded so that 'Independents' scored a value of 3, in the middle of the range, and 'other' was coded as missing. Surprisingly, as Figure 2.3 illustrates, identification with the president's party did not have a significant effect on support for humanitarian intervention at the bivariate level.

Media coverage

The media are often perceived as playing a significant role in the formation of public opinion. In a classic work, Bernard Cohen (1963) categorized the press as observer, participant and catalyst. He found that the media create an environment in which the policymaker must simultaneously conduct business with two actors, the media as a counterpart and an opinionated viewing public. As a catalyst, the media act as international witnesses and allow the public to observe human tragedy almost in real time. When people watch refugees dying, children in pain and communities destroyed, the viewing public might push their leaders to act. Daniel Goure argues that in the case of the US, the media have served as a catalyst to the extent that US interventions resembled 'foreign policy for soccer moms' (Goure 1999). Daniel Schorr concurs to some extent, stating that international media coverage influences perceptions, public opinion and policy, creating an environment for 'edge-of-seat diplomacy' where policymakers must make an effort to quell the images of people suffering (1998: 11). According to this argument, leaders respond to public opinion to satisfy a particular constituency with intervention (Goodman 1992; Kennan 1993).

While the media are frequently portrayed as exerting a powerful impact on public opinion, several scholars argue that what is commonly referred to as the 'CNN factor' is exaggerated. James Burk (1999) rejects the CNN thesis, arguing that in fact experts and foreign policy leaders provide the media with their information. In a similar vein, Philip Powlick and Andrew Katz (1998) argue that public opinion is a 'dog that could bark'; however, it must first be activated by elite debate and media coverage.

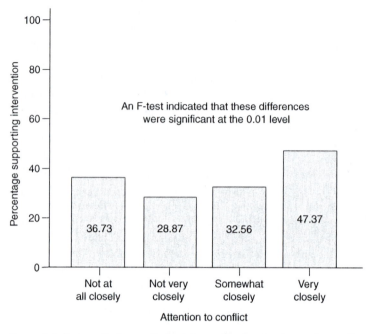

Figure 2.4 Support for humanitarian intervention by attention to the media
(source: Program on International Policy Attitudes 1999).

Given that the relationship between the media and public opinion is the subject of much debate, we aimed to assess the relationship between attention to the media and support for intervention in Kosovo. The PIPA survey asked respondents: '*As you may know, NATO is bombing Serb targets to pressure Yugoslav President Milošević to stop ethnic cleansing in Kosovo. How closely are you following the situation in Kosovo? (1) not at all closely; (2) not very closely; (3) somewhat closely; (4) very closely.*'[6] As Figure 4 demonstrates, at the bivariate level there is a significant though modest relationship between respondents' attention to the media and support for humanitarian intervention.

Risk assessment

Scholars have also noted that public support for various types of foreign policy initiatives is contingent upon risk assessment. According to this view, the public is quite rational and weighs the potential benefits of a mission (e.g., providing food to refugees, protecting national interests) against the costs likely to be incurred (e.g., casualties, monetary contributions). Furthermore, a prudent public is also prone to consider in its calculations the likelihood that a mission will be successful. After considering the benefits, costs and potential for success, the public renders a positive or negative verdict for the mission at hand.

Prior to 9/11, conventional wisdom held that Americans would not tolerate casualties (Luttwak 1994; Mueller 1996). Indeed, this perception heavily influenced the way in which the US intervened in Kosovo. Still, recent work has begun to question this accepted view. Steven Kull and Clay Ramsey (2001) found that while policymakers and the media frequently cite Americans' refusal to accept sustained casualties, actual polling data reveal a very different story. Burk (1999) concurs, arguing that public support for intervention does not always depend upon the risk of casualties. Peter Feaver and Christopher Gelpi (2003) provide additional evidence that the public considers more than just casualties when forming opinions. They find that the casualty hypothesis is misstated, and that in fact there is considerable tolerance for casualties in 'high intensity realpolitik missions'. They conclude that the public is 'defeat phobic, more than casualty phobic' (Feaver and Gelpi 2003).

Feaver and Gelpi's work highlights the importance of a more crucial component of risk assessment – the likelihood of success. Public evaluations are not contingent solely on costs (such as casualties), but also on the objectives of the mission and its potential for success. Richard Eichenberg provides empirical evidence supporting the importance of success in determining citizens' attitudes. In an expansive study of twenty-two cases in which the US contemplated, threatened or used force, he finds that the success or failure of the mission was crucial to understanding public support for military intervention. Indeed, he found that the success or failure of a mission provided the necessary 'context in which the impact of casualties must be understood' (Eichenberg 2005: 141).

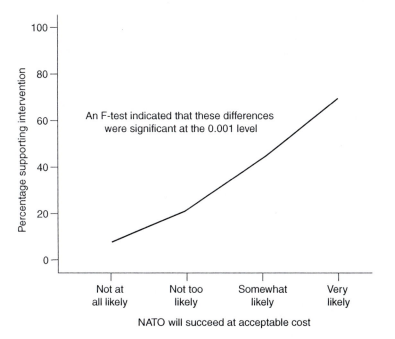

Figure 2.5 Support for humanitarian intervention by likelihood of success
(source: Program on International Policy Attitudes 1999).

The PIPA survey provides a ready operationalization for the theory of risk assessment. The survey asked respondents: '*If further bombing does not prove to be effective and NATO decides to intervene with ground troops, how likely do you think it is that the operation will succeed at an acceptable cost? (1) not at all likely; (2) not too likely; (3) somewhat likely; (4) very likely.*' As Figure 2.5 depicts, there is a strong and significant correlation between risk assessment and support for humanitarian intervention at the bivariate level. This provides preliminary evidence that the public does like a winner.

Historical milieu

Finally, we turn now to a variable that has not been extensively studied in the literature – the impact of prior experiences with humanitarian intervention, or historical milieu. According to Alynna J. Lyon and Chris Dolan, historical milieu can function 'as the "lens" through which previous events shape and inform the public and policy elite consciousness' (2007: 50). It is reasonable to expect that support for current operations might be colored by recent episodes of success and failure. Bruce Jentleson dubs this the 'halo effect', in which a recent successful military intervention can create the perception that future venues will garner the same success (1992). Historical milieu may produce a rally effect, in that the sheen or success from a previous engagement inspires optimism about another engagement.

At the same time, after examining the recent record of global humanitarian interventions and peacekeeping operations, it seems that instead of a 'halo' there might be more of a 'hangover' effect.[7] While the major world powers were optimistic about humanitarian operations following the end of the Cold War, this optimism was tempered by a few debacles (e.g., Somalia) where it was difficult to get in, tough to manage and tougher to get out. There is a growing understanding that such operations are complex endeavors, and in many cases may not assist in conflict resolution. In fact, the recent success rate for such interventions is mixed. Cases such as Somalia, Rwanda, Sri Lanka and Haiti do not present pictures of success. In many of these places, violence continues and at times has escalated despite the presence of outside troops, peacekeepers and other international commitments. In some respects, these failures are a function of the broadening ambitions that have moved beyond the original mandate to supervise ceasefires into the area of conflict resolution and even governance (UNMIK is an example of such mission expansion).

In light of the growing evidence that humanitarian intervention missions do not always go smoothly, these 'hiccups' may undermine public support for such operations (Fortna 2004). Indeed, Kull notes, 'many Americans are leery about contributing to international efforts' when they are perceived as ineffective. In the case of Bosnia in 1995, Kull cites an April 1995 PIPA poll that found 75 percent of Americans viewed the operations as 'ineffective and even dangerous' (Kull 1995–1996: 105).

If historical milieu does matter, then previous engagement in Bosnia seems like the most likely suspect for explaining support for operations in Kosovo three years later, due to its geographical proximity and overlap of actors.[8] Indeed, some of the key actors in Bosnia were the same international organizations pushing for action in Kosovo, including the United Nations and NATO. The record of these two organizations differed sharply. In July 1995, inaction by the United Nations force UNPROFOR/UNPF in the town of Srebrenica made international headlines as UN 'safe areas' became execution sites for Bosnian men and boys. Several months later, under US leadership and after the Dayton Accords Agreement, a NATO-led Implementation Force (I-FOR) replaced UNPROFOR. Surveys by the Program on International Policy Attitudes (PIPA) found that the Bosnia operation was viewed as successful as it progressed. In September 1997 only 27 percent perceived it as successful, whereas in March 1998 49 percent believed that the operation had 'improved the chances of finding a way to permanently end the fighting there' (Richman 1998). In some respects this presents a dual historical milieu, as the Bosnian legacy is mixed. In terms of the United Nations the public perceptions are negative, whereas NATO's operations are evaluated as more effective and successful.

In measuring prior experiences with humanitarian intervention it is imperative to focus on the public's perception of these operations, rather than objective indicators of success or failure. For example, if the goal is to determine individual levels of support for humanitarianism, it is imperative to ensure that measurement of prior experience with humanitarian intervention is also at the individual level. Individuals will vary substantially in their evaluations of past

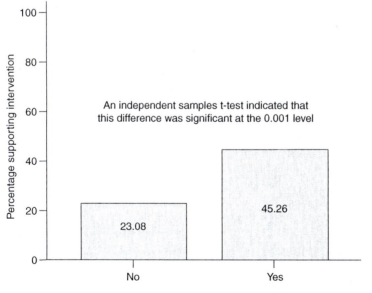

Figure 2.6 Support for humanitarian intervention by perceptions of the Bosnia mission (source: Program on International Policy Attitudes 1999).

policy initiatives; therefore, to account for such variation, one must ask individuals themselves to evaluate past humanitarian missions.

In the case of Kosovo, we determine whether Americans were influenced by images of either a 'halo' or a 'hangover' with the following survey question: '*Do you believe that sending US and other NATO forces to Bosnia has improved the chances of finding a way to permanently end the fighting there, or not? (1) yes, has improved chances or (0) no, has not improved chances.*' We hypothesize that respondents who view the Bosnia mission more favorably will be more supportive of intervention in Kosovo. Figure 2.6 provides some evidence for this hypothesis, as it illustrates that there is a significant correlation between perceptions of the Bosnia mission and support for operations in Kosovo at the bivariate level.

To test whether historical milieu, along with the other variables highlighted here, can significantly predict public support for humanitarianism, we must test these variables in a multivariate model. While the bivariate analyses are useful for illustrating the relationships between each independent variable and the dependent variable, it is imperative to test these variables in multivariate models to ensure that the findings are robust. Our multivariate models also included variables to measure the socioeconomic status of respondents, as such factors are typically included in public opinion research.[9]

Multivariate analyses

Since the dependent variable is dichotomous, we rely upon binomial logistic regression for this portion of the analysis. The dependent variable is measured through the following survey question: '*Some people feel that NATO should send ground troops into Kosovo at this point. Do you favor or oppose this idea? (1) favor; (0) oppose.*' It is important to remember that respondents answered this survey question approximately six weeks after the bombing campaign was initiated and approximately one month prior to the peace accords.

As Table 2.2 indicates, in most cases the variables measuring socioeconomic status are not significant predictors of support for humanitarian intervention in terms of support for troops; age is insignificant across the models while education is significant only when included with the variable measuring the perception of strategic interest. Respondents' income also performs inconsistently, as it is significant in only three of the models. In those cases, wealthier respondents are more likely to support intervention. In almost all cases, men were more supportive of troops than women. Respondents' sex is insignificant when included in the strategic interest model, yet in all other cases men are more likely to support intervention than women.

While the inclusion of the socioeconomic variables allows us to control for important characteristics, our main variables of theoretical concern are those measuring policy objectives, elite cues, attention to the media, likelihood of success, and historical milieu. Interestingly, identification with the president's party was not a significant predictor of attitudes towards humanitarian inter-

Table 2.2 Support for humanitarian intervention

Independent variables	Model 1: media and party ID	Model 2: success	Model 3: Bosnia	Model 4: moral reason for intervention	Model 5: strategic interest
Constant	0.177**	0.013***	0.113**	0.052**	0.083**
	(0.540)	(1.021)	(0.859)	(0.878)	(0.878)
Age	0.912	0.854	0.999	0.880	0.832
	(0.108)	(0.179)	(0.165)	(0.167)	(0.179)
Education	0.907	0.934	0.908	0.961	0.779*
	(0.095)	(0.161)	(0.142)	(0.144)	(0.146)
Income	1.159*	1.240*	1.121	1.105	1.352**
	(0.076)	(0.130)	(0.117)	(0.113)	(0.121)
Sex	1.733**	1.802*	1.672*	2.142**	1.190
	(0.196)	(0.325)	(0.302)	(0.292)	(0.300)
Party identification	1.053	0.927	1.047	1.041	0.984
	(0.073)	(0.127)	(0.109)	(0.110)	(0.117)
Attention to the media	1.271*	1.087	1.196	1.271	1.610*
	(0.124)	(0.209)	(0.197)	(0.198)	(0.215)
Likelihood of success		3.289***			
		(0.189)			
Halo/hangover			2.212**		
			(0.304)		
Moral reason for intervention				4.328***	
				(0.400)	
Strategic interest reason for intervention					2.023*
					(0.332)
N	476	224	220	240	225
Nagelkerke Pseudo R Squared	0.049	0.347	0.090	0.162	0.124

Notes
Our multivariate model is handicapped by the manner in which the data were collected, as many questions were asked of only half of the sample during the administration of the survey. Thus, it is not possible to include all of the variables together in the same model. While this is not ideal, we aim to circumvent this problem by including split sample variables separately.
This table reports odds ratios, with standard errors in parentheses.
All models are significant. *$P<0.05$; **$P<0.01$; ***$P<0.001$.

vention. In the multivariate models partisanship was insignificant, as Republicans, Democrats and Independents registered comparable levels of support for intervention. These findings could be influenced by Clinton's domestic political troubles. During the Kosovo intervention, President Clinton had been embroiled in a series of scandals, leading to his eventual impeachment. Thus, his political standing was weakened, perhaps diluting the impact of his cues in support of American involvement in Kosovo. Before dismissing the importance of elite cues, however, it is imperative to provide a more stringent test of elite influence, perhaps one that measures support for the actual elite in question (i.e., President Clinton) rather than a more diffuse measure of identification with the elite's party. While such a measure is not available in our dataset, this does seem like a fruitful endeavor for future research.

Attention to the media also yielded surprising results, as it is significant only in Models 1 and 5. Model 1 does not include measures of risk assessment, policy objective or historical milieu. Model 5 does include our measure of strategic policy objectives. However, when other factors such as likelihood of success, perception of Bosnia, and humanitarian rationale for intervention are included in the models with the media variable, the effects of the media disappear.[10] We find it interesting that, at least in the tests here, media attention has only a mild impact on public attitudes. One possible interpretation of this finding is that the likelihood of success, perceptions of Bosnia, and humanitarian concerns out-weigh any effect caused by the media. Still, it is important to recognize that the media could frame these other factors by highlighting the failures of a given intervention, or stressing the humanitarian need for a mission.

At the same time, we do find very strong support for the likelihood of success. As individuals view success as increasingly likely, they are more than twice as supportive of humanitarian engagement as those who perceive failure as immi-nent. Furthermore, as the Nagelkerke Pseudo R Squared indicates, the model including the likelihood of success variable performs quite well.

Perceptions of Bosnia were also significantly linked to support for operations in Kosovo. Those who saw halos around this previous mission were 121 percent more likely to support efforts in Kosovo. It is important to remember that while perceptions of Bosnia are closely tied to those of Kosovo, other humanitarian missions outside of the Balkans (e.g., Somalia and Haiti) may also have an effect. Furthermore, our analysis found that the principal policy objective of the mission was also significant in predicting support. Respondents who thought that the US had a moral justification for intervening in Kosovo were more than three times as likely to support the operation as those who did not.

Findings

This study of American public opinion and humanitarian intervention finds support for many of the variables highlighted in the literature. Overall, we find that the CNN thesis is exaggerated, that party affiliation is not a significant pre-dictor of support,[11] and that the amount of media attention has an inconsistent impact on public attitudes. The key factors influencing public attitudes towards humanitarian intervention appear to be policy objectives, historical milieu and the belief in operational success.

The results concerning historical milieu are quite intriguing. They suggest that when assessing risk, respondents do not think solely in terms of the imme-diate costs and benefits of the mission at hand. Factors such as monetary cost, casualties, and likelihood of success of the present/proposed mission appear to be influenced by respondents' evaluations of what has happened in the past. In the case of Kosovo, previous missions in the region exerted a significant impact on respondents' support for operations in Kosovo.[12] Our results indicate that when formulating opinions on humanitarian interventions in the Sudan, for example, the public may evaluate the success of missions such as those in Afghanistan and Iraq, as these latter operations have both been framed in humanitarian terms at different times.

There are additional alternative explanations for public support for humanitarian missions that also merit further exploration. In particular, the impact of multilateral versus unilateral operations deserves closer scrutiny. The literature suggests that multilateral operations tend to be viewed more favorably than unilateral ones, as the former share the costs of missions with other countries.[13] For example, Senator McCain's earlier comments on the need for European contributions to peacekeeping forces implied that the burden of any operation in Kosovo would need to be shared with other European powers. Moreover, as most humanitarian operations are multilateral endeavors, it is important to expand this analysis to other countries to determine if results from this American sample are applicable to other populations.

Another alternative explanation of support for humanitarian missions highlights the importance of the international organization leading the effort. For example, is the public more supportive of a NATO versus a UN operation? Furthermore, would the impact of the sponsoring nation vary from country to country? Again, this alternative explanation is beyond the scope of this study, but opens an interesting venue for future research. When considering a humanitarian intervention in Sudan, for example, the support of allies and the inclusion of the United Nations may be important items in determining public support for such a commitment of force.

Conclusions

Given the increasing demands for humanitarian operations in places like the Democratic Republic of Congo, Lebanon, Sudan, Somalia (again), Nepal, Afghanistan and potentially Iraq, understanding the factors that propel a population to support international operations will remain important for decades to come. Since humanitarian operations have the potential to promote regional and international stability, factors such as public opinion that could influence the creation and commitment to such operations deserve further exploration. Indeed, some evidence suggests that policymakers themselves would benefit from a closer study of public attitudes, as there are those that argue policymakers consistently misread public opinion (Destler 2001).

Our findings also indicate that the American public finds morality-based rationales for intervention appealing. While the strategic implications of intervention were significant, Americans also responded positively to intervention appeals framed on moral grounds. Almost 75 percent of Americans found moral arguments for intervention in Kosovo persuasive, and these individuals were significantly more likely to support intervention. This is consistent with recent polls indicating that strong support for humanitarian intervention in Kosovo is not a relic from the pre-9/11 years. A 2005 poll conducted on attitudes towards Sudan found that 84 percent of Americans believed that 'the US should not tolerate an extremist government committing such attacks and should use its military assets, short of putting US troops on the ground, to help stop them'. There was strong support for the creation of a no-fly zone over Darfur (80 percent) as well as for the use of NATO involvement to provide logistical support for the African Union's beleaguered peacekeeping force (76 percent) (International Crisis Group 2005). A 2007 survey conducted by The Chicago Council on Global Affairs reported that Americans strongly agreed that the United Nations Security Council has either the 'responsibility' (48 percent) or the 'right' (35 percent) to intervene in the domestic affairs of some countries, supporting 'the use of military force to protect people from severe human rights violations, such as genocide, even against the will of their own government'. In addition, 65 percent of Americans polled supported contributing troops to a peacekeeping effort in Darfur (Whitney and Kull 2007). Both the 2005 and 2007 polls found extensive support for the United States to play a leadership role in Sudan. Thus, 'there would appear to be much greater public backing for America to play a leadership role in stemming this catastrophe than has been the conventional wisdom in Washington' (International Crisis Group 2005: 1).

While the American public appears to demonstrate consistent support for engagement in humanitarian crises like that of Sudan, the US government has been slow to act. This disparity between public preferences and public policy could be due to a variety of factors, one of which could be the receptivity of elites to public opinion. The impact of public opinion on policy elites does appear to vary, as some administrations appear to be more sensitive and vulnerable to public attitudes. At the same time, one is hard pressed to imagine a president committing troops in the name of humanitarianism without domestic public support. Thus, the significance of public opinion may wax and wane over time, yet it remains an essential factor in creating and supporting American humanitarian initiatives.

Kosovo presents an important case, especially because some find that it set the stage for later US interventions into Iraq and Afghanistan. In addition, Kosovo illustrated how ending the violence does not always end the suffering, as a temporary relief operation morphed into a long-term international commitment. Ultimately, the United Nations also began operations in Kosovo, focusing on poverty reduction, the rule of law, nation-building, policing and refugee return. As humanitarian missions become more complicated, the likelihood of success diminishes. The fact that the solutions to violence are often complicated and require a long-term commitment may ultimately undermine public support for such engagements. The public may be increasingly reluctant to support such endeavors as they become aware that these conflicts are difficult to organize, legally precarious, tough to manage and almost impossible to leave. In addition, concurrent with public support for humanitarian interventions, states and international organizations are more reluctant to intervene. The result is a growing tension between sovereignty, practical experience, changing norms, rising public expectations and human need.

Notes

1 Humanitarian intervention is defined as 'coercive action by one or more states involving the use of armed force in another state without the consent of its authorities, and with the purpose of preventing widespread suffering or death among the inhabitants' (Roberts 2002). Traditional peacekeeping is based on state consent and actor neutrality, and is usually administered by the United Nations.
2 For an examination of the role that donor commitment plays in the success of peacekeeping operations, see Johansen (1998).
3 Steven Kull (1995) describes similar findings, as he reports that 66 percent of Americans supported US troop commitment to UN peacekeeping operations even in cases where there were no strategic interests.
4 In this graph (as well as all subsequent graphs), the dependent variable is measured through the following survey question: '*Some people feel that NATO should send ground troops into Kosovo at this point. Do you favor or oppose this idea? (1) favor; (0) oppose.*' It is important to remember that respondents answered this survey question approximately six weeks after the bombing campaign was initiated and approximately one month prior to the peace accords.
5 At the same time, it is important to note that a widely covered impeachment proceedings and a trial by the US Senate had concluded only weeks before the Kosovo operations. These events may have diminished the 'trust' in the president and decreased the influence of President Clinton's cues to the American public.
6 Originally, responses were coded so that higher values corresponded to lower levels of attention paid to Kosovo. We have recoded these values for purposes of presentation.
7 In an examination of the United States, Jentleson has referred to this phenomenon as 'Vietnam-taught risk aversion'.
8 According to Eichenberg (2005), American support for the Bosnian intervention was at 42 percent prior to engagement and actually rose four points during the intervention.
9 Age was measured according to the following categories: (1) 18 to 29; (2) 30 to 45; (3) 46 to 65; (4) Over 65. Respondents were asked to indicate their highest level of education: (1) Less than high school (no degree); (2) High school graduate; (3) Some college; (4) Four-year college degree; (5) Advanced degree. The question measuring income read '*Here is a range of household incomes. Just stop me when I read an amount that is more than the correct category for your household; (1) $15,000 (2) $25,000 (3) $45,000 (4) $70,000 (5) $100,000 (6) More than $100,000.*' Sex of respondent was coded as (1) men, (0) women.
10 Again, before one could completely dismiss the importance of the media, one would have to include the media variable in a fully specified multivariate model. While such a model is not possible given the confines of the data collection of this particular survey, it is imperative to test the effects of the media in subsequent analyses
11 At the same time, we do want to acknowledge that a more specific question measuring allegiance with particular elites (e.g., Clinton and McCain) could yield different results. Our measure of elite influence was an indirect one, measuring identification with a particular party. Still, it is interesting that there were no visible party differences between Republicans and Democrats, particularly given that elites in each of these parties had distinct views on Kosovo and those views were expressed publicly.
12 The relationship between risk assessment and historical milieu needs further exploration, as the limitations of our data did not allow for a thorough examination of the relationships between these variables. To determine how generalizable this finding is, it will need to be tested in additional cases. In addition, further analysis is needed to determine if the geographic proximity is also significant.
13 This variable could be of some importance; however, we were not able to test its relevance here, as our case selection held this variable constant – Kosovo was a multilateral effort.

References

Aldrich, J. H., Gelpi, C., Feaver, P., Reifler, J., Sharp, K. (2006) 'Foreign Policy and the Electoral Connection', *Annual Review of Political Science*, 9: 477–502.

Almond, G. (1960) *The American People and Foreign Policy*, New York, NY: Praeger.

Berinsky, A. J. (2007) 'Assuming the Costs of War: Events, Elites, and American Public Support for Military Conflict', *Journal of Politics*, 69/4: 975–997.

Boulding, K. E. (1959) 'National Images and International Systems', *Journal of Conflict Resolution*, 3: 120–131.

Burk, J. (1999) 'Public Support for Peacekeeping in Lebanon and Somalia: Assessing the Casualties Hypothesis', *Political Science Quarterly* 114: 53–78.

Clinton, W. (1999) 'Statement by the President to the Nation', Office of the Press Secretary, The White House, 24 March.

Cohen, B. C. (1963) *The Press and Foreign Policy*, Princeton, NJ: Princeton University Press.

Delli Carpini, M. and Keeter, S. (1996) *What Americans Know about Politics and Why It Matters*, New Haven, CT: Yale University Press.

Der Meulen, J. V. and Soeters, J. (2005) 'Considering Casualties: Risk and Loss during Peacekeeping and Warmaking', *Armed Forces and Society* 31/4: 483–486.

Destler, I. M. (2001) 'The Reasonable Public and the Polarized Policy Process', in A. Lake and D. Ochmanek (eds) *The Real and the Ideal: Essays on International Relations in Honor of Richard H. Ullman*, Lanham, MD: Rowman & Littlefield.

Eichenberg, R. C. (2005) 'Victory Has Many Friends: US Public Opinion and the Use of Military Force, 1981–2005', *International Security*, 30/1: 140–177.

Everts, P. (2001a) 'Introduction', in P. Everts and P. Isernia (eds) *Public Opinion and the International Use of Force*, New York, NY: Routledge.

Everts, P. (2001b) 'War without Bloodshed? Public Opinion and the Conflict over Kosovo', in P. Everts and P. Isernia (eds) *Public Opinion and the International Use of Force*, New York, NY: Routledge.

Feaver, P. and Gelpi, C. (2003) *Choosing Your Battles: American Civil–Military Relations and the Use of Force*, Princeton, NJ: Princeton University Press.

Fortna, V. P. (2004) 'Does Peacekeeping Keep Peace? International Intervention and the Duration of Peace after Civil War', *International Studies Quarterly*, 48/2: 269–292.

Foyle, D. (2003) 'Foreign Policy Analysis and Globalization: Public Opinion, World Opinion, and the Individual', *International Studies Review* 5/2: 155–202.

Fromkin, D. (1999) *Kosovo Crossing: American Ideals Meet Reality on the Balkan Battlefields*, New York, NY: The Free Press.

Goodman, W. (1992) 'How Much Did TV Shape Policy? *New York Times*, 8 December.

Goure, D. (1999) 'A Post-Clinton Foreign Policy', *World and I*, 14/9: 58.

Hurwitz, J. and Peffley, M. (1987) 'How Are Foreign-Policy Attitudes Structured – A Hierarchical Model', *American Political Science Review*, 81/4: 1099–1120.

International Crisis Group (2005). 'Do Americans Care about Darfur? An International Crisis Group/Zogby International Opinion Survey', *International Crisis Group*, Africa Briefing No. 26.

Jentleson, B. W. (1992) 'The Pretty Prudent Public – Post Post-Vietnam American Opinion on the Use of Military Force', *International Studies Quarterly*, 36/1: 49–74.

Jentleson, B. W. and Britton, R. L. (1998) 'Still Pretty Prudent: Post-Cold War American Public Opinion on the Use of Military Force', *Journal of Conflict Resolution*, 42/4: 395–417.

Johansen, R. (1998) 'Enhancing United Nations Peace-keeping', in C. Alger (ed.) *The Future of the United Nations System: Potential for the Twenty-first Century*, New York, NY: United Nations University Press.

Kagan, D. (1998) 'McCain Says Administration May Mislead Congress on Kosovo Involvement', *CNN Morning News*, 7 October.

Katz, E. (1957) 'The Two-Step Flow of Communication', *Public Opinion Quarterly*, 21: 61–78.

Kennan, G. F. (1993) 'Somalia, Through a Glass Darkly', *New York Times*, 30 September.

Kull, S. (1995) 'The US Public Isn't Averse to Peacekeeping', *Christian Science Monitor*, 87/144: 19.

Kull, S. (1995–1996) 'What the Public Knows that Washington Doesn't', *Foreign Policy*, 101: 102–115.

Kull, S. and Ramsay, C. (2001) 'The Myth of the Reactive Public: American Public Attitudes on Military Fatalities in the Post-Cold War Period', in P. Everts and P. Isernia (eds) *Public Opinion and the International Use of Force*, New York, NY: Routledge.

Luttwak, E. N. (1994) 'Where Are the Great-Powers – at Home with the Kids', *Foreign Affairs*, 73/4: 23–28.

Lyon, A. and Dolan, C. (2007) 'American Humanitarian Intervention: Toward a Theory of Coevolution', *Foreign Policy Analysis*, 2/1: 46–78.

Mueller, J. E. (1996) 'Policy Principles for Unthreatened Wealth-Seekers', *Foreign Policy*, 102: 31.

Newman, R. W. (1986) *The Paradox of Mass Politics: Knowledge and Opinion in the American Electorate*, Cambridge, MA: Harvard University Press.

Page, B. I. and Shapiro, R. Y. (1984) 'Presidents as Opinion Leaders – Some New Evidence', *Policy Studies Journal* 12/4: 649–661.

Page, B. I. and Shapiro, R. Y. (1992) *The Rational Public: Fifty Years of Trends in Americans' Policy Preferences*, Chicago, IL: University of Chicago Press.

Powlick, P. and Katz, A. (1998) 'Defining the American Public Opinion/Foreign Policy Nexus', *Mershon International Studies Review*, 42/1: 29–61.

Program on International Policy Attitudes (1999) *Americans on Kosovo*, 13–17 May 1999.

Richman, A. (1998) 'US Public's Views on Peacekeeping Missions: The Bosnia Case', *USIA Electronic Journal*, 3/2.

Roberts, A. (2002) 'The So-Called "Right" of Humanitarian Intervention', *Yearbook of International Humanitarian Law*, 3: 3–51.

Rosenau, J. (1961) Public Opinion and Foreign Policy; an Operational Formulation, New York, NY: Random House.

Schorr, D. (1998) 'CNN Effect: Edge-of-Seat Diplomacy', *Christian Science Monitor*, 27 November.

Whitney, C. and Kull, S. (2007) 'French and Americans Ready to Contribute Troops to Darfur Peacekeeping Operation', *The Chicago Council on Global Affairs*. Available: www.thechicagocouncil.org/media_press_room_detail.php?press_release_id=61 (accessed 10 June 2009).

Wilson Quarterly (2000) 'What Will America Risk?' 24/4: 97.

3 Kosovo and the advent of sovereignty as responsibility

Alex J. Bellamy

Each individual state has the responsibility to protect its populations from genocide, war crimes, ethnic cleansing and crimes against humanity.

(2005 World Summit Outcome Document, paragraph 138)

Introduction

Ten years on, NATO's 1999 intervention in Kosovo remains a seminal moment in the history of sovereignty. For some, the intervention represented the emergence of a new 'solidarist' conception of world order – within Europe at least – where the rights of sovereign legitimacy would only be conferred upon states that fulfilled their responsibility to protect their citizens from genocide and mass atrocities (see, for example, Wheeler 2000; Bellamy 2008). For others, the use of force without the authorization of the UN Security Council represented a fundamental challenge to the post-1945 international legal order (see, for example, Chomsky 1999). Although they are often portrayed as such, these two propositions are not mutually exclusive. New norms emerge as a result of state practice, and sometimes that practice involves acts contrary to established patterns of legitimate behaviour. Norms change when new practices are accepted as the appropriate standard (see, for example, Byers 1999). As such, an act such as NATO's intervention in Kosovo might simultaneously contribute to changing ideas about the nature of sovereignty and disrupt an international order predicated on a different conception of sovereignty.

This chapter investigates the contribution made by NATO's intervention in Kosovo to the emergence of sovereignty as responsibility. It argues that the debate about the merits of NATO's actions helped define international attitudes on the nature and scope of sovereignty as responsibility. In so doing, it revealed a broad constituency of states that were prepared to acknowledge that sovereignty did not give states a blank cheque to treat their citizens however they liked. The principal debate over Kosovo revolved not around Yugoslavia's entitlement to abuse its own citizens or the appropriateness of international engagement per se, but around the gravity of the government's abuses in Kosovo and the necessity of armed intervention. The widespread acknowledgement of sovereign responsibility that accompanied the Kosovo war provided a catalyst for new thinking about the use of armed force for humanitarian purposes and the infusion of the doctrine of sovereignty as responsibility into the debate about humanitarian intervention. This, in turn, influenced the emergence of a new humanitarian politics that focuses on the prevention of genocide and mass atrocities and protection of endangered populations, and situates the use of force within a broader spectrum of measures designed to achieve these commonly agreed ends. This new politics was crystallized by the global commitment to the Responsibility to Protect at the (2005) World Summit. This chapter seeks to demonstrate that NATO's intervention in Kosovo helped embody principles of sovereignty as responsibility and provided a catalyst for their further development.

The chapter proceeds in three parts. The first section examines the emergence of sovereignty as responsibility, briefly charting its historic roots before considering the work of Francis Deng and Roberta Cohen on Internally Displaced Persons in the 1990s and the adoption of sovereignty as responsibility by UN Secretary General Kofi Annan a year before NATO's intervention in Kosovo. The second section focuses on the international debate about the legitimacy of the intervention in Kosovo, and examines what this tells us about the scope of sovereignty as responsibility and the extent of international support for the principle. The third section focuses on Kosovo as a catalyst for the further development of sovereignty and responsibility, embodied in the emergence, transformation and adoption of the Responsibility to Protect by international society.

Sovereignty as responsibility

In a now famous article in *The Economist*, former UN Secretary General Kofi Annan set out two concepts of sovereignty. Alongside traditional conceptions of sovereignty that grant states a virtual carte blanche to treat their citizens however they see fit on the (false) assumption that governments reflect the will of their people, Annan identified a second form of sovereignty that entailed responsibilities. According to Annan (1999a, 1999b):

> [S]tate sovereignty, in its most basic sense, is being redefined.... States are now widely understood to be instruments at the service of their peoples, and not vice versa. At the same time individual sovereignty, by which I mean the fundamental freedom of each individual, enshrined in the Charter of the UN and subsequent international treaties, has been enhanced by a renewed and spreading consciousness of individual rights. When we read the Charter today, we are more than ever conscious that its aim is to protect individual human beings, not to protect those who abuse them.

This account of sovereignty was prefaced on the idea that sovereignty is ultimately derived from individual human rights; 'individual sovereignty' in Annan's parlance. According to this view, sovereignty thus entails both rights

and responsibilities. Only those states that cherish, nurture and protect the fundamental rights of their citizens and thereby fulfil their sovereign responsibilities
are entitled to the full panoply of sovereign rights. By this view, sovereignty is
not 'suspended' or 'overridden' when international society acts against (or to
assist) a government that fails in its responsibilities by abusing its citizens on a
massive scale. Instead, sovereignty is protected and promoted because such
international activism seeks to create the conditions necessary for individual
sovereigns to determine their own fate. Sovereignty as responsibility, therefore,
rests on two foundations. First, individuals everywhere have inalienable human
rights that may never be rescinded. These rights are natural (inherent in human
beings), equal (the same for everyone) and universal (Hunt 2007: 20). Second,
where governments abuse those rights, others acquire a responsibility to protect
individuals from these abuses.

This is often presented as a new conception of sovereignty, particularly by
its critics (but also its proponents). But the doctrine was first explicitly written
down by Thomas Jefferson and proclaimed in America's Declaration of Independence, promulgated on 4 July 1776. The first lines of the Declaration made
it clear that governments that fail to protect the fundamental rights of their citizens or that wantonly abuse those rights fail in their sovereign responsibilities.
This gave the people, as individual sovereigns, the right and duty to overthrow
the government and replace it with one more conducive to the satisfaction of
their rights. These ideas were repeated thirteen years later by the French
National Assembly, which, in 1789, proclaimed the 'Rights of Man and the
Citizen' (Bukovansky 2002). Of course, these ideas were not widely supported
in their own time. American independence was won through force of arms, not
the power of persuasion. The French Revolution gave way to the Terror, Napoleonic despotism and imperial expansion. Paradoxically, however, the Napoleonic Wars simultaneously discredited the idea of popular sovereignty and
spread it to new parts of Europe, ultimately inspiring Italian, Hungarian and
even German nationalists. Although its meaning and fortunes ebbed and flowed,
sovereignty as responsibility survived into the twentieth century and under-
pinned the decolonization movement. It is not coincidence that the contemporary constitutions of states such as India and Russia bestow upon the state a duty
to protect its citizens.

Sovereignty as responsibility was given new impetus after the Cold War,
principally as a result of renewed interest in basic human rights. One of the
clearest early signs of the emergence of sovereignty as responsibility was the
world's changing practice of recognition. Under the 1933 Montevideo Convention on the Rights and Duties of States (Article 1), the recognition of sovereign
statehood was linked to four objective criteria: permanent population, defined
territory, a government, and the capacity to enter into foreign relations with other
states. Although there were notable exceptions, such as the recognition of states
with contested borders (such as Israel), these four criteria guided the practice of
recognition during the Cold War. This changed after the Cold War. When Yugoslavia dissolved, recognition of its successor states was made contingent on

guarantees about their commitment to protecting human rights, minority rights and acceptance of international monitoring (see Crawford 2006: 395–402). In a very direct sense, recognition was related to the successor states' ability and willingness to discharge their sovereign responsibilities.

The renewed emphasis on human rights evident in this changing practice of recognition also lay behind the adoption of the language of sovereignty as responsibility by UN officials. The immediate catalyst was Boutros Boutros-Ghali's appointment of Francis Deng, a well-respected former Sudanese diplomat, as his Special Representative on Internally Displaced People (IDPs) in 1993. In appointing Deng and highlighting the problem of IDPs, Boutros-Ghali was responding to both urgent humanitarian need and a vexing political dilemma. As wars became less a matter between states and more a struggle between competing state and non-state actors, so the proportion of civilians killed and displaced increased. When Deng was appointed, there were some 25 million IDPs globally (Weiss 2007: 90). If these civilians had crossed an international border they would be entitled to claim refugee status, providing that their host was a signatory to the 1951 Refugee Convention or accepting the help of the UNHCR (see Davies 2007). As IDPs, however, they were afforded no special protection and remained vulnerable to the whims or failings of their home state (Deng 2004: 18). In order to argue his way around the use of sovereignty to deny assistance to IDPs, Deng and his collaborators put forward an account of sovereignty as responsibility, describing sovereignty as a state's responsibility to protect its neediest citizens. Where a state was unable to fulfil its responsibilities, it should invite and welcome international assistance to 'complement national efforts' (Deng 2004: 20).

Deng argued that international involvement aided rather than inhibited the realization of national sovereignty. The best way for a vulnerable or failing state to protect its sovereignty, he argued, was by inviting international assistance. For Deng, sovereignty as responsibility was partly a diplomatic tool for engaging recalcitrant states in the protection of IDPs. At its heart, the concept was based on Deng's 'positive' take on sovereignty, insisting that:

> Sovereignty carries with it certain responsibilities for which governments must be held accountable. And they are accountable not only to their national constituencies but ultimately to the international community. In other words, by effectively discharging its responsibilities for good governance, a state can legitimately claim protection for its national sovereignty.
>
> (Deng *et al.* 1996: 1)

According to Deng and his collaborators, troubled states could work with international actors to improve their citizens' living conditions or they could obstruct international efforts and forfeit their sovereignty (ibid.: 28).

But at what point could a state be judged to have forfeited its sovereignty, and what body had the right to decide? Deng and his collaborators were sketchy on these questions, but usefully suggested that sovereignty as responsibility implied the existence of a 'higher authority capable of holding supposed sovereigns accountable' and that this higher authority should place the common good ahead of the national interests of its members. Clearly, the UN Security Council is closest to fitting the bill, but it falls a long way short of Deng's ideal. The important point to note for our purposes, however, is that in his discussions with over thirty governments, confronting serious internal displacement issues, not a single leader challenged the assertion that sovereigns had responsibilities towards their own citizens.

In the late 1990s, two permanent members of the Security Council, the United States and United Kingdom, put forth their own ideas about sovereignty as responsibility which did little to promote consensus about Deng and Annan's ideas. For American policymakers associated with the Clinton and Bush administrations, responsible sovereignty was tied not just to human rights, but also to security imperatives such as WMD non-proliferation and anti-terrorism cooperation. A key advocate of the American conception of sovereignty as responsibility was Richard Haass, President of the Council on Foreign Relations and former Director of Policy Planning in Colin Powell's State Department. Haass argued that sovereignty should be conditional on human rights as well as a commitment to WMD non-proliferation and counter-terrorism (Haass 2002). Two years later, Stewart Patrick, one of Haass' colleagues at the State Department, elaborated, insisting that:

> Historically, the main obstacle to armed intervention, humanitarian or otherwise, has been the doctrine of sovereignty, which prohibits violating the territorial integrity of another state. One of the striking developments of the past decade has been an erosion of this non-intervention norm and the rise of a nascent doctrine of 'contingent sovereignty'. This school of thought holds that sovereign rights and immunities are not absolute. They depend on the observance of fundamental state obligations.
>
> (in Elden 2006: 15)

As Elden argues, Haas' conception of responsible sovereignty extended to judgements about state capacity (2006: 15). Thus, a state that was willing but unable to control terrorists within its borders could be subject to international intervention. This doctrine of sovereignty later became part of the US defence strategy, with the (2005) National Defence Strategy declaring that:

> It is unacceptable for regimes to use the principle of sovereignty as a shield behind which they can claim to be free to engage in activities that pose enormous threats to their citizens, neighbors, or the rest of the international community.... The US, its allies, and partners must remain vigilant to those states that lack the capacity to govern activity within their borders. Sovereign states are obliged to work to ensure that their territories are not used as bases for attacks on others.
>
> (Department of Defence 2005)

This doctrine partly informed Clinton's decision to intervene in Kosovo in 1999, and was subsequently associated with the 2001 intervention in Afghanistan and 2003 invasion of Iraq. As is now well known, this link between sovereignty as responsibility and George W. Bush's unpopular foreign policy created significant obstacles for those seeking to forge a global consensus on the Responsibility to Protect principle (see Evans 2004; Bellamy 2005).

NATO's 1999 intervention in Kosovo provided the catalyst for Tony Blair to put forth his own ideas about sovereignty as responsibility. From early 1998, when the Kosovo crisis erupted, Blair took a hawkish position. Having strongly criticized his Conservative predecessors for standing aside during the Bosnian bloodbath, Blair was a determined advocate of using force to prevent or halt Serbian ethnic cleansing in Kosovo. Shortly after NATO began its bombing campaign in 1999, Blair travelled to the United States to help Clinton shore up domestic support for the war. It was there that he gave a landmark speech, the first draft of which was penned by the British academic Sir Lawrence Freedman, which set out his 'doctrine of the international community' and conception of sovereignty as responsibility.

Blair famously argued that sovereignty should be reconceptualized because globalization was changing the world in ways that made traditional sovereignty anachronistic. According to Blair, global interconnectedness created a global responsibility to deal with egregious human suffering. Sovereigns acquired responsibilities to international society because domestic problems caused by massive human rights abuse, for example, spread across borders. According to Blair (1999):

> The most pressing foreign policy problem we face is to identify the circumstances in which we should get actively involved in other people's conflicts. Non-interference has long been considered an important principle of international order. And it is not one we would want to jettison too readily.... But the principle of non-interference must be qualified in important respects. Acts of genocide can never be a purely internal matter.

In order to balance respect for non-interference with concern for human rights, Blair proposed five tests to ascertain the legitimacy of intervention, setting in train a debate about criteria to guide decisions about armed intervention which crystallized in the work of the International Commission on Intervention and State Sovereignty.

In late 1999, the British Foreign Office circulated a draft paper on criteria to govern intervention to members of the Security Council (Kampfner 2003: 50–53). The paper went through several revisions, but was never made publicly available before being quietly dropped at around the same time as the controversy sparked by Annan's endorsement of the need to rethink the relationship between sovereignty and intervention erupted (see below) (Wheeler 2001: 564).

The adoption of variants of sovereignty as responsibility by the United States and United Kingdom attracted heavy criticism and undermined efforts to build consensus around Annan, Deng and Cohen's variant. Critics argued that the United States and United Kingdom were abusing and selectively applying a partial account of human rights to justify armed intervention in weak and mainly postcolonial states. Tellingly, however, criticisms like this predated the adoption of sovereignty as responsibility by Washington and London. When Deng first started talking about sovereignty as responsibility, he attracted withering criticism. During a 1993 debate in the UN Human Rights Commission, China stressed human rights and fundamental freedoms as a 'lofty goal of mankind', but delivered a broadside on sovereignty as responsibility. It argued against external interference in the internal affairs of states on the grounds that it represented 'self-interested' concepts of human rights and ideologies held by 'a few countries'. China argued:

> the practices of distorting human rights standards, exerting political pressure through abuse of monitoring mechanisms, applying selectivity and double standards have led to the violation of principles and purposes of the UN Charter, and the impairing of the sovereignty and dignity of many developing countries. Thus the beautiful term of human rights has been tarnished.

According to China, advocacy of sovereignty as responsibility amounted to nothing more than an attempt to legitimize the interference of the strong in the affairs of the developing world:

> The urgent issue is to remove as soon as possible the imposition of their own human rights concepts, values and ideology by a few countries who style themselves as "human rights judges": and the interference in internal affairs of other countries by using human rights as a means of applying political pressure. The victims of such practice are developing countries whose people suffered from violation of human rights and fundamental freedoms for a long time before and are now making great efforts to safeguard their sovereignty and independence for their survival and development.
>
> (UN Commission on Human Rights 1993)

Cuba joined the assault, linking Deng's work on IDPs to a doctrine of humanitarian intervention that constituted an attempt 'to forcibly impose certain ideological conceptions of human rights on a number of countries, chiefly, though not exclusively, in the Third World' (UN Commission on Human Rights 1993). Advocates of traditional sovereignty worried that by propounding sovereignty as responsibility, the West was setting itself up as both judge and jury in relation to a doctrine that lent the veneer of legitimacy to coercive interference in the affairs of sovereigns. This doctrine permitted the world's powerful states to impose their particular conception of human rights on the rest. Moreover, it allowed them to further their own self-interests by interfering in the affairs of others under the banner of human rights.

Within this context, Deng and Cohen recognized that they needed to clarify the legal standing and rights of IDPs as a foundation for building a case for their protection. This was achieved through the 'Guiding Principles' on IDPs set out in 1998. Deng and Cohen had rejected the idea of developing a new treaty on IDPs because international consensus was unlikely and treaty negotiations would be protracted. Instead, they worked with legal experts to define IDPs, identify the rights that they already enjoyed under existing human rights instruments, place those rights into the context of displacement and present them in the form of 'Guiding Principles'. The principles recognized that primary responsibility for displaced people rested with the local authorities but that consent to international aid should not be 'arbitrarily withheld', especially when the local authorities were unable or unwilling to provide the necessary assistance – a formula later borrowed by the ICISS.[1]

The 'Guiding Principles' have played an important role in improving the protection of IDPs. Kofi Annan (2005: paragraph 210), for example, described them as 'the basic international norm for protection', and the (2005) World Summit recognized them as 'the minimum international standard for the protection of internally displaced persons'. More concretely, the principles were endorsed by the UN's Inter Agency Standing Committee and regional organizations such as the OSCE and AU. ECOWAS called upon its members to disseminate and apply them, and several countries (Burundi, Colombia, the Philippines and Sri Lanka) have incorporated the principles into national law (Cohen 2006: 470). Of course the adoption of Guiding Principles does not necessarily translate into actual protection, but their adoption points towards growing acceptance of sovereignty as responsibility. The question of how much acceptance, and the agreed scope, of sovereignty as responsibility is taken up in the following section, which focuses on the international debate about NATO's 1999 intervention in Kosovo.

Kosovo

This section evaluates what the international debate about NATO's intervention in Kosovo can tell us about sovereignty as responsibility, in particular about its scope and the depth of international support for it. Focusing mainly on debates within the UN Security Council, it makes two principal arguments. First, all but NATO's staunchest critics accepted that the Yugoslav government was responsible for protecting its Kosovar Albanian citizens from killing and ethnic cleansing, and that it was legitimate for international society to be engaged in the crisis. In other words, there was broad support for the basic tenets of sovereignty as responsibility. Second, the sharpest disagreements concerned not the principle itself, but the most appropriate way of acting upon it. The first disagreement revolved around the practical question of the capacity of military force to resolve the crisis, and the second concerned the locus of appropriate international authority for the use of force. As such, although not apparent at the time amidst the controversy sparked by the intervention, Kosovo helped lay the foundations for the grand consensus on sovereignty as responsibility, reached in 2005, by highlighting the fact that international disagreement was focused more on the modalities than on the principle of sovereignty as responsibility.

The background to the Kosovo crisis is well known, and will not be rehearsed here (see Judah 2000; Bellamy 2002). From the outset of the crisis, the European response, if somewhat indecisive, was rapid and based on the presumptions that ethnic cleansing and other human rights abuses were illegitimate and that external actors had a legitimate role to play in bringing abuses to an end, protecting vulnerable civilians and holding the perpetrators of abuse to account. Whilst US Secretary of State Madeleine Albright immediately intimated the possibility of military intervention, German Foreign Minister Klaus Kinkel advocated a multi-pronged approach that involved strengthening NATO's presence in Macedonia and the WEU's mission in Albania and embarking on a joint EU–OSCE peace process (in Bellamy 2008: 246). Kinkel's proposed diplomatic route prevailed, and European efforts were supported by a relatively early UN Security Council Resolution 1160 (31 March 1998) (UN Security Council 1998a).

Resolution 1160 was adopted under Chapter VII of the Charter, recognizing that the emerging conflict in Kosovo posed a 'threat to international peace and security'. The resolution called for an end to the violence, imposed an arms embargo on Yugoslavia, voiced support for the non-violent opposition movement in Kosovo and called upon both sides to cooperate with international efforts to broker a negotiated settlement. Significantly, the Resolution also condemned both the Yugoslav authorities and the KLA. For our purposes, the significance of Resolution 1160 lay not in the specifics of what it said about the crisis but in its recognition that the situation in Kosovo warranted international engagement because, in part, the Yugoslav authorities were failing in their sovereign responsibilities. To be sure, the Resolution's adoption at a relatively early stage in the crisis caused significant unease within the Russian and Chinese governments in particular, both of which abstained, arguing that the situation in Kosovo was a domestic matter that fell within Yugoslavia's jurisdiction (UN Security Council 1998a). China argued that Security Council intervention in internal matters such as this was likely to set a negative precedent for the future. Their concerns forced the resolution's drafters to insert passages reaffirming Yugoslavia's sovereignty and territorial integrity. On the other hand, the majority of Council members argued that human rights abuses in Kosovo constituted a clear threat to regional peace and security (see Wheeler 2000: 259; Welsh 2008: 548–549).

Although Russia had expressed concerns about international engagement in what it saw as a domestic matter, its position began to change after the passage of Resolution 1160, leaving China isolated as the only member of the Security Council arguing against Council activism on the grounds of domestic jurisdiction. In other words, from mid-1998 onwards China was more or less alone in arguing that the manner of Yugoslavia's treatment of its own citizens was not a matter of international concern. This gradual transformation of Russia's position on Kosovo is a critical part of the broader process of widening the consensus on sovereignty as responsibility, and is worth considering in detail.

Immediately after the passage of Resolution 1160, Russia began to work on a pathway for lifting the sanctions against Yugoslavia. Milošević assured Russian diplomats that his Interior Ministry forces had been withdrawn from the province as requested by the Security Council, and this was enough to persuade Russia to begin arguing the case for lifting sanctions on the grounds that Yugoslavia was in compliance with the Council's requests (Russian Federation 1998a, 1998b). Russia still opposed international mediation on the grounds that the Kosovo conflict was a domestic matter, but by engaging in diplomacy that linked the lifting of sanctions with Yugoslav compliance with the Security Council's demands, Russia was forced to tacitly accept some of the tenets of sovereignty as responsibility; most clearly, the idea that international recognition was properly connected to domestic behaviour.

It became clear relatively quickly that, despite its assurances to the Russian government, Yugoslavia was not in compliance with the Security Council's request that it withdraw Interior Ministry forces from Kosovo. In April 1998, the EU reported that although government violence had decreased, Interior Ministry units had not been withdrawn and were being used to restrict movement inside Kosovo (EU 1998). Amidst heightened calls in the West for tougher sanctions and armed intervention, Russian President Boris Yeltsin stepped in to persuade Milošević to comply with the resolution. Yeltsin convinced Milošević to comply with three of the Council's four demands. This included a commitment to negotiate on all aspects of the Kosovo problem, including the question of autonomy; an agreement to refrain from further violence against the civilian population of Kosovo; and a commitment to grant unimpeded access to humanitarian organizations such as the ICRC and UNHCR. Milošević also agreed to withdraw paramilitary forces from Kosovo once the KLA ceased violent attacks (see Youngs 1998: 28). At one level, this was a major diplomatic coup that outmanoeuvred the West. At a deeper level, however, it represented an intensifying of Russia's entanglement in sovereignty as responsibility. Negotiating a cessation of hostilities, and commitments to protect civilians and accept unimpeded humanitarian by emphasizing a sovereign's responsibility to its own people (and international society), is precisely the stuff of sovereignty as responsibility as envisaged by Deng and Cohen.

Yeltsin's diplomatic triumph was short-lived. Having promised to restrain Yugoslav forces in Kosovo, Milošević permitted the Yugoslav army to reinforce its positions in the province and, within a month of the deal, the army's tanks were being employed against villages on the outskirts of Pristina. In response, the Russian position vis-à-vis Yugoslavia palpably hardened and was made manifest by its vote in support of a tougher UN Security Council Resolution, 1199 (23 September 1999) (UN Security Council 1999a). Resolution 1199 was passed with fourteen votes in favour and a Chinese abstention.

Like its predecessor, Resolution 1199 was passed under Chapter VII, and specifically identified the 'deterioration' of the situation in Kosovo as a threat to international peace and security. The resolution demanded (rather than requested) a cessation of hostilities, and that the leadership of both sides take urgent steps to 'avert the impending humanitarian catastrophe'. The Council also insisted that it would consider further measures in the event of non-compliance. Although Russia supported the Resolution, it stressed that it did not authorize military force or impose further sanctions (UN Security Council 1998b). China was now alone in arguing that it could not support the resolution, but felt the need to supplement its argument that the crisis in Kosovo was a domestic matter and therefore not a threat to international peace and security with the pragmatic argument that threatening Yugoslavia with punitive measures 'would adversely affect the possibilities of a peaceful settlement to the conflict' (UN Security Council 1998b).

My point here is that prior to NATO's intervention in Kosovo, there was a broad consensus (though not unanimity) that Yugoslavia was not entitled to treat its citizens however it saw fit and had a duty to alleviate human suffering in Kosovo. Specifically, Resolution 1199 imposed on Yugoslavia obligations to 'cease hostilities' and 'take immediate steps to improve the humanitarian situation', and made the Yugoslav authorities accountable to the Security Council by deciding that further measures would be considered in the case of non-compliance. Of course, the consensus that Yugoslavia had sovereign responsibilities did not translate into agreement on the most effective and legitimate means of ensuring that the Yugoslav government complied with its responsibilities. This point was made abundantly clear by the debate that followed the launch of NATO's intervention in early 1999.

A day after NATO launched Operation Allied Force in March 1999, Russia introduced a draft resolution demanding an immediate cessation of hostilities against Yugoslavia. In line with Russia's position on Resolution 1199, the draft resolution limited itself to criticizing the use of force as a breach of Article 2(4) of the Charter and recalling the Council's primacy on matters of international peace and security, and did not imply a position on the question of Yugoslavia's actions in Kosovo (UN Security Council 1999b). Nonetheless, the resolution was heavily defeated by twelve to three, with only Russia, China and Namibia voting in favour. Among the states voting against the resolution were Argentina, Bahrain, Brazil, Gabon, Gambia and Malaysia. Whilst the vote cannot be understood as retrospective endorsement or authorization for the intervention, it was indicative of broader sentiment regarding Yugoslavia's failure to fulfil its responsibilities in Kosovo.

Russia's criticism of NATO centred on two arguments, both of which focused on the intervention's modalities rather than the appropriateness of international engagement with domestic human rights issues. The first was that NATO did not have the authority to make determinations about when to use force in circumstances like this. Only the UN Security Council had that authority. As Sergei Lavrov told the Council – somewhat ironically, given his 2008 defence of Russian intervention in Georgia on human rights grounds,

> the members of NATO are not entitled to decide the fate of other sovereign and independent States. They must not forget that they are not only members

of their alliance, but also Members of the United Nations, and that it is their obligation to be guided by the United Nations Charter.

(UN Security Council 1999a)

Two days later, Lavrov extended his argument by suggesting that the unilateral use of force by NATO challenged the Council's authority and thereby threatened international order more generally:

members of the Security Council bear a special responsibility not only to their peoples but to all Members of the United Nations, upon which decisions of the Council are binding under the Charter. Today's vote is not just on the problem of Kosovo. It goes directly to the authority of the Security Council in the eyes of the world community.

(UN Security Council 1999c)

Stressing that it did not condone 'violations of international humanitarian law by any party', Russia's second argument was that NATO's intervention was likely to make the humanitarian crisis in Kosovo worse and hinder attempts to broker a peace settlement. Tacitly recognizing that Yugoslavia was indeed violating humanitarian law, Lavrov insisted that 'it is possible to combat violations of the law only with clean hands and only on the solid basis of law'. 'Lawlessness' he argued 'would spawn lawlessness' (UN Security Council 1999a). The use of force undermined political and diplomatic efforts to yield a settlement to the crisis and caused 'severe humanitarian consequences' (UN Security Council 1999c).

This basic claim – that it was not the principle of sovereign responsibility but the modalities of unilateral armed intervention that was the nub of the problem – was further emphasized by Namibia, which joined China in supporting Russia's draft resolution. Indeed, Namibia's argument opened with a relatively clear endorsement of sovereignty as responsibility. Its Ambassador opened by pointing out that

the current crisis in the Serbian province of Kosovo ... is a source of great concern to us. The degree of brutality perpetrated on the civilian population, the massacre of women, children and the elderly, the displacement of people from their homes, kidnappings and the wanton destruction of property continue to take place in Kosovo.

(UN Security Council 1999a)

However, Namibia argued, military action against Yugoslavia 'may not be the solution'. Such action was unlikely to serve the cause of peace in Kosovo, and could destabilize the wider region (UN Security Council 1999a). As with Russia, Namibia doubted neither Yugoslavia's responsibilities towards its own citizens nor the appropriateness of international engagement. Under doubt were the practical merits of NATO's course of action. Other states such as India and

Belarus that joined the Security Council debate made broadly similar points (UN Security Council 1999a, 1999c).

Among NATO's prominent critics, only China continued to question the legitimacy of international engagement in what it saw as an essentially 'domestic' matter, though in the March 1999 debates China augmented this claim with arguments about the Security Council's primacy even at the expense of adopting a somewhat contradictory position. Thus, China continued to maintain that 'the question of Kosovo, as an internal matter of the Federal Republic of Yugoslavia, should be resolved among the parties concerned in the Federal Republic of Yugoslavia themselves', and reaffirmed its opposition to 'interference in the internal affairs of other States, under whatever pretext or in whatever form' (UN Security Council 1999a). China also joined Russia in criticizing NATO's decision to bypass the Security Council. The slight contradiction that crept into China's position was its statement that a political settlement for Kosovo should guarantee 'the legitimate rights and interests of all ethnic groups in the Kosovo region' (UN Security Council 1999a). This implies that the Yugoslav government was not entirely free to determine the terms of the peace settlement, and that it is indeed legitimate for external actors to expect that the 'legitimate rights and interests' of ethnic groups be respected by sovereigns.

It goes without saying that NATO and its allies defended the intervention by arguing that ethnic cleansing by government forces in Kosovo created a moral imperative to act. Interestingly, though, many of the non-aligned states that joined with NATO in voting down Russia's draft resolution referred to Yugoslavia's failure to fulfil its responsibilities as the primary reason for their votes. Clearest in this regard were Argentina, Gambia and Malaysia, all of which used language reminiscent of sovereignty as responsibility. Argentina argued that states have an 'obligation to protect and ensure respect' the fundamental legal norms set out by international humanitarian law, an obligation it considered all the more urgent in the case of Kosovo given evidence of genocide committed four years earlier in Bosnia (UN Security Council 1999c). Gambia, meanwhile, plainly stated that 'it is the responsibility of any Government to protect its citizens', maintaining that it regretted the fact that the Security Council had been unable to establish a consensus on how to protect the people of Kosovo. Presaging its decision to vote against Russia's draft, Gambia insisted that 'we cannot remain indifferent to the plight of the murdered people of Kosovo' (UN Security Council 1999a). Similarly, Malaysia regretted the Council's inability to reach a consensus but insisted that 'the Yugoslav leadership bears full responsibility' for the failure of the political process. 'Such a tragic situation', Malaysia argued, 'calls for appropriate and prompt action by the international community' (UN Security Council 1999c).

Although the Non-Aligned Movement stood firmly opposed to NATO's use of force without Security Council authorization, the Organization of the Islamic Conferences issued a letter to the Security Council expressing sympathy with NATO's cause, condemning the ethnic cleansing of Kosovar Albanians, demanding an immediate cessation of hostilities, and insisting that the Yugoslav government accept the terms of the Rambouillet Peace Plan (UN Security Council 1999d). A significant number of states, including Mexico, South Africa and India, expressed concern that the Yugoslav government had failed to fulfil its responsibilities to its own citizens, and disquiet about the unilateral use of force without UN Security Council authorization (see Schnabel and Thakur 2000).

In summary, with the benefit of hindsight it seems clear that the furore about the legitimacy and legality of NATO's intervention in Kosovo masked the emergence of a deeper consensus around the concept of sovereignty as responsibility enunciated by Deng and Cohen. All except one member of the Security Council (China) accepted that the Yugoslav government had a responsibility to protect its Kosovar Albanian citizens from grave breaches of international humanitarian law, and that, as the government was at best struggling and at worst manifestly failing to fulfil its responsibilities, it fell to the Security Council to adopt measures aimed at ending the violence and settling the dispute in a manner that protected the 'legitimate rights and interests' of Kosovo's ethnic groups. The underlying debates in 1999 did not primarily relate to this first-order question of whether sovereigns have responsibilities to protect the fundamental rights of their citizens and whether international society has a duty to act when a sovereign is struggling or failing to fulfil those responsibilities, but to second-order questions about the most efficacious way of protecting those fundamental rights and the appropriate sources of authority for the use of force. As such, beneath the vitriol and furore sparked by NATO's intervention, and American and British attempts to develop a doctrine of sovereign responsibility that would legitimize armed intervention (see above), was an emerging consensus about sovereignty as responsibility. In order to clarify and codify that consensus as a prelude to encouraging states to formally recognize their sovereign responsibilities, hard questions about the scope of those responsibilities, the range of available measures to fulfil those responsibilities, and decision-making about the use of force to protect fundamental rights needed answers. The controversy sparked by NATO's intervention in Kosovo prompted a range of actors to begin seeking answers to these questions. The next section briefly charts those efforts.

Towards responsibility to protect

This section briefly examines the role of Kosovo as a catalyst for the subsequent development of sovereignty as responsibility. In the months and years that immediately followed the intervention, the broad consensus on sovereignty as responsibility was obscured by debates about the 'right' of humanitarian intervention and the relative weight of sovereignty and human rights, obscuring ideas that posited sovereignty and human rights as two sides of the same coin (see Reus-Smit 2001). This was reflected in the creation of an International Commission on Intervention and State Sovereignty (ICISS) charged with reconciling the two. In reformulating the debate's language, the ICISS revived Deng and Cohen's conception of sovereignty as responsibility (though without directly mentioning it), and thus tapped into a pre-existing consensus about the basic responsibilities that sovereigns owe to their citizens. This basic idea laid the foundations for a new grand consensus on sovereignty, announced in 2005, which went a long way towards addressing the questions of scope, appropriate measures and legitimate authority left over from Kosovo. This whole process was propelled by NATO's intervention in Kosovo.

To understand the immediate dilemmas posed by NATO's intervention, it is worth focusing on their impact on the UN Secretary General's efforts to build international consensus around the notion of responsible sovereignty articulated in his *Economist* article discussed earlier. It was clear from the outset of the Kosovo crisis in 1998 that there would be little likelihood of consensus in the Security Council about armed intervention, owing to NATO's determination to proceed and Russian and Chinese opposition. It was in this atmosphere that Annan took on the role of 'norm entrepreneur' and delivered his 1998 lecture to the Ditchley Foundation on the subject of 'intervention'. On the one hand, Annan recognized that the UN's failure to halt the bloodletting in Rwanda and Bosnia had badly hurt the organization and undermined its credibility. On the other hand, he believed in the sanctity of the UN Charter, including Article 2(4). He also recognized that it would be difficult, if not impossible, to persuade a majority of member states of the case for humanitarian intervention. Trying to balance these two imperatives, the Secretary General insisted that certain responsibilities were inherent to sovereignty and embedded in the UN Charter (Annan 1998). Annan then appealed to supporters of traditional sovereignty by highlighting the dangers associated with licensing individual states to decide the case for intervention for themselves. 'Surely', he continued,

> the only institution competent to assume that role is the Security Council of the United Nations. The Charter clearly assigns responsibility to the Council for maintaining international peace and security. I would argue, therefore, that only the Council has the authority to decide that the internal situation in any state is so grave as to justify forceful intervention ... humanity is ill-served when the Council is unable to react quickly and decisively in a crisis.

The real challenge, Annan maintained, was to prevent crises from emerging in the first place. To do this, member states should work through UN bodies and agencies to tackle the underlying causes of humanitarian crises. This, of course, was precisely what Deng was getting at.

The 'Ditchley formula', as it became known, was put to the test by the crisis in Kosovo. The intervention sparked fierce debate within Annan's office. Some, such as his American special advisor John Ruggie, Edward Mortimer, and Annan's deputy, Iqbal Rizza, supported NATO and recommended that the Secretary General do likewise. Others, such as Kieran Prendergast (Head of the Department of Political Affairs) and Sashi Tharoor (future candidate for Secretary General), criticized the violation of Article 2(4) and argued that Annan should do the same (Traub 2006: 97). The two sides squabbled over the wording of UN memos and reports, over the culpability of the KLA and the extent of ethnic cleansing. Trying to pick his way through the morass, the Secretary General issued an even-handed statement the day after the intervention began (in Meisler 2007: 177–178).

Many non-aligned countries saw Annan's statement as a tacit endorsement of NATO, but NATO countries themselves were disappointed by the Secretary General's decision not to offer forthright support. As such, relations between the UN and NATO remained tense. Albright took offence at an Annan statement deploring the loss of civilian lives. When Yeltsin proposed that Annan be invited to broker a political settlement, Clinton rejected it on the grounds that he would not permit the UN to negotiate on NATO's behalf (Meisler 2007: 179). To make matters worse, the perception that Annan had tacitly supported the intervention did nothing for the Secretary General's ambition to sell a new doctrine of responsible sovereignty.

In the wake of Kosovo, Annan created a working group, including people from both sides of the debate, to explore the question of the post-Kosovo security framework. Over time, the group became more sceptical about Annan's association with humanitarian intervention. Lakhdar Brahimi, a diplomat of high standing and Chair of the UN's Panel on Peace Operations, argued that by associating itself with humanitarian intervention, the UN risked being abused by powerful states to the detriment of the organization as a whole. On the other side, Edward Mortimer pointed out that it was the UN's failures in Rwanda and Bosnia that had done more than anything else to discredit the organization (Traub 2006: 99). Grasping for a way to meaningfully bridge the divide, Mortimer agreed that it was necessary to find a new way of talking about intervention that emphasized 'relieving human suffering' rather than military action and the legal rights of interveners (ibid.: 100). The Secretary General, in other words, needed to adopt the concept of sovereignty as responsibility advocated by Deng six years earlier.

Over the coming months, Annan tackled the issue head-on, writing the 'two concepts of sovereignty' essay described earlier and using his opening Address to the 1999 General Assembly to set the terms of the forthcoming debate. Tacitly adopting Deng's approach to sovereignty, Annan argued that states were the servants of their people and that the 'sovereignty of the individual' was enhanced by growing respect for human rights. State sovereignty therefore implied a responsibility to protect individual sovereigns. The role of the UN was to assist states in fulfilling their responsibilities and strengthening their sovereignty. The question, however, was one of how to determine the 'common interest' in hard cases. In a case such as Kosovo, did sovereignty as responsibility require intervention, and, if so, who was entitled to decide?

The Secretary General did not have to wait long for the debate to begin, and the adoption of sovereignty as responsibility did little to stem the tide of opposition. The third speaker after Annan, President Abdelaziz Bouteflika of Algeria, issued a strong rebuke to the Secretary General, insisting that his country was extremely sensitive to any undermining of our sovereignty, not only because sovereignty is our final defence against the rules of an unjust world, but because we have no active part in the decision-making process in the Security Council nor in monitoring the implementation of decisions.... We firmly believe that interference in internal affairs may take place only with the consent of the State in question.

(in Traub 2006: 101; Meisler 2007: 186)

Later that day, Theo-Ben Gurirab, the Namibian Ambassador and President of the General Assembly, used a toast at a diplomatic cocktail party to further criticize Annan's speech in a move described as 'an astonishing breach of etiquette' (Traub 2006: 101).

The key problem was that using the language of sovereign responsibility in the context of a debate about armed intervention in Kosovo challenged the underlying consensus evident in debates about the Yugoslav government's behaviour in its southern province by connecting sovereignty as responsibility with the potential legitimization of unilateral military intervention – something that Deng and Cohen had studiously avoided. Within this context, it is not surprising that the ICISS was primarily focused on the question of intervention and that this had the effect of limiting support for the Responsibility to Protect among states concerned about its potential to be a 'Trojan horse' for military intervention (see Bellamy 2005, 2009a, 2009b).

The main findings and recommendations of the 2001 ICISS report, in particular its concept of 'Responsibility to Protect', are well known and need not be rehearsed again (ICISS 2001). Although it did not specifically refer to Deng and Cohen, the report was essentially a re-articulation of sovereignty as responsibility. Its findings were premised on the notion that when states are unwilling or unable to protect their citizens from grave harm, the principle of non-interference 'yields to the responsibility to protect'. The Responsibility to Protect was intended as a way of escaping intractable debates about humanitarian intervention by focusing not on what interveners are entitled to do ('a right of intervention') but on what is necessary to protect people in dire need and the responsibilities of various actors to afford such protection. Taking a lead from Annan and Deng, the ICISS argued that the Responsibility to Protect was about much more than just armed intervention. In addition to a 'responsibility to react' to massive human suffering, international society also had responsibilities to use non-violent tools to prevent such suffering, and rebuild polities and societies afterwards. Rather than viewing sovereignty and human rights as antagonistic, the Responsibility to Protect sees them as mutually supporting.

Despite these efforts, the Responsibility to Protect continued to be associated with unilateral intervention, undermining consensus on the concept itself as well as masking the underlying consensus on sovereignty as responsibility evident in international debates about Kosovo. It is important to recognize that the persistent association of the Responsibility to Protect with humanitarian intervention was not a product of a failure to point out the differences. From the very outset,

ICISS and its principal supporters have been at pains to distinguish the two and to embed non-consensual force within the broader continuum of measures (Evans 2004; Thakur 2006). In his own blueprint for UN reform, 'In Larger Freedom', Annan tried to put clear distance between the Responsibility to Protect and humanitarian intervention by separating the commitment to the Responsibility to Protect principle from a proposal that judgements about the use of force be guided by criteria. By so doing, Annan hoped to reinforce the view that the Responsibility to Protect was not primarily about the use of force but, in the words of William Pace and Nicole Deller (2005: 25), 'a normative and moral undertaking requiring a state to protect its own citizens'. Yet, despite Annan's efforts, the association persisted for three principal reasons.

First, the Responsibility to Protect had its genesis in a debate about unilateral armed intervention, and there were notable attempts to use the concept to justify the 2003 invasion of Iraq. Second, many commentators and academics fail to properly distinguish the Responsibility to Protect from unilateral armed intervention. There are too many instances of this to permit anything more than illustrative examples. For instance, Alicia Bannon (2006: 1158) argued that the Responsibility to Protect 'strengthens the legal justification for limited forms of unilateral and regional action – including military action – if the United Nations fails to act to protect populations from genocide and other atrocities'; Stephen John Stedman, who served as an advisor to Kofi Annan with responsibility for actualizing the Secretary General's reform agenda, argued that Annan's agenda included 'a new norm, the responsibility to protect, to legalize humanitarian intervention' (Stedman 2007: 933). Of course, this is precisely what Annan hoped to avoid by distinguishing so carefully between the Responsibility to Protect and the use of force. Finally, despite protestations to the contrary, the ICISS report was – in fact – primarily concerned with humanitarian intervention, and not with setting out and advocating a broad continuum of measures to prevent and halt genocide and mass atrocities. The prevention and rebuilding aspects were covered by the report in only sixteen pages, compared with thirty-two pages given to intervention. The report was therefore clearly more interested in intervention than in the prevention and rebuilding aspects of the continuum.

The association between the Responsibility to Protect and unilateral intervention was a key barrier to consensus, and masked the deeper consensus on sovereignty as responsibility. It is important, however, to distinguish between two groups of states who remained sceptical about, if not outright opposed to, the Responsibility to Protect and sovereignty as responsibility. For some of the more radical opponents of sovereignty as responsibility, such as Cuba, Algeria, Iran, Zimbabwe, Sudan and Venezuela, the issue was one of forestalling any moves to relinquish sovereignty to international actors, and not just one of concerns about non-consensual armed intervention. We should distinguish this unreconstructed defence of absolutist sovereignty levelled by a few states from the concerns raised by more influential states such as India, the Philippines and Russia. For these states, deep-seated scepticism towards intervention did not necessarily translate into a rejection of sovereignty as responsibility, just unease with its modalities. This is perhaps best demonstrated by noting the shift in China's position. Whereas China had stood alone in the Council arguing that Kosovo was a domestic matter, in its 2005 position paper on UN Reform China insisted that 'massive humanitarian' crises were 'the legitimate concern of the international community' (Government of China 2005).

The key to forging a new grand consensus on sovereignty as responsibility lay in addressing the source of these concerns. Most states that express scepticism towards unilateral intervention are not principally concerned with armed interventions genuinely inspired by humanitarian concerns and aimed at preventing or reversing genocide and mass atrocities. After all, sceptics such as India, China, Pakistan and Bangladesh are among the largest contributors to UN peace operations, and have allowed their forces to engage in armed enforcement operations to protect civilians in eastern Congo, Haiti and elsewhere. Similarly, during the 1994 genocide in Rwanda no state argued that Rwandan sovereignty precluded armed intervention. What concerns states like India is that unilateral intervention, if legitimized in principle, will be used to justify non-genuine humanitarian interventions – in other words, the use of force for principally self-interested reasons (see Pattison 2007: 308–314).

After the Responsibility to Protect was put on the international agenda by Kofi Annan's call for it to be adopted by the General Assembly, the negotiating process revealed a relatively small group of states that were opposed to the underlying principle and able to use a combination of influence within the Non-Aligned Movement (NAM) and G77, and heightened post-Iraq sensitivities about unilateral intervention, to create powerful obstacles to its adoption. The negotiations also revealed that the Responsibility to Protect had many more supporters than opponents, and that many of those supporters – such as South Africa, Rwanda, Ghana, Zambia, Nigeria, Chile, Guatemala, Mexico and Argentina – were members of the Non-Aligned and G77 blocs that had typically sought to limit the advance of sovereignty as responsibility. A majority of states, and most NAM/G77 members, sat somewhere between these two positions and shared the Chinese and Indian positions noted earlier. That is, they accepted the Responsibility to Protect in principle but remained concerned about the potential for it to be abused by great powers, opposed to efforts that may weaken the rules governing recourse to force, and sceptical about the West's commitment to the full range of the Responsibility to Protect continuum, especially prevention. This in turn raised concerns that the Responsibility to Protect would open the door to self-interested Western interventionism rather than to genuine collective efforts to rid the world of genocide and mass atrocities (see Wheeler 2005). In some regions, most notably Southeast Asia and Africa, these concerns have translated into the view that the Responsibility to Protect is best administered by relevant regional organizations paying due respect for regional norms and security cultures (see, for example, Morada 2006).

Given this and the broad consensus on sovereignty as responsibility evident in the debate about NATO's intervention in Kosovo, it is not surprising that agreement was reached on the adoption, in 2005, of the Responsibility to Protect. Key to forging that consensus was clarification of the principle's scope and the question of where the authority to use force lay. By limiting the scope to genocide, war crimes, ethnic cleansing and crimes against humanity, and insisting that only the Security Council was permitted to authorize the use of force, proponents of the Responsibility to Protect succeeded in allaying fears that a statement of principle on sovereignty as responsibility would open the door to unilateral intervention.

Conclusion

With the benefit of hindsight, it is clear that NATO's intervention in Kosovo played an important role in embodying and catalysing the principle of sovereignty as responsibility. Security Council debates about the merits of NATO's decision to intervene focused on second-order questions about the modalities for intervention and revealed a deeper consensus about sovereignty as responsibility, with only China arguing that the crisis was an entirely domestic affair. However, the furore about the legitimacy and legality of intervention masked this deeper consensus, and the invocation of sovereignty as responsibility immediately after the intervention linked the two together. This linkage made it difficult to persuade states to commit to sovereignty as responsibility and the Responsibility to Protect for fear of tacitly legitimizing unilateral armed intervention. In this sense, Kosovo damaged the prospects of sovereignty as responsibility in the short term. In the longer term, however, the impetus it created for resolving apparent tensions between sovereignty and human rights most clearly manifested in the ICISS and the activism of Kofi Annan helped progress and clarify the scope and meaning of sovereignty as responsibility and the appropriate licensing authority for the use of force. The product was the grand consensus on sovereignty set out in paragraphs 138–140 of the (2005) World Summit Outcome Document and, in particular, the commitment to sovereignty as responsibility quoted at the very beginning of this chapter. Whatever its other merits or failings, NATO's intervention in Kosovo played an important part in helping to identify and forge this consensus.

Note

1 Principles 3 and 25 of the Guiding Principles on Internal Displacement. For a detailed explanation and commentary, see Kalin (2000).

References

Annan, K. (1998) 'Intervention', Ditchley Foundation lecture, 26 June.
Annan, K. (1999a) 'Two Concepts of Sovereignty', *The Economist*, 18 September.
Annan, K. (1999b) 'Annual Report of the Secretary-General to the General Assembly', 20 September.
Annan, K. (2005) 'In Larger Freedom: Towards Development, Security and Human Rights for All', A/59/2005, 21 March.
Bannon, A. L. (2006) 'The Responsibility to Protect: The UN World Summit and the Question of Unilateralism', *Yale Law Journal*, 115: 1156–1165.

Bellamy, A. J. (2002) *Kosovo and International Society*, New York, NY: Palgrave Macmillan.

Bellamy, A. J. (2005) 'Responsibility to Protect or Trojan Horse? The Crisis in Darfur and Humanitarian Intervention after Iraq', *Ethics and International Affairs*, 19/2: 31–54.

Bellamy, A. J. (2008) 'Geopolitics and Solidarity on the Borders of Europe: The Yugoslav Wars of Succession', in J. M. Coicaud and N. J. Wheeler (eds) *National Interest and International Solidarity: Particular and Universal Ethics in International Life*, Tokyo: UN University Press.

Bellamy, A. J. (2009a) *Responsibility to Protect: The Global Effort to End Mass Atrocities*, Cambridge: Polity.

Bellamy, A. J. (2009b) 'Realizing the Responsibility to Protect', *International Studies Perspectives*, 10/1: 18–35.

Blair, T. (1999) 'Doctrine of the International Community', speech to the Economic Club of Chicago, Hilton Hotel, Chicago, 22 April.

Bukovansky, M. (2002) *Legitimacy and Power Politics: The American and French Revolutions in International Political Culture*, Princeton, NJ: Princeton University Press.

Byers, M. (1999) *Custom, Power and the Power of Rules: International Relations and Customary International Law*, Cambridge: Cambridge University Press.

Chomsky, N. (1999) *The New Military Humanism: Lessons from Kosovo*, London: Pluto Press.

Cohen, R. (2006) 'Developing an International System for Internally Displaced Persons', *International Studies Perspectives*, 7/2: 87–101.

Crawford, J. (2006) *The Creation of States in International Law*, 2nd edn, Oxford: Oxford University Press.

Davies, S. E. (2007) *Legitimising Rejection? International Refugee Law in Southeast Asia*, The Hague: Martinus Nijhoff.

Deng, F. M. (2004) 'The Impact of State Failure on Migration', *Mediterranean Quarterly*, 15/4: 16–36.

Deng, F. M., Kimaro, S., Lyons, T., Rotchild, D. and Zartman, I. W. (1996) *Sovereignty as Responsibility: Conflict Management in Africa*, Washington, DC: The Brookings Institution.

Department of Defence (2005) 'The National Defense Strategy of the United States of America', March. Available: www.globalsecurity.org/military/library/policy/dod/nds-usa_mar(2005).htm (accessed February 2009).

Elden, S. (2006) 'Contingent Sovereignty, Territorial Integrity and the Sanctity of Borders', *SAIS Review*, 26/1: 11–24.

EU (1998) 'European Union Report on the Situation in Kosovo', annex to United Nations press release, S/1998/361, 21 April.

Evans, G. (2004) 'When is it Right to Fight?', *Survival*, 46/3: 59–82.

Government of China (2005) 'Position Paper of the People's Republic of China on the United Nations Reform', June 7. Available: www.china-un.org/eng/smhwj/2005/t199101.htm (accessed September 2009).

Haass, R. N. (2002) 'Defining US Foreign Policy in a Post-Cold War World', The 2002 Arthur Ross Lecture, 22 April.

Hunt, L. (2007) *Inventing Human Rights: A History*, London: W. W. Norton.

ICISS (Independent Commission on Intervention and State Sovereignty) (2001) *The Responsibility to Protect*, Ottawa: International Development Research Centre.

Judah, T. (2000) *Kosovo: War and Revenge*, London: Yale University Press.

Kalin, W. (2000) 'Guiding Principles on Internal Displacement: Annotations', *American*

Society of International Law Studies in Transnational Legal Policy, 32, Washington, DC: American Society of International Law/Brookings Institution.

Kampfner, J. (2003) *Blair's Wars*, London: The Free Press.

Meisler, S. (2007) *Kofi Annan: A Man of Peace in a World of War*, London: John Wiley.

Morada, N. M. (2006) 'R2P Roadmap in Southeast Asia: Challenges and Prospects', UNISCI Discussion Papers, No. 11, May.

Pace, W. R. and Deller, N. (2005) 'Preventing Future Genocides: An International Responsibility to Protect', *World Order*, 36/4: 15–30.

Pattison, J. (2007) 'Humanitarian Intervention and International Law: The Moral Importance of an Intervener's Legal Status', *Critical Review of International, Social and Political Philosophy*, 10/3: 301–319.

Reus-Smit, C. (2001) 'Human Rights and the Social Construction of Sovereignty', *Review of International Studies*, 27/4: 519–538.

Russian Federation (1998a) 'Statement by the Spokesman of the Ministry of Foreign Affairs of the Russian Federation', 2 April.

Russian Federation (1998b) 'Memorandum by the Russian Federation', 14 April.

Schnabel, A. and Thakur, R. (eds) (2000) *Kosovo and the Challenge of Humanitarian Intervention: Selective Indignation, Collective Action, and International Citizenship*, Tokyo: UN University Press.

Stedman, S. J. (2007) 'UN Transformation in an era of Soft Balancing', *International Affairs*, 83/5: 933–944.

Thakur, R. (2006) *The United Nations, Peace and Security: From Collective Security to the Responsibility to Protect*, Cambridge: Cambridge University Press.

Traub, J. (2006) *The Best Intentions: Kofi Annan and the UN in an Era of American Power*, London: Bloomsbury.

UN Commission on Human Rights (1993) 'Responses of Governments and Agencies to the Report of the UN Special Representative for Internally Displaced Persons', E/CN.4/1993/SR.40.

UN Security Council (1998a) Security Council 3868th Meeting, S/PV.3868, 31 March.

UN Security Council (1998b) Security Council 3930th Meeting, S/PV.3930, 23 September.

UN Security Council (1999a) Security Council 3988th Meeting, S/PV.3988, 24 March.

UN Security Council (1999b) 'Belarus, India and Russian Federation: Draft Resolution', S/1999/328, 26 March.

UN Security Council (1999c) Security Council 3988th Meeting, S/PV.3989, 24 March.

UN Security Council (1999d) 'Letter dated 7 April 1999 from the Permanent Representative of the Islamic Republic of Iraq to the UN addressed to the President of the Security Council', S/1999/394, 7 April.

Weiss, T. G. (2007) *Humanitarian Intervention: Ideas in Action*, Cambridge: Polity.

Welsh, J. M. (2008) 'The Security Council and Humanitarian Intervention', in V. Lowe, A. Roberts, J. Welsh and D. Zaum (eds) *The United Nations Security Council and War: The Evolution of Thought and Practice since 1945*, Oxford: Oxford University Press.

Wheeler, N. J. (2000) Saving Strangers: Humanitarian Intervention in International Society, Oxford: Oxford University Press.

Wheeler, N. J. (2001) 'Legitimating Humanitarian Intervention: Principles and Procedures', *Melbourne Journal of International Law*, 2/2: 550–567.

Wheeler, N. J. (2005) 'Legitimating Humanitarian Intervention: A Reply to Farer's Five Part Test', *International Relations*, 192: 237–241.

Youngs, T. (1998) 'Kosovo: The Diplomatic and Military Options', House of Commons Research Paper 98/93.

4 Conflicting rules

Global constitutionalism and the Kosovo intervention

Anthony F. Lang, Jr

Introduction

The air campaign launched against the Federal Republic of Yugoslavia on 24 March 1999 was intended to force the Yugoslavian authorities to respect the rights of Albanians living in Kosovo, a region that had enjoyed semi-independent status within Yugoslavia. Reports of violations of the rights of the Albanian community had been widely disseminated in the Western media for a full year prior to the initiation of the campaign. Rather than the United Nations Security Council, the military campaign was undertaken by NATO forces, led primarily by the United States and United Kingdom. Both US President Bill Clinton and UK Prime Minister Tony Blair argued strongly that the air campaign was undertaken to enforce the rules of the international community, specifically those concerning the human rights of minority groups in multi-ethnic communities. The air campaign remained largely that – an air war without the use of ground troops. It officially ended on 10 June 1999, when the regime of Slobodan Milošević agreed to a peace plan.

The intervention generated a voluminous amount of commentary, both for and against. In terms of the jus ad bellum conditions of the war, those in favour argued it was necessary to enforce international norms concerning human rights and the prevention of genocide. Those opposed argued that it violated international law concerning the role of the Security Council and the core international norm of sovereignty. In terms of jus in bello issues, some voiced concerns about the failure of NATO nerve to use its full military might, especially ground troops, in a cause that they considered to be just. Others argued the exact opposite – the force used in the air campaign was too excessive in a situation where both sides were violating human rights norms. In essence, the disagreements on all counts revolved around questions of norms, rules and laws – that is, ethical disagreement.

Much of the criticism of the military campaign has focused on the motives of the intervening states. The general critique of Kosovo has been that the United States in particular, and the United Kingdom to a lesser extent, were motivated to undertake the war by classical realist concerns revolving around power, especially the control of Russia, China and an emerging European Union. The protestations about a just war, a humanitarian war or a war for humanity are, according to this argument, simply covers for more nefarious motives. Danilo Zolo has presented this position most forcefully: from the realist perspective, the sincerity of the ideological convictions of individual political or military decision-makers is irrelevant. It is important, instead, to grasp to what extent ethical motivations can play a role of persuasion in a war. From this point of view, to qualify a war as 'humanitarian intervention' is a typical ploy for self-legitimization by those who wage that war. As such, it is part and parcel of war itself, an instrument of military strategy in the strict sense, used to obtain victory over the enemy (Zolo 2002: 38).[1] This critique taps into a commonsense understanding of ethics, one in which authenticity is the highest virtue and hypocrisy is the highest vice. Nevertheless, this chapter will not focus on this set of issues in analysing the intervention in Kosovo, mainly because I do not find this critique to be particularly decisive. If one considers the fact that almost any action results from a set of mixed motives, coupled with the fact that governments have a combined set of motives stretching from diverse individuals to institutions, a criticism based on motives does not tell us much about ethics and international affairs.[2]

Instead, in this chapter I turn to the idea of rules as a way to understand the intervention in Kosovo. Two sets of rules have been invoked by supporters and critics of the intervention: (1) that military force should be used to enforce rules concerning human rights and genocide; and (2) that the rules barring aggression and intervention should take precedence over the rules concerning human rights. Both sides in the debate over Kosovo have relied upon these rules in their critiques of each other. Moreover, these rules continue to play a central role in debates about military actions in Afghanistan, Iraq, Sudan, Georgia and elsewhere.

These rules have been invoked in the Kosovo case, and elsewhere, in a strangely non-political sense. That is, they have been abstracted from any larger political structure by which they can be understood, interpreted and enforced. In response to the reliance on an apolitical understanding of rules, I propose an alternative: understanding the Kosovo intervention within the context of a global constitutional order. This is not an argument that we should abandon rules in favour of a Schmittian decisionist approach to politics. Instead, the idea of constitutionalism focuses on the importance of judgements undertaken by a global judiciary in accordance with a broadly understood rule-governed system. This form of judgement would, of necessity, draw upon rules, but it would not be a formulaic recitation of rules in response to conflict. Rather, it would require the practice of interpretation by judicial institutions that can provide insight into when force can be used. Alongside this practice of interpretation, judgements by judicial authorities need to be balanced by the political activities of legislative authorities and the administration of judgement by executive authorities. In other words, my critique of the Kosovo intervention is that it failed to conform to a constitutional framework that might have given it more legitimacy. My critique is thus not whether the war conformed to a pre-existing set of rules, but whether or not it took place within a constitutional order at the global level. Its importance in shaping the current international order gives it even more significance.

The chapter proceeds as follows: the next section distinguishes norms, rules and laws, and then explains how the enforcement of rules raises particular problems at the global level. The subsequent section lays out the two competing sets of rules concerning Kosovo – rules concerning human rights, and rules concerning the use of military force. The chapter then addresses some of the factual debates surrounding the situation in Kosovo, particularly rights claims, before turning to the factual debates surrounding the use of force in relation to UN Security Council resolutions that had been passed prior to the bombing campaign. The next section makes the case that the core problem was not lack of clarity about the rules but a failure to adjudicate on matters of rules and facts both in Kosovo and in the international system more broadly. This leads to the concluding section, in which I argue for a global constitutional order within which such disputes might be legitimately addressed by a sound prosecutorial and judicial structure.

The concept of rules in international relations

One way in which the Kosovo conflict was presented was that the intervention was illegal but moral. This distinction has led to much confusion about the relationship between law and morality. A standard response has been that when positivist legal theory structured international law in the mid-nineteenth century, morality was decisively separated from law. As Terry Nardin has argued, the belief that positivism is amoral misunderstands the nature of both law and morality (Nardin 1998, 2008). Nevertheless, this view continues to structure arguments about Kosovo, with even former UN Secretary General Kofi Annan claiming the war may have not been legal but it was moral.

This chapter will not explore the nature of positivist legal theory in order to clarify this problem. Rather, I turn to a concept that exists between morality and law: rule.[3] A rule is an action-guiding directive that applies to more than one agent. There exists a wide range of rules in the international realm. One could argue that there are, in fact, two types of rules: formal (or legal) and informal (Lang *et al.* 2006). Informal rules derive from traditions of statecraft, such as allies should work together and not betray each other in order to balance against an adversary. Formal rules coalesce around the UN Charter in the current international security order. Both types of rules play an important role in the international order, by providing guidelines and patterned behaviour.[4]

It is important to stress that even within formal rules there exists a wide variety of rules, not all of which state the same thing. Thus, while rules can provide some guidelines, they also leave open space for interpretive strategies, some of which create great uncertainty. The combination of both informal and formal rules, and the wide range of rules in both spheres, creates a complex international order. For some, the variety of rules means that they have no force, since actors (especially powerful ones) can pick and choose whatever rules they want at whatever moments they need. Rules become no more than a patina covering over the pursuit of self-interest.

But, even within this diversity, rules provide a means of thinking about international order that other concepts do not. One could say that rules not only regulate the behaviour of actors, they also constitute their agency and the structures within which they engage each other. The rules that have constructed the international order, then, are not simply regulative rules about what can and cannot be done (although they are that as well). They are constitutive rules that define the very nature of international politics. As a result, they are one of the primary languages through which international affairs takes place. State and even non-state actors employ the language of rules to explain what they are doing. The language of rules makes international relations possible.

Understanding how rules both regulate and constitute international relations leads to a greater appreciation of what rules can and cannot do. Some theorists, such as Peter Katzenstein and other constructivists in International Relations (IR), argue that the regulative and constitutive functions of rules should be kept separate (Katzenstein 1996). When rules are constitutive, they construct the world by providing names and concepts that structure basic social interactions. The classic example of a constitutive rule in international relations is sovereignty; there is no single rule that says sovereigns can or cannot do this or that, but the definition of what a sovereign state is creates certain conditions that allow for certain types of behaviours. When rules are more regulative they dictate certain kinds of behaviours as permissible, such as the rule that states cannot go to war unless they are acting in self-defence.

Constitutive rules can be seen throughout most spheres of life. Such rules do not need any authority figure to enforce them, but become part of the very nature of our interactions. Regulative rules, on the other hand, need an authority figure to enforce them. This is especially true if we think of such rules as not necessarily (although occasionally) corresponding with the needs and wants of individual agents at all times. The function of a regulative rule is to guide behaviour in a social context so that individuals can moderate their own desires in accordance with the needs of the community as a whole. Regulative rules are closer to laws.

If, then, our focus is on regulative rules only, or if the functions of regulative and constitutive rules are kept separate, then international rules may not have much force. This has long been the critique of rules and laws from those who see the international realm as anarchic; without a sovereign, there can be no real regulative rules or laws. But, clearly, the regulative and constitutive functions of rules overlap with each other. Nicholas Onuf argues that a rule is simultaneously regulative and constitutive, suggesting that our attempts to distinguish them results more from the perspective of the analyst than from the reality of how rules function in daily life. Onuf locates the importance of rules in social life and international affairs, exploring their role in situations of anarchy, or when there is a lack of a clearly defined ruler (Onuf 1989: 51). Although there is no hierarchy, or formal system of rule, Onuf does not accept that the international system or social reality more broadly should be characterized as anarchic. Instead, he introduces the term 'heteronomy' (adapted from Kant). Heteronomy is the condition of being under a rule, and is the opposite of autonomy, or the ability to act freely.

The concept of heteronomy, as Onuf employs it, describes a condition in which individuals believe they are autonomous but where they are, in fact, constrained to some extent by the rules that constitute their reality (Onuf 1989: 206–219). Drawing on the speech act theory of John Searle, Onuf describes a situation in which an agent promises to act in a certain way, a promise that is transformed into a duty, a process that then binds that agent in a way that he may not recognize as regulative. The agent feels autonomous in that he has made the promise, but the promise now binds him in an important way. Onuf demonstrates that rules play a central role in constructing the international system around us. They do not need a sovereign authority, but they still bind and constrain agents through the heteronomy function. By constructing the world around us, rules are central to the ways in which international relations operate.

Other theorists of IR and International Law (IL) draw upon the idea of rules to establish the structure of the international system (Kratochwil 1989). Constructivist IR theorists occasionally draw on the idea of rules, but more often turn to the cognate idea of a norm to theorize the constructed nature of international relations. While some authors conflate the two terms, the difference between them is important. Norms, as socially shared commonplaces that structure our reality, do not have the same command function as rules. While this may be a matter of nuance, the idea of a rule comes closer to what we see as important in structuring social interactions where individuals do not necessarily share the same interests – a description of just about every social and political situation that exists. As a result, rules are more central to political organization and order than norms.

Rules are also similar to laws, although, again, the differences between them are important. Many IL theorists begin with the point that laws are essentially rules, but with something added to them. H. L. A. Hart is perhaps the most well-known advocate of this position. Hart argued that law is a form of rule, but only if there are two types of rules, what he calls the primary and secondary: Rules of the first type impose duties; rules of the second type confer powers, public or private. Rules of the first type concern actions involving physical movement or changes; rules of the second type provide for operations which lead not merely to physical movement or change, but also to the creation or variation of duties or obligations (Hart 1994: 81). When a political system includes both primary and secondary rules, it is a legal system. The combination can be seen in the way that a legislature works; a legislature passes pieces of legislation that determine actions (primary rules) while the constitution elaborates how the legislature makes those laws (secondary rules). The advantage of Hart's theory of law is that it avoids the need for a sovereign authority that decides the law; by making the determination of law dependent upon the secondary rules, he gives space for a wider range of different political systems, including (potentially) an international legal system.[5]

While there are certainly similarities between law and rules, to focus purely on law would miss some important regulative and constitutive phenomena at the global level – phenomena that a number of theorists have recently explored. Anne-Marie Slaughter argues that the international system is governed by a series of regulatory structures that result from inter-governmental cooperation. Rather than creating formal institutions, regimes, or new international laws, these interactions remain in the realm of regulations (Slaughter 2004). David Malone, in a recent study of how the UN Security Council has dealt with Iraq for the past fifteen years, argues that the Council has increasingly taken on what he calls a 'legal regulative' role in its operations. While he uses the term legal here, his focus is more on regulatory structures, particularly in the sanctions regime that operated from 1991 through 2003 (Malone 2006). David Kennedy has examined how lawyers, military officers and humanitarian activists have been cooperating more and more to develop the regulations and rules that govern the conduct of military force. Their cooperative efforts have produced the rules that govern the conduct of forces in the field in a wide variety of situations, stretching from peacekeeping operations to the war against Iraq (Kennedy 2006).

In the international security realm, which at times appears to be the most anarchic and least rule-governed, rules play a central role in organizing the system. Interventions like Kosovo, the response to 9/11, and the war in Iraq have been interpreted as a radical destruction of the rules (Murphy 2004; Sands 2005). Indeed, as David Chandler has argued, one can trace a trajectory from the intervention in Kosovo to the conflicts in Afghanistan and Iraq; the undermining of the rule against intervention without Security Council authorization appears in the Kosovo conflict and, Chandler argues, reinforced the tendency of states like the United States and United Kingdom to draw upon moral arguments in support of their actions (Chandler 2002).

Rules, in other words, both constitute the reality of international affairs and regulate the behaviour of agents in those affairs. As a result, rules both enable action and constrain it. They enable actions by creating the conditions in which we can do certain things; in international affairs, the idea that states are the agents authorized to use military force both internally and externally means that the rule of sovereignty creates the possibility for police enforcement and war. They constrain actions by stating what can and cannot be done in certain contexts; in international affairs, the rule of sovereignty coupled with the rules outlawing aggression limits the ability to wage war. When you have a situation like this, the idea that one 'breaks a rule' by using force or 'enforces the rules' by using force is more complicated than a simple appeal to the rules. To decide what it means to conform to the rules requires an institutional framework by which facts and rules can be judged – a constitutional framework.

Enforcement of rules

The debate over Kosovo arose from a debate not only about what rules apply, but also about what should happen when rules are violated. NATO countries argued that the Yugoslav authorities had broken rules concerning human rights norms as they have been spelled out more broadly and then reinforced in a series of Security Council resolutions. Once these rules were broken, there was a need to punish the violators. At the same time, when NATO forces undertook their air campaign, many argued that the countries involved had violated the rules concerning non-intervention and aggression. But, because of the power of those engaging in these actions, there was no agent that could 'punish' the NATO countries for their actions. When no agent can enforce the rules, a rule-governed system will break down.

This suggests that the question of enforcing the rules must be considered more carefully. The question of enforcing rules in a system without a clearly defined authority structure leads to questions of rule-following. Rule-following and rule-breaking are two possible responses to the rules. One might first ask why participants in a specific context decide to follow or violate rules. Such questions lead one to assumptions about human behaviour – assumptions that range from complete self-interest to complete altruism. Of course, no one person or group operates at either extreme. Yet questions about rule-following suggest questions about motivations, which are tied to questions about broader modes of social and political life.

A different way to put this is that following or breaking rules are not decisions made in isolation. Rule-following and violating involves not just an individual's decisions, but also a strategic interaction between the agent and some larger society, polity or authority. How does such interaction determine or explain decisions to follow or violate rules? One way is through coercion, which is often the model adopted by rationalists to explain decisions to follow the rules. In the current international system, military coercion has become a tool employed by the international community (or primarily, as some would argue, the United States) in places such as Iraq and the former Yugoslavia. The international community, through the WTO, has constructed a system of coercive trade sanctioning to enforce rules of a liberal economic order. And the emergence of various international criminal tribunals and the ICC implies that individuals can be coerced into complying with human rights norms through the threat of punishment.

Other means to convince agents to follow rules do not result from coercion. One possible alternative is the theory of compliance, which suggests that rules are followed as a result of the construction of normative structures that attain legitimacy and are thus accepted by all agents involved (Chayes and Chayes 1995). This model relies on the constructivist logic suggested above, in which rules are not seen as constraints on behaviour but as part of the larger social context in which individuals operate.

Breaking the rules usually leads to sanctions being imposed, especially by the strong on the weak. In domestic legal systems, punishments are imposed upon those who do not follow the rules, after a procedure that determines that the rules have been violated. The international realm is different because it lacks a clearly defined central authority to determine violations and impose sanctions. Yet the lack of a central authority does not mean sanctions are not possible. Hans Kelsen argued that the concept of a sanction is inherent in the concept of law, including international law. For Kelsen, war and military reprisal could be considered forms of punishment, as long as such military actions are undertaken in response to a violation of the important legal norms (Kelsen 1946). According to social contract theorists such as John Locke and Hugo Grotius, when agents are in a state of nature, anyone can impose sanctions on those who violate the rules (Lang 2008: 25–44). In the current international system, sanctions and punishments are not imposed by clearly defined authorities but by quasi-authoritative structures composed of the agents themselves (often the most powerful agents).

According to the compliance or constructivist approach, violations of the rules might lead to questions being raised about the identity of the agent as member of a particular group. In international politics, the discourse of 'civilized' states sometimes is employed in this way. That is, when some states engage in policies that violate the core principles of the society, they are castigated as outside the boundaries of normal states. Recent American discourse about 'rogue' states is one example of this, as are attempts to label the United States a 'rogue' by those who believe it violates international law with impunity (Chomsky and Said 1999). But do judgements such as these lead to the enforcement of rules? Or, rather, are they examples of a moralistic discourse that does not create conformity with rules but enemies?

If there is no sanctioning authority, does the violation of rules have any consequences? For my purposes here, the consequences of rule violation for the entire system or society must be considered. The violation of certain kinds of regulative rules will force changes in societal and political relations among agents. When core rules or constitutive rules are violated, however, this may cause the entire system to collapse. Such collapse would, undoubtedly, be the worst possible outcome for a rule-governed system. One might ask, however, whether or not the need to live in rule-governed systems means the collapse of one system will lead to near automatic creation of a new system of rules, one that either reflects the interests of the most powerful, or, hopefully, is a more fair and just set of rules. This said, history tells us that such collapses do occur, and that they are often followed by determined efforts to develop new and 'better' rules and rule-bearing institutions. The twentieth century's great wars and subsequent efforts to reconstitute the international order provide telling examples. They also beg the question whether profound changes in rules and institutions can only be instigated after upheavals, or whether they can be achieved gradually and peaceably.

It is this concern with the larger political order that lies behind my analysis of Kosovo. As I will suggest below, rules were most certainly violated in the context of the Kosovo intervention, both by the Yugoslav authorities and by the NATO powers. The violations by those in Yugoslavia did indeed deserve a sanction. But the response to those violations by the NATO authorities undermined the larger international order. The NATO powers took on the rule of executioner rather than adjudicator in their response to violations. Using an analogy from criminal law, there was a punishment imposed without a trial or even sentencing procedure. Admittedly, in a time of crisis it is difficult to think of long-term consequences and institutional creation. Nevertheless, the failure of the great powers to draw upon the global constitutional order that existed (in a way) is perhaps their greatest failure. The next sections address the case of Kosovo in more detail.[6]

Breaking human rights rules

Human rights have become a central part of the international political order. This centrality has only become concrete in terms of international legal instruments during the past sixty years. Nevertheless, some conception of political rights has long been part of political thought (Hayden 2001). The concept of natural law, the idea that ethical norms can be found in the ability of humans to reason and live in community, provides perhaps the most important starting point for theories of human rights (d' Entrèves 1994). The idea that individuals have rights arises from this natural law tradition in the early modern period through such thinkers as Thomas Hobbes and John Locke (Tuck 1979). The idea of rights for these thinkers was related to the idea of somehow 'owning' the self that could not be infringed upon by others (Macpherson 1962). This basic idea has become known as political rights, or negative rights; those which stipulate what protections an individual has. The idea that rights should include some provisions for the sustenance of life arose in response to the writings of Karl Marx and others, who saw that rights that were so closely linked to protecting the individual sustained an unfair distribution of resources (Marx 1843). This critique eventually led to the idea of second-generation rights, or positive rights; the provision of goods that the government is obligated to provide to its citizens in the realm of economics. A third generation of rights has emerged more recently, focused on the rights of groups to things like self-determination and cultural protections.

These three types of rights have become a central part of the rules of the international order. While they existed as ideas and shaped political structures and debates prior to the twentieth century, they were only made a concrete part of the international legal order after the Second World War. As David Forsythe has described, this process of making human rights a concrete reality in terms of law has been a complex and often tortured one (Forsythe 2006). The Universal Declaration of Human Rights was adopted by the UN General Assembly on 10 December 1948, creating what some have called an international bill of rights. This was followed by the adoption by the General Assembly in 1966 of two binding treaties, the International Covenant on Civil and Political Rights and the International Covenant on Economic, Social, and Cultural Rights. It was not until ten years later that enough signatories had ratified the treaties, hence making them operative.[7]

As a result of this legal regime, it is not difficult to state that there exists a set of rules governing human rights in the current international order. Objections to those rules do occur, sometimes motivated by cultural differences, but in general there exists a clear set of human rights rules governing how individuals should be treated. In some cases, such as the European Union, rules made at the supra-national level have a concrete impact in legal disputes in member states; in the United Kingdom, for instance, the EU human rights laws have forced certain changes in the way the British legal system deals with constitutional questions (King 2007: 127–135).

The other relevant set of rules concerns genocide. The rule barring genocide is obviously connected to human rights, but is not necessarily the same thing. The concept of genocide is not a simple one, for to claim that an act is one of genocide raises important questions concerning intention, group rights, and responsibility. Martin Shaw has argued that understanding genocide in the context of legal rules misunderstands its essentially sociological and political nature (Shaw 2007). Yet after the Second World War, and especially as a result of the Nuremberg Trials that followed the war, the crime of genocide soon became a central part of the international legal order. In 1948 the Convention on the Prevention and Punishment of Genocide was opened for signatures, and it came into force in 1951. It defined genocide, and clearly stated that it is not simply an international crime but one that governs the way states treat their own citizens.

The legal instruments detailing human rights and genocide provide a basic framework of rules. The question is whether or not those rules were violated in Kosovo. This question became the key dividing point in debate within the West about whether or not the intervention was justified. Tim Judah claims that while the NATO governments emphasized violations of human rights rules in Kosovo, this was not really the central issue:

> ... many Kosovars successfully convinced many Westerners that the question of Kosovo was one of human rights. In fact, it was not. At the heart of the matter was a fundamental struggle between two people for control of the same piece of land. In our times, however, human rights have become an influential factor in shaping international politics. This is not to say that the Kosovars did not suffer grievous human rights abuses at the hands of Serbian authorities. They did. But it is to say that, with the benefit of hind-sight, we can see how the question of human rights became another weapon in the arsenal of the Kosovars.
>
> (Judah 2000: 84)

Others, such as Michael Ignatieff, took the opposite view. Ignatieff argued that the activities of the Serb authorities in relation to the Albanian Kosovars most certainly constituted abuses of human rights and perhaps even genocide:

> A defenceless people [Kosovar Albanians] have been driven from their homes and their arrival in Albania and Macedonia is destabilizing a strategi-cally important region.... Having spent a week in the camps in Macedonia,

talking to families evicted from Pristina, I am in no doubt that ethnic cleansing was systematically planned before the NATO bombing.

(Ignatieff 2000: 77)

Tony Blair's speech in Chicago in April 1999 argued that the situation in Kosovo demanded intervention as a result of the 'ethnic cleansing' that had been taking place over the past ten years in the region. While more emotive than analytical, and about a wider set of issues than just Kosovo, the speech provided a clear statement that in Kosovo rules had been broken (Blair 1999).

The facts concerning violations of human rights in Kosovo are not that much in dispute. Human rights of Kosovar Albanians had been progressively deteriorating since the early 1980s. In 1974, a constitution was implemented in Yugoslavia that gave substantial autonomy to the Albanian community in Kosovo. This constitutional structure, however, soon led to concerns among the Serbian community in the region that their rights were being overturned. Yet, when Slobodan Milošević came to power in the late 1980s, he managed the abrogation of the 1974 constitution, severely undermining the previous independence of the Kosovar Albanian community. Alex J. Bellamy describes the use of cultural and economic policy to reinforce the power of the Serbian community (Bellamy 2001: 114–117). Violations of human security followed, with the largely Serbian judicial authorities in Kosovo allowing torture as a means of coercing confessions on revolutionary activity by the Albanian community. Human Rights Watch detailed how Serbian authorities used 'terrorism' charges to systematically abuse the human rights of Albanian citizens in Yugoslavia (Human Rights Watch 1998). The OSCE Kosovo Verification Mission, put in place in 1998, verified 'an escalating number of human-rights abuses including: right to life, right to liberty, freedom from torture and ill treatment, and freedom of movement' (Walker 2001: 134). Based on this evidence, it would seem that human rights abuses were clearly taking place in the Kosovo region – abuses in large part inflicted by the largely Serbian federal government against Albanians.

The question of whether or not genocide took place is more complex. In the background of many critiques of Milošević and the Serbs more generally is the claim that they committed genocide not only in Kosovo against the Albanians but also in Bosnia-Herzegovina against the Muslim and Croat populations. In one interpretation of this debate, Tim Dunne and Daniela Kroslak argue that what took place in Kosovo was ethnic cleansing rather than genocide, the difference hinging on the act of dispossession rather than destruction (Dunne and Kroslak 2001: 36). Ethnic cleansing seems to be a better description of what happened in Kosovo, for Serb forces were engaged in a process of removing Albanians from their homes more than systematic killing of them in concentration camps.

Overall, then, the rules supporting the human rights of individuals were certainly violated in Kosovo, while it is more difficult to make the case that genocide was committed. It would require a much longer and more empirically grounded analysis to make either of these cases with certainty; I have only tried here to lay out the basic issues. Before moving to how an adjudication of such questions might come about, let me turn to the other set of rules that played a role in the Kosovo intervention: those governing non-intervention.

Breaking non-intervention rules

The rules governing non-intervention constitute an important part of the international legal order. Intervention as a distinct practice in international affairs did not exist until there was a state into which military troops could be interjected (Lang 2009a). This means that the concept of intervention makes little sense prior to the emergence of the sovereign state system, or Westphalian order that emerged in the late seventeenth century. As the sovereign state system developed, however, intervention of any kind came to be understood as more of a problem than a help to the suffering of others. In the eighteenth and nineteenth centuries positivist international law grew in importance, creating an international normative order that privileged the state as the vehicle most centrally concerned with the good life. As international law developed during the nineteenth century, intervention became progressively illegal, for to violate the boundaries of the sovereign state was to violate the international order. Non-intervention came to be seen as a defining principle of international society, one that continued to define the twentieth century international order (Vincent 1974).

This normative order was turned into a set of rules as the General Assembly undertook efforts to protect the sovereignty of developing states in the context of the Cold War. In 1965, the General Assembly passed a resolution that stated clearly:

> No state has the right to intervene, directly or indirectly, for any reason whatsoever, in the internal or external affairs of any other State. Consequently, armed intervention and all other forms of interference or attempted threats against the personality of the State or its political, economic, and cultural elements are condemned.
>
> (General Assembly Resolution 2131: 1965)

This resolution was reaffirmed by the General Assembly in 1970 and 1981. In all these resolutions, the affirmation of non-intervention was without doubt. As one international lawyer noted,

> The Assembly has thus construed the Charter as imposing a rule of per se invalidity with respect to intervention. The rule admits of no exceptions: Intervention is always unlawful, regardless of the identity of the state undertaking the intervention, and regardless of its motive or effects.
>
> (Glennon 2001: 21)

The practice of international affairs during the twentieth century may have undermined this legal rule at times, but the general consensus was that the rule barring intervention was a central one to international relations.

When the Cold War ended in 1989, the rule began to be challenged. Particularly as the United Nations took on a more active role responding to international crises and state failure, the rule that the sovereign state was sacrosanct came under further strain. This weakening of the rule was not exactly welcomed by the international community, although many saw it as a chance to respond to human rights abuses taking place around the world. The Secretary General of the UN, Boutros Boutros-Ghali, captured something of this spirit in his Agenda for Peace, a 1992 report commissioned by the Security Council in which he laid out the need for more aggressive forms of peace enforcement – that is, missions undertaken for the purpose of not simply monitoring a cease-fire, but also making peace through the halting of one side in a conflict. One of the most famous sections from that report speaks directly to the change in sovereignty: 'The time of absolute and exclusive sovereignty, however, has passed; its theory was never matched by reality' (Boutros-Ghali 1992). While this sentence was preceded by one that stated the importance of the state, nevertheless it captured an emerging shift in the international order.

Interventions in Somalia (1992–1994) and Bosnia-Herzegovina (1994–1999) defined this new United Nations activism in peacekeeping. The active role of the UN in Cambodia in 1992 and 1993 in order to rebuild state institutions torn apart by war demonstrated that sovereignty would not stop the international community from reconstructing the very essence of statehood – the functions of policing, economic distribution and constitution writing. The failure to act in Rwanda in the 1994 genocide only reinforced the belief of some that the rule concerning non-intervention was preventing action to save those in need of rescue. By the time of the 1998 and 1999 conflicts in Kosovo, the rule concerning international intervention had been sufficiently weakened that military action was seen as a further step in the protection of those subject to the horrors of war.

But the intervention in Kosovo also solidified for some the need to reaffirm the rule against intervention. In bypassing the Security Council and making the case that their intervention was based more on moral purpose than legal justification, the NATO powers generated a backlash among some in the international community concerning the centrality of intervention. Soon after the Kosovo intervention, the Canadian government organized a working group to develop a new approach to intervention. The commission produced a document that has become the touchstone of a new approach to intervention, The Responsibility to Protect (International Commission on Intervention and State Sovereignty 2001). The report sought to shift the discourse of international humanitarian action and international security more broadly away from debates on the right to intervene towards a discourse surrounding the 'responsibility' of various actors to provide for human security. While it responded to the weakening of the rule concerning intervention, the report in fact sought to recreate a new rule concerning intervention. The report is an attempt to reinterpret the rules to conform to new international security challenges, particularly those concerning intervention. It begins with the principle of non-intervention, and then construes its task as being the definition of those circumstances when that 'rule' can be overridden; in other words, the creation of a rule for breaking the rules (International Commission on Intervention and State Sovereignty 2001: 31–32). Its section on authority emphasizes that the Security Council must remain the only source of legitimate authority in the international system. Challenging or evading the UN Security Council will 'undermine the principle of a world order based on international law and universal norms' (International Commission on Intervention and State Sovereignty 2001: 48). In 2004, a UN report continued to insist that the current rules of the UN system simply needed to be better enforced rather than abandoned. This report resurrected collective security as a central principle of the international security order. The report's subtitle, 'our shared responsibility', suggests a possible move away from a rule-governed international security order. But, when considering the dangers of preventive military action, the report falls back upon the UN Charter, stating boldly; 'We do not favour the rewriting or reinterpretation of Article 51 [states cannot use military force without Security Council authorization]' (United Nations 2004: 63).

These changes in the rules concerning intervention and sovereignty suggest a state of confusion at the heart of international relations. The justification of the Kosovo intervention generated more confusion, as it raised questions about the enforcement of rules through the Security Council. The United States argued that three Security Council Resolutions passed during 1998 concerning the obligations of Yugoslavia in regards to Kosovo had been violated (SC Resolutions 1160, 1199, and 1203). As a result of these violations, the United States claimed, it was authorized to undertake military action to ensure that the will of the Council was enforced (Glennon 2001: 30–32). This built upon another set of rules in the international order: all states are obliged to follow the dictates of the Security Council that is responsible for peace and security in the international order.

What changed was that the United States reinterpreted the enforcement function of the Security Council to allow itself to undertake military action through NATO. The argument that previous Security Council resolutions authorize military action when it had not been explicitly cited in those resolutions was a new and radical interpretation of the rules. More importantly, this same line of argument was invoked by the United States to authorize its military action against Iraq in 2003; that is, Iraq had failed to live up to its previous obligations in accordance with the Security Council, and thus the United States was authorized to enforce the mandate of the Council (Lang 2006).

The Kosovo intervention, in other words, resulted in part from a shift in the rules concerning intervention, but also from a reinterpretation of how another set of rules, those concerning the authority of the Security Council, should be interpreted. The shifting rules by themselves created enough uncertainty in the international order to leave space for the Kosovo intervention, while the American reinterpretation of the rules concerning enforcement further opened the space for a new set of rules.

Making judgements about the rules

While the rules governing non-intervention had been shifting, there remained a strong enough standard barring intervention. At the same time, the rules concerning human rights had become a much more central part of the international order. The Kosovo intervention can be read as a moment when these two sets of rules came into direct conflict. Which rules apply in this case?

In a domestic political setting, rules come into conflict in a number of situations. In some cases, the conflicts can be settled by those whose responsibility is to enforce the rules: the executive. Usually, these are cases in which a bureaucratic interpretation of a regulation or rule can shift to allow for new circumstances. In some cases, the conflict cannot be settled so easily by an executive, leading the legislature to create a new set of rules to govern the situation. This may mean abrogating old rules or changing the current rules through the creation of a new set. The most common response to conflicting rules is for a judicial body, an appellate court of some sort, to reinterpret the existing rules to apply to specific cases in which the conflict originated. This adjudication role can take place at a number of levels in a judicial system, sometimes taking place at the summit of the legal order. When such judgements take place at this high a level, this can sometimes lead to a new constitutional interpretation. In very rare cases, a conflict among rules that are central to the system as a whole will cause a rethinking of the entire constitutional order, resulting in a new constitution. This comes about through an extralegal process; that is, such changes in the legal order are not really legal processes, but changes that recreate the order anew. More often than not this large-scale change will come about in a violent way, as in a revolution. Occasionally it is a peaceful transition, although such transitions usually follow an outbreak of violence as the system undergoes a radical shift.

Does this largely constitutional description apply at the international level? In some ways, it does. First, there is a proto-constitutional order at the global level. Such an order is not simply the UN Charter, but includes a wide range of legal and political structures by which international relations takes place. This order structures the rule-making process by which treaties, customs, resolutions from international and regional organizations, and legal opinions from select juridical bodies structure the international legal order.

Second, various executives seek to enforce the rules of this constitutional order, with the most important being the UN Security Council. The Council's role in enforcing peace and security resulted in part from the great powers being given a privileged place in its composition. Other executive bodies exist, not the least of which are the sovereign states acting in concert in certain situations. Admittedly, to say that states within the order are also the executives that enforce that order may sound contradictory. Yet the real individuals in the order are people, so the states can be considered institutions that should enforce the rules governing peoples' lives. As the international system has become progressively more globalized, the interactions of individuals cross boundaries, but those interactions are still rule governed by state authorities.

The more difficult institution to identify is a legislative one. International law does not result from a single legislature, although certainly resolutions from either the UN General Assembly or the UN Security Council create law-like rules. The General Assembly looks most like a legislature, but most do not see it as such. In some cases, such as definitions of contested concepts like terrorism, aggression and intervention, the General Assembly acts as a legislator. But the fact that Security Council resolutions also result in legislative-like actions, and that states obviously make laws that structure international affairs, means the General Assembly is not the final legislative structure in the international system.

Judicial institutions do exist, including a 'constitutional court' of sorts in the International Court of Justice. The recent emergence of international criminal tribunals and the International Criminal Court has created a new body of international criminal law, but the ultimate appeals court remains the ICJ.

And there have been 'revolutions' that have recreated the international constitutional order. In the twentieth century, the aftermaths of the two World Wars were the clearest examples of such constitutional moments. What is perhaps surprising is that there has not been a similar constitutional revolution in the past twenty years. Since the end of the Cold War, shifts have been taking place in the rule-governed system of the international order; however, no single event has redefined that order.

What does all this mean for the Kosovo intervention? The Kosovo intervention took place at a moment when global constitutional change was accelerating. The weakening of a fundamental rule in the international order, non-intervention, was being accompanied by a rise in emphasis on the moral dimensions of human rights and humanitarianism. As these two movements intersected, no large-scale change took place in the order, but rather a powerful group of actors was able to take advantage of the existing gaps in the order. As noted at the beginning of this chapter, I am not interested in what motivated their actions as a way to make judgements about those actors; rather, what is interesting is how the shifting rules allowed their action to come about. It is too easy to say that their power allowed them to simply override the rules, for that is not what they did. The great powers are bound by constitutive rules, something that can be understood through the heteronomy concept that Onuf developed. Rather, in their attempt to enforce the rules outside of a constitutional context, they fundamentally altered the rules. Now that we are over ten years past that moment, with the intervening interventions and wars, its importance seems even more evident.

Could a different outcome have been possible? I want to suggest that if the order was truly constitutional, a different outcome would have certainly been possible. The one thing that was absent from the Kosovo debate was a role for a judicial body to make a judgement about both the facts and the laws concerning the intervention. International bodies certainly played a key role here; the OSCE monitored the 'facts' concerning human rights violations, and the Security Council generated the 'laws' concerning the situation in Kosovo with the three resolutions from 1998. But when it came to which set of facts and rules were to be applied in this particular situation, no judicial structure was invoked or even tried to play a role in deciding what should happen. Some would say the practical reasons for the failure of an institution like the ICJ to act here is its slow procedural process that takes years to decide on any case before it. As individuals suffer human rights violations, no one has time to wait. Others might argue that the Security Council played the role of a judicial body in this situation. It did deliberate about the possible options. Yet, even if it had acted, the Security Council would then be combining the roles of judicial and executive body into one institution – a combination that throughout the history of liberal politics has long been feared.

In other words, the international order was not constituted so that formal judgement could play a role. This hole in the international constitutional order led to the rigid reliance on rules by both supporters and critics of the intervention; without a legitimate judicial structure that could consider both facts and laws, the international community was left with nothing but rules. Rules, however, do not interpret or enforce themselves. They can be useful in political polemics, which have characterized the debate about Kosovo. What was needed was not a new rule but a new judgement to make possible the continued existence of a rule-governed political order.

Conclusion

This chapter has suggested that the core problem of the Kosovo intervention was not misguided motives or a failure to protect innocents (although both of these elements certainly existed). Rather, the core problem was a lack of a truly constitutional order at the global level. Some parts of such an order do exist, but the failure of a judiciary to respond to the conflicting sets of rules is perhaps the most revealing part of the intervention. Such a perspective is, admittedly, a long-term one rather than a reflection on the real suffering that took place in Kosovo and Serbia. But that suffering might well have been avoided if there had existed an international order within which conflicting rules could be adjudicated rather than simply deployed in a political battle. Indeed, it is when law and deliberative politics break down that violence becomes possible. One can only hope that a lesson to be learned from Kosovo is the need for a constitutional order within which judgements play a more central role.

Notes

1 For a similar critique that focuses on motives, see Chomsky (1999).
2 For more on motives, and the related concept of intentions, as they relate to humanitarian intervention, see Nardin (2006: 10).
3 This section draws upon Lang (2009b: 4–7).
4 See Arend (1999) for one international legal theorist's use of the concept of rules.
5 Although Hart denied that the international system was a truly legal one according to his theory; see Hart (1999: 213–237).

6 Parts of this section were drawn from Lang (2006).
7 For the texts and a brief legal background on these legal instruments, see Buergental (1995).

References

Arend, A. C. (1999) *Legal Rules and International Society*, Oxford: Oxford University Press.

Bellamy, A. J. (2001) 'Human Wrongs in Kosovo: 1974–1999', in K. Booth (ed.) *The Kosovo Tragedy: The Human Rights Dimension*, London: Frank Cass Publishers.

Blair, T. (1999) 'Doctrine of the International Community', speech to the Chicago Economic Club, 24 April. Available: www.number10.gov.uk/Page1297 (accessed February 2009).

Boutros-Ghali, B. (1992) *An Agenda for Peace: Preventive Diplomacy, Peace-making and Peacekeeping*, New York, NY: United Nations Publications. Available: www.un.org/Docs/SG/agpeace.html (accessed February 2009).

Buergental, T. (1995) *International Human Rights in a Nutshell*, 2nd edn. St Paul, MN: West Publishing Co.

Chandler, D. (2002) *From Kosovo to Kabul: Human Rights and International Intervention*, London: Pluto Press.

Chayes, A. and Chayes, A. H. (1995) *The New Sovereignty: Compliance with International Regulatory Agreements*, Cambridge, MA: Harvard University Press.

Chomsky, N. (1999) *The New Military Humanism: Lessons from Kosovo*, London: Pluto Press.

Chomsky, N. and Said, E. (1999) *Acts of Aggression: Policing Rogue States*, London: Seven Stories Press.

D'Entrèves, A. P. (1994) *Natural Law: An Introduction to Legal Philosophy*, with a new introduction by C. J. Nederman, New Brunswick: Transaction Publishers.

Dunne, T. and Kroslak, D. (2001) 'Genocide: What to Remember, or Forget, or Forgive?', in K. Booth (ed.) *The Kosovo Tragedy: The Human Rights Dimension*, London: Frank Cass Publishers.

Forsythe, D. (2006) *Human Rights in International Relations*, 2nd edn, Cambridge: Cambridge University Press.

General Assembly (1965) 'Declaration on the Inadmissibility of Intervention in the Domestic Affairs of States and the Protection of Their Independence and Sovereignty', Resolution 2131, 21 December.

Glennon, M. J. (2001) *Limits of Law, Prerogatives of Power: Interventionism after Kosovo*, New York, NY: Palgrave.

Hart, H. L. A. (1994) *The Concept of Law*, 2nd edn, Oxford: Oxford University Press.

Hayden, P. (ed.) (2001) *The Philosophy of Human Rights*, St Paul, MN: Paragon House.

Human Rights Watch (1998) 'Federal Republic of Yugoslavia: Detentions and Abuse in Kosovo', Human Rights Watch Reports 10 (10). Available: www.hrw.org/reports98/kosovo2 (accessed February 2009).

Ignatieff, M. (2000) *Virtual War: Kosovo and Beyond*, New York, NY: Metropolitan Books.

International Commission on Intervention and State Sovereignty (2001) *The Responsibility to Protect*, Ottawa: International Development Research Centre.

Judah, T. (2000) *Kosovo: War and Revenge*, New Haven, CT: Yale University Press.

Katzenstein, P. (1996) 'Introduction', in P. Katzenstein (ed.) *The Culture of National Security*, New York, NY: Columbia University Press.

Kelsen, H. (1946) *General Theory of Law and State*, Cambridge, MA: Harvard University Press.

Kennedy, D. (2006) *Of War and Law*, Oxford: Oxford University Press.

King, A. (2007) *The British Constitution*, Oxford: Oxford University Press.

Kratochwil, F. (1989) *Rules, Norms and Decisions: On the Conditions of Practical and Legal Reasoning in International Relations and Domestic Affairs*, Cambridge: Cambridge University Press.

Lang, A. F. Jr (2006) 'Normative Causes and Consequences: Understanding and Evaluating the War with Iraq', in R. Hinnebusch and R. Fawn (eds) *The Iraq War: Causes and Consequences*, Boulder, CO: Lynne Rienner Publishers.

Lang, A. F. Jr (2008) *Punishment, Justice and International Relations: Ethics and Order after the Cold War*, London: Routledge.

Lang, A. F. Jr (2009a) 'Humanitarian Intervention', in P. Hayden (ed.) *The Ashgate Research Companion to Ethics and International Relations*, Burlington, VT: Ashgate.

Lang, A. F. Jr (2009b) 'Rules and International Security: Dilemmas of a New World Order', in A. Beattie and A. F. Lang, Jr (eds) *War, Torture and Terrorism: Rethinking the Rules of International Security*, London: Routledge.

Lang, A. F. Jr and Beattie, A. (eds) (2009) *War, Torture and Terrorism: Rethinking the Rules of International Security*, London: Routledge.

Lang, A. F. Jr, Rengger, N. and Walker, W. (2006) 'The Role(s) of Rules: Some Conceptual Clarifications', *International Relations*, 20: 274–294.

Macpherson, C. B. (1962) *The Political Theory of Possessive Individualism: From Hobbes to Locke*, Oxford: Clarendon Press.

Malone, D. (2006) *The International Struggle Over Iraq: Politics in the UN Security Council, 1980–2005*, Oxford: Oxford University Press.

Marx, K. (1843) 'On the Jewish Question', in R. C. Tucker (ed.) *The Marx–Engels Reader*, 2nd edn, New York, NY: W. W. Norton.

Murphy, J. (2004) *The United States and the Rule of Law in International Affairs*, Cambridge: Cambridge University Press.

Nardin, T. (1998) 'The Positivist Tradition in International Law', in D. Mapel and T. Nardin, (eds) *International Society: Diverse Ethical Perspectives*, Princeton, NJ: Princeton University Press.

Nardin, T. (2006) 'Introduction', in T. Nardin and M. Williams (eds) *Humanitarian Intervention,* New York, NY: New York University Press.

Nardin, T. (2008) 'Theorising the International Rule of Law', *Review of International Studies*, 34: 385–401.

Onuf, N. (1989) *World of Our Making: Rules and Rule in Social Theory and International Relations*, Columbia, SC: University of South Carolina Press.

Sands, P. (2005) *Lawless World: America and the Making and Breaking of Global Rules*, London: Allen Lane.

Shaw, M. (2007) *What is Genocide?*, Cambridge: Polity Press.

Slaughter, A.-M. (2004) *A New World Order*, Princeton, NJ: Princeton University Press.

Tuck, R. (1979) *Natural Rights Theories: Their Origin and Development*, Cambridge: Cambridge University Press.

United Nations (2004) *A More Secure World: Our Shared Responsibility*, Report of the High Level Panel on Threats Challenges and Change, 2 December. Available: www.un.org/secureworld/report.pdf (accessed September 2009).

Vincent, R. J. (1974) *Non-Intervention and International Order*, Princeton, NJ: Princeton University Press.

Walker, W. G. (2001) 'OSCE verification experiences in Kosovo: November 1998–June 1999', in K. Booth (ed.) *The Kosovo Tragedy: The Human Rights Dimension*, London: Frank Cass Publishers.

Zolo, D. (2002) *Invoking Humanity: War, Law and Global Order*, translated by F. Poole and G. Poole, London: Continuum.

5 De facto states in the Balkans

Shared governance versus ethnic sovereignty in Republika Srpska and Kosovo[1]

Rick Fawn and Oliver P. Richmond

Introduction

The state of representation of de facto entities in the Balkans, in particular the Republika Srpska (RS) and Kosovo before its unilateral declaration of independence on 17 February 2008, indicates that such entities have capacities that belie their lack of formal sovereign status. Indeed, ascribing only states with representational capacity is misleading, as local actors may develop tools that can be used to simulate governance and sovereignty in material ways often deemed not to be part of their repertoire or role. Furthermore, their relationship with international actors forms a crucial part of their identity, both in its exclusionary and in its more pluralistic forms. These issues have been of essential importance in the management of peace in both Bosnia and Kosovo. Far from being eased or eradicated in, respectively, more than twelve or eight years since open war, the de facto state quality of the RS and of pre-independence Kosovo remains strong and challenges regional order. The prospect of EU accession for the whole of the West Balkans – now often seen as the panacea for regional peace and prosperity – is at best a project to be fulfilled in the coming decade, as the European Commission acknowledged in its 2007 enlargement report (European Commission 2007). And as the likelihood grew that Kosovo would be recognized by several major Western states, but not by the UN Security Council, the importance of who recognizes de facto states and how they function in the Balkans has also increased.

Though the continuation of Herceg-Bosna – an ethnically Croat de facto state in wartime Bosnia – as an entity was blocked by international pressure, the RS and Kosovo have presented far more difficult challenges. They were not legally sovereign, but nevertheless have functioned similarly. This is a phenomenon we term 'ethnic sovereignty', where entities may develop or simulate as many of the qualities of formal sovereignty as possible given international constraints. The ways and reasons for these entities to function as such represent part of their efforts to attain a level of sovereignty recognized by the international community. This means they both defend their current status, and try to attain more status by direct and indirect means. Indeed, this recognition game (Mitchell 1992: 277) – whereby each party seeks a high quality of international recognition so as to simulate de jure sovereignty, while also working to undercut the ability of their counterpart to do the same – colours their internal development as well as their relationship with the international custodians of their settlements. Conversely, actors to which sovereignty has already been ascribed, such as Croatia, Albania and Serbia, are active differently, either to support ethnic sovereignty, or to curtail it, according to which entity is being dealt with. Even where actors are recognized sovereign states, without any direct trusteeship or shared sovereignty from international actors, a recognition game continues to prevent the dissolution of their juridical sovereignty. This complex dynamic surrounding sovereignty in the Balkans disguises the continuing fragility of the regional peace process where vertical relationships with internationals are more significant than horizontal relationships among local actors. Whether the 'post-modern' courtship between the EU and Balkan actors will alter this remains uncertain, though international actors regard themselves reluctantly as indispensable in the region in the long term (Diez *et al.*, 2008).

Ethnic sovereignty in the Balkans means that the relationships between local states, entities and internationals are riven by inconsistencies that slow progress on peace. Shared sovereignty between local and international actors and the predominance of forms of trusteeship and shared sovereignty means that relations between the entities are generally, though of course not entirely, ignored. Entities focus far more on their relations with influential international actors, such as British or American diplomats and donor governments, the European Commission, the Organization for Security and Cooperation in Europe (OSCE), international financial institutions (IFIs) and UN agencies, at the expense of local relations. The RS and Kosovo present related but still illustratively different cases; neither was meant to have any foreign relations, or indeed even foreign presence of its own, and yet each has managed some. Kosovar leaders even exploited international peacemaking institutions to strengthen the case for sovereignty. In both cases, such strategies have disrupted the peace process and even destabilized it. Simultaneously, particularly in Kosovo, developing the entity's relations with regional actors is integral to that peace.[2]

Both the fact of the efforts of non-state entities in Balkans to engage in foreign relations and the prescription that they, particularly Kosovo, before any international recognition, do so to enhance regional peace raises a conceptual problem with Krasner's shared sovereignty framework between local elites and international organizations and actors. This framework expects local actors to follow international prescriptions for peace without contesting their roles or international objectives, which is unlikely. Instead, we propose a corrective notion called 'shared governance', where an additional focus is on the local actors' relations with each other. The relation of local actors with internationals should therefore be conditional upon shared governance – accepting a level of interdependence with neighbouring entities – in order to prevent an exploitation of the international presence, or devious objectives related to long-term spoiling or revisions of the original peace settlement.[3] This does not, of course, bypass the deeper problem posed by international actors that exert hegemonic and conditional influence in locales of which they have only limited understanding, though it is assumed here that the developing practices of international intervention and peacebuilding cannot be rejected, even on these grounds. International actors need to become aware of the dynamics caused by their relations with local actors, which may outweigh regional connections. Indeed, the continued predominant form of shared sovereignty in the region might cause a dependency of local actors on internationals and competition, fair or foul, for their attention. Making local and regional relations the key focus of international peacebuilding approaches, rather than shared sovereignty, would make local peace settlements far more durable.

International custodians have both denied de jure sovereignty while also contributing to the conditions for de facto sovereignty. They have also denied some aspects of governance for local actors (such as foreign policy), and have failed to emphasize the need for local interaction between entities in their efforts to develop good relations between themselves and local entities. This creates an under-explored paradox that discourages local ethnic entities from collaborating or even communicating with each other. This situation creates significant obstacles for the implementation of peace settlements because the entities are primarily concerned about their international relations. It also represents a complex situation that requires, but has lacked, detailed or systematic investigation, and that carries implications for other post-conflict settlements, given the widespread dependence upon international custodianship for the development of a new, liberal peace. This varies according to which actor is examined: for example, in Kosovo prior to independence, local representatives regarded the EU as significant in their goal of statehood, but generally saw UNMIK and the UN Security Council as obstacles, both to this and to self-government.

These entities' situations and their aspirations for sovereignty can be determined by examining, where relevant, their political and material resource bases and their interaction with outside actors, including kin states, NGOs and international organizations. This process contrasts with the intended practices of the international custodians for Bosnia and Kosovo, including the OSCE, the EU, NATO and the UN. While other studies have concentrated on 'democratization' in Bosnia or on international trusteeship there and in Kosovo, we concentrate on ethnic and shared sovereignty, and their implications for the peace settlement.

We analyse the role of international custodians in this controversial process of state creation/simulation.[4] The following sections examine the relevant theoretical arguments on ethnic and shared sovereignty, and point to a new framework of 'shared governance' in the context of an empirical analysis of sovereignty in Bosnia and Kosovo.

The claims of shared sovereignty and international trusteeship

For international custodians of peace processes, ranging from official mediators to the UN system, agencies, and NGOs, the tasks of building states and peacebuilding are particularly problematic in situations where disputants contest territorial sovereignty, international recognition and identity. In this contest, some local actors, often representing traditional, pre-conflict elites, have considerable agency, and aim at goals outside of the formal aim of the peace process (Newman and Richmond 2006). Where communities establish claims for an ethnicized version of sovereignty, as in Cyprus amongst both communities, for example, resting on the simulation of the institutions of state within an ethnically homogeneous territorial context, a 'shared sovereignty' may emerge. This is not shared between the coexisting communities but between each entity, formal or informal, and various international bodies such as the UN and the EU. As Krasner has argued: 'in some cases, decent governance may require some new form of trusteeship, almost certainly de facto rather than de jure' (2004: 85; see also Krasner 2005). Shared sovereignty as a response to ethnic sovereignty represents a softer version of (neo-colonial) international and transitional administration. The 'liberal peace' is constructed in the context of a broad range of forms of highly interventionary governance (Duffield 2001: 11; International Commission on Intervention and State Sovereignty 2001; Mandelbaum 2002: 6; High Level Panel on Threats Challenges and Change 2004; Paris 2004; Richmond 2005). International actors and institutions, and dominant liberal states, act as 'bio-powers' that have the capacity to shape social interactions,[5] and effectively run a regime system of governance that defines personal, community, social, economic and political interactions (MacGrew 1997: 1–24; Lipschutz 2002; Paris 2002: 642–645; Shaw 2002; Dillon 2003: 135).

Some Balkan entities have turned to aspirations of EU integration, both to reinforce their claims for ethnic sovereignty, and to develop a shared sovereignty framework with international actors that is acceptable to local elites, local populations and international actors. Simultaneously, the EU framework is seen as potentially undermining formally existing entities on the grounds of ethnicity, through the norms, discursive change, and practical pluralism of regional integration (Diez 2005). This demonstrates that major international actors have a set of norms, regimes and expectations that they seek to develop in a local context. These actors do not necessarily concur on these frameworks, which are driven by the most influential actors in the peacebuilding consensus (Richmond 2004). To impose these frameworks would be a form of trusteeship and neo-colonialism; to establish them in association with local actors would be much more acceptable both to international actors and, ideally, to local actors.

Following this line of thought, shared sovereignty, as Krasner calls it, implies a multilateral framework for peacebuilding that focuses on internationals directing and taking substantial responsibility for local reform. It assumes that local actors have very limited capacity and, perhaps foremost, that the best chance for cooperation lies between them and internationals, rather than between different regional entities. Such cooperation is, instead, deferred into the future when the reforms the internationals introduce have taken root and disputants have resolved their underlying differences.

Ethnic sovereignty and the agency of local entities

The other side of this debate concerns the agency of local actors and entities, despite the international exercise of trusteeship or shared sovereignty. Sovereignty is not merely exercised by states, but also to some degree by individuals, as Kofi Annan has pointed out, and increasingly by de facto states, through vertical multilateral contacts between official and unofficial actors (Annan 1999). Even in situations such as the Balkans, where much decision-making capacity has been, or still is, exercised by international actors, a form of ethnic sovereignty exists that local entities exercise in a limited but still effective manner in terms of their own interests if not those of a viable liberal state.

In this contest it is clear that some local actors, often representing traditional, pre-conflict elites, have considerable agency, and are able to manipulate their work to attain goals outside the formal aims of the peace process. Worse, such ethnic claims may prompt other disputants to harden their positions. Next, it may also produce political entities incapable of reaching a formal and self-sustaining peace settlement with their adversaries. Finally, it reproduces a polity based upon a mixture of dependence upon international actors, domestic manipulation of those internationals, local defiance of international will, and local particularism expressed with the indirect assistance of international custodians.

While the view that '[S]overeign rights attach to those entities that enjoy sovereign status' has been common, increasingly entities need not have sovereign status to gain de facto sovereignty (James 2000: 336). De facto sovereignty exists at three levels of analysis, including (i) how official actors and state representatives view this de facto or ethnic sovereignty; (ii) how ethnic groups view state sovereignty; and (iii) how the internationals present and the international community respond to such claims.[6] This requires the ability to identify the status ascribed to de facto states by other states and internationals present in the region; examine the official rhetoric used by each entity; its internal coherence, including its ethnic composition; its ability to administer itself; its capacity to project images of de facto state competence; and the political and material sources for these activities, including intended and unintended support from kin states, NGOs and intergovernmental organizations; to examine the responses of representatives of the states, and many so-called internationals present, to such claims. It is important to be able to identify the level of ethnic sovereignty and understand its impact on the implementation of peace settlements. Even non-state entities have some leverage on the peace settlement by engaging in a subtle renegotiation of it with the international custodians, by threatening to withdraw, or engaging in spoiling behaviour.

Ethnic sovereignty occurs when ethnic groups claim sovereignty and try to act as if they were sovereign at the military, political, social and institutional levels. It is a form of quasi sovereignty constituting, perhaps, more than a degree of statehood. Often the only resources such groups are denied are international relations, external legitimacy and regional economic integration. Clearly, the exercise of ethnic sovereignty may lead to non-pluralist entities whose internal legitimacy is probably far greater than their external legitimacy. Ethnic sovereignty is derived from within ethnic groups, but it may be endorsed by implication by international roles in implementing a peace settlement. A self-constructed 'web of meaning', of which perception of sovereignty is an important part, partially defines actors' objectives (Neufeld 1993). It is this that claims of sovereignty represent from the point of view of ethnic groups. Thus, ethnic sovereignty can be defined as a form of status accrued from internal and sometimes external sources, and derived from reorganization along the lines of a state project. It arises even as ethnic groups are under pressure from host states, and even though the orthodoxy of the international system dictates the normative inadmissibility of such claims.

Ethnic sovereignty develops as follows: military and political actors define secession as a key objective, normally on popular demand, through the demarcation of a specific identity group. This group may span state boundaries or be solely sub-state. The next step for them is to develop a case for the legitimacy of this position, normally resting upon aspirations towards the terms of sovereignty noted, for example, by the 1933 Montevideo Convention.[7] These actors endeavour to show how their current situation disadvantages them, leading to violent domination by their host state. Domestically, the group must then organize military, bureaucratic, political, social and economic cohesion through the development of institutional structures of statehood. Establishing a constitutional framework and holding elections are an important part. In international terms, they must establish relationships, often using the medium of peacemaking actors, with other states, IOs, ROs, international agencies and financial institutions. Even NGOs and academics may be seen as significant in this search for validation and legitimacy.

Increasingly, such entities claim to be building a liberal peace, which in itself is regarded by internationals as an automatically legitimate endeavour. Establishing liberal institutions domestically, and developing such relationships internationally, are clearly seen to ascribe levels of sovereignty. Where both these domestic and international dynamics occur, an unrecognized state can be said to exist that exercises ethnic sovereignty. This is unofficial sovereignty in its classical sense, where, as in many conflict zones, all that differentiates these quasi states from many other weak, underdeveloped and war-torn states is their lack of clear representation in international bodies. Non-state actors, once in this situation, are then part of a 'recognition game' – a simulation of sovereignty and even of the liberal state itself – a charade that at its most extreme can reignite violence (Mitchell 1992: 277). In more critical analytical terms, this development of ethnic sovereignty represents an inevitable subjective claim of sovereignty based not on international recognition but on internal cohesion on identity grounds through which identity groups are able to subvert the formulaic, problem-solving mechanisms proposed by liberal states and their governance frameworks.

Major states and donors are clearly the most visible part of this process. Courting the attention of the permanent members of the UN Security Council, and ideally creating a debate to support the goal of sovereignty, are ideal objectives. Lesser goals include developing lines of communication between such actors so that non-state actors can claim both limited recognition from P5 members or their officials, as well as some say over how their resources may be deployed in their particular locale. Similarly, such non-state actors may court relationships with such international bodies as the World Bank, UNHCR and UNDP for similar reasons. NGOs, often seen to be providers of key resources in the absence of government, play a similar role. They can provide resources, expertise and experience in economic, political and social development and governance that local actors require to approximate a polity recognizable from the outside as liberal and democratic, with a free market, and adhering to international cosmopolitan norms. Ironically, many international actors have laid themselves open to such manipulation over the last decade by developing and adopting procedures and objectives whereby their intervention in conflict zones is legitimated, and aimed at democratization, development, human rights promotion and the establishment of the rule of law. These are the very components that non-state actors see as vital if they are to mount a credible claim for an embryonic form of sovereignty.

Such sovereign claims produce their own dilemmas for ethnic groups, internationals and states. This may lead to the creation and recreation of bounded mono-ethnic and non-pluralist entities, ironically exploiting liberal and humanitarian norms. Indeed, the impact of ethnic sovereignty on peace settlements could, as our case studies below show, produce the following effects: empower groups that do not intend to cooperate with the peace settlement; create a relationship of dependency between moderate groups and the internationals present; redirect attention from the peace settlement to the issue of status; reformulate the relations between custodians and internationals engaged in a peace settlement because the latter organizations or states dare not jeopardize their relationships with disputants; and delineate new and unintended limits to a peace settlement through the implementation process. This implies that the exercise of ethnic sovereignty means that the disputants are engaged in a renewed attempt to renegotiate the original peace agreement and the mandate of international actors therein.

This also indicates differing levels of ethnic sovereignty and of state sovereignty. The role of custodians, mediators and peacebuilding inevitably rests upon their capacity to strengthen disputants' claims for sovereignty, either directly or indirectly. More directly, custodians become involved in the support of state sovereignty, which means that they cannot become involved in any activities that might hinder its development. They will be expected to support the capacity of the state actor to operate both domestically and internationally, and not to hinder mainstream nationalist policy. State actors tend to be very active in these circumstances in developing a foreign policy capacity, and are at pains to demonstrate that they control their domestic situation, while providing all or most societal groups with sufficient rights and opportunities. Ethnically sovereign actors tend to be relatively domestically organized, but more dependent upon internationals for any international or foreign policy status. Both state and non-state claimants of disputed sovereignty tend to see the roles of third parties – mediators, institutions, militaries and NGOs – as deriving their legitimacy from the support they provide directly or indirectly for their own case.[8]

Perhaps the most important implication of these dynamics is that in order to have any kind of relationship with a third party, in a peace process, and later in a resultant agreement's implementation, disputants need to be organized into recognizable negotiating institutional entities that are capable of demonstrating that they represent and carry a large constituency. At the next level, they need to be able to negotiate and implement any peace agreement, while retaining the support of their constituency through a (seemingly) democratic process. This implies that disputants and third parties in a peace process must cooperate in the construction of an institutional framework for an agreement to be reached and implemented. Thus, peace processes are about building liberal state-like entities, even where one actor is not officially constructed as a state. Herein lies an incentive for non-state actors engaged in peace processes to build state-like institutions with the help of third parties, even where this may not be acceptable to the international community. The chapter now turns to an examination of these processes, and their implications, in the cases of the RS and Kosovo.

Shared or ethnic sovereignty in Bosnia

This section considers how actors in Bosnia have acted in the light of the concepts of shared sovereignty and ethnic sovereignty. Elements of these have existed simultaneously; the important issue is how much of each exists and why and what the overall implications are for the intended peace. We consider several major issues, including the forms of governance, internal and external, intended by Dayton, and the RS's ability to circumvent them.

The results of the Bosnian peace settlement highlight three broad features relevant to our hypothesis. First, the international agreement created – in principle – structures of governance that were intended to bring the three principle ethnic constituencies together. In addition, the agreement intended to create of Bosnia a unified international actor with the normal attributes of sovereign statehood. Dayton laid – again, in principle – the foundations for cooperation between Bosnia's entities. It also created mechanisms for shared governance within the state and across the region, although these were not by the choice of the IC. These were more the recognition of existing relations resulting from the conflict than the ideal of relations with all regional actors. These elements, however, may have looked like shared governance and cooperation across the region in theory, but in practice were concessions to secure a basic peace and were implemented on a selective and sometimes counterproductive basis.

Second, what has happened since Dayton is also illustrative of how international actors have also been able to curb and manage some aspects of ethnic sovereignty. Nevertheless, actors in Bosnia that defined themselves on an ethnic basis (also encouraged by the approach of Dayton) have still defied the peace process and used it to develop political features of their own, and to engage in political relations they were not meant to possess. Third, they have been able to thwart efforts to create shared governance across the region by interfering with the web of relations intended by the international actors, both by creating their own and by disregarding those desired by the internationals.

The RS illustrates ethnic resistance to some international practices and the need to encourage conditions for shared governance. Its ability to assert its claims to ethnic sovereignty has changed over time, largely due to international pressures. From the outset, Dayton created shared sovereignty; Annex 10 stipulated that the High Representative could reverse policies of local leaders that were deemed to challenge the Accord. Because of circumstances, the capacities of the internationals in Bosnia, particularly those of the OHR, were increased (formally, as through the Bonn Powers; informally, as exercised by particular High Representatives, particularly Paddy Ashdown). The OHR's power became a substitute for real, locally owned and controlled governance,[9] though after Ashdown's departure the OHR tried, unsuccessfully, to pass responsibility to local actors and institutions. Indeed, the institution of the OHR was supposed to end by June 2007; it not only continues (somewhat reluctantly), but its newest officeholder, Miroslav Lajčàk, introduced proposals in October 2007 for far-reaching structural changes to Bosnia's governance (to which we return below).[10]

Bosnia as a state – as distinct from its entities – is a primary case in theory of shared governance being created by the international peacemakers across its entities in order to prevent ethnic sovereignty from taking hold after Dayton. This was closely patrolled by something akin to a shared sovereignty framework, which was calculated to defer crucial areas of authority to the OHR. The essence of Dayton was to provide some local autonomy, but to weld together the different peoples of the country. The post-war agreements included measures to make Bosnia appear as an integrated state with representative domestic structures and full international legal status. Those structures together would create incentives for the three principle ethnic groups to cooperate with each other and, through national structures, to interact in a coherent way with other sovereign actors and international bodies. The basis, however, for regional cooperation was neglected, while an expectation of economic development – implying trade and investment – was nevertheless made.

Among the domestic structures was a common parliament and a shared presidency, in which each of the three ethnic constituencies had representation. Local actors were meant to interact with each other through these mechanisms. Of course, the international community's 'focus on civil society is meant to overcome the limits of external regulation and to emphasize indigenous and community-based contributions to peacebuilding'. The result has been the opposite, with any local participation instead coming from the international presence and a 'failure to address the structural problems that affect the country' that in turn hinders 'the formation of an open and democratic society' (Belloni 2001: 168). Some success for Dayton must be acknowledged, as the expectation thereafter was that Bosnia was heading for a three-way partition (*The Economist* 1996: 43).

These national mechanisms were meant to give Bosnia, as in any 'normal' sovereign state, the means and form for interaction with the international political and financial community. To an extent this has worked; witness a Bosnian Foreign Ministry and Bosnian embassies. A common foreign policy has been made and is also represented at various bodies, from regional initiatives to the UN. The success of this measure in practice is open to interpretation. By some accounts, the Muslim leadership supported the unified Bosnia state as proposed under Dayton as it 'hoped and still hopes to be able to lay claim to this common state, thereby monopolizing foreign policy as well as the administration of foreign credits' (Meier 1999: 244–245).

Simultaneously, however, the Bosnian state was too weak, partly because of its fragmented armed forces, to participate in Partnership for Peace (PfP), NATO's outreach program offered from 1994 to almost all post-communist states. Only in 2005, and through the lobbying of the High Representative, was Bosnia considered for participation in PfP (it joined, with Montenegro and Serbia, on 14 December 2006). Mechanisms created by Dayton for a unified Bosnia have instead become tools for its ethnic constituencies:

> The political elite compete for spoils and use historically fine-tuned tactics in manipulating the international donors and administrator with the result of deep corruption, insider privatization, getting internationals to eliminate one's rivals and plenty of cooperation among leaders of the three national communities if necessary to keep the game going.
>
> (Woodward 2001: 253)

The RS is even more illustrative of the weaknesses of the peace and of the need to develop shared governance across the region, as opposed to ethnic or even shared sovereignty, which increasingly appear to have promoted each other's dominance of the politics of peace.

The case of the RS

In contrast to Kosovo, the RS was losing de facto statehood at least until final status talks for Kosovo began in 2006, when some connections began to be made between Kosovo's independence from Serbia, and the RS's from Bosnia. Unlike Kosovo, before the 1990s the RS never possessed any distinct identity or administrative experience. Thus, the entity has a much greater challenge to create – and maintain – de facto statehood than Kosovo had before its unilateral declaration of independence. In addition, the international community, unlike on Kosovo, was united on Bosnia remaining a single state. The RS lacks institutional precedent, and faces international consensus for Bosnian unity and substantial international efforts to restrain and unravel its authority. Indeed, the RS is thoroughly a product of the Bosnian war. Kosovo had both the status and physical infrastructure of a province in federal Yugoslavia between 1974 and 1989. In addition, no-one disputes that the area had some cultural identification.

Indeed, this is part of the contest over Kosovo – that, for Serbian nationalists, a Kosovar identity was allowed to develop in what they assert is a Serbian heartland. For Kosovar Albanians, the area has been a natural cultural–political home. Even opponents of the Kosovars recognize that they gained administrative experience running the province during the socialist federation.

While Serbs have lived in the territories now known as the RS, they have never done so exclusively, preventing any immediate claim to statehood on an ethnic basis. Furthermore, the RS only came to have any acknowledgement as a political unit in 1992. In addition, the contours of that entity lack precedent and, because of the previous multi-ethnicity of that area, it can hardly be seen as an exclusively Serbian homeland (though such claims are made). The RS was named in the Dayton agreement as one of the 'entities' essentially to bring the Bosnian Serbs into the peace. Few outside the conflict see this move, as perhaps as necessary as it was at the time, as more than a reward for wartime aggression and violence. The international community, however, had to work against Bosnian Serb intentions to form a separate state from the territory they forcibly secured during the war. As international negotiator David Owen observed, Bosnian Serb leaders wanted the RS to be an entirely independent state and to have no connections whatsoever to Muslim Bosnia, creating 'in effect a Muslim-free area' (Owen 1996: 102–103). Dayton's weaknesses are extensive, and rarely is it considered a reasonable or effective recipe for a permanent post-conflict settlement. Before stepping down, Ashdown called Dayton 'a superb agreement to end a war, but a very bad agreement to make a state' (Vulliamy 2005).

Since the formal recognition of the RS's existence within Bosnia-Herzegovina (BiH), international officials have stated bluntly that the RS is a 'para-state' built on war crimes and ill-gotten gains. Furthermore, the RS's supporters were committed to resisting international efforts to roll back its autonomy because they would lose these material gains, and the crimes that made them possible would be given additional light.[11] (A similar view is presented by many Serbs, including those in senior official positions, towards Kosovo.) Thus, the RS's leadership challenges international peacebuilding by having strong reasons to further develop the entity's cultural and institutional identity, a trend that has gained significance since the OHR has scaled down its involvement.

The principles of Dayton and shared sovereignty

From a worst-case scenario of mass murder and population displacements, international negotiators secured agreement at Dayton that created a fragile Bosnian state with two 'entities' and an additional layer of authority at the lower, cantonal, level. To ensure Bosnian Serb participation, Dayton acknowledged the RS's existence, giving a legal – if intended to be only temporarily – identity to the RS. From this stemmed the phenomenon of ethnic sovereignty. Indeed, a fundamental criticism of Dayton is that it empowered collective rights over individual; ethnic sovereignty is its result. The RS was given institutions intrinsic to a state that the RS leadership have used as fully as possible, even if state-wide political institutions and economic mechanisms were also created, such as a single currency, customs services and taxation. Such centralized provisions aimed to create a common Bosnian structure, and ideally an identity, and to limit the functional capacity of the entities.

Each community was also granted organizations traditionally associated with statehood – foremost, and remarkably, armed forces. While that was undone easily, each community could also establish and maintain separate police forces. Unlike the separate armies, these forces remained in place for a decade after the Dayton Peace Agreement. Support for the retention of its police force has been seen, by both RS leaders and international officials, as more important to the RS's existence than the military. Ethnically based paramilitaries provided 'protection', and committed atrocities, during the 1992–1995 war, so it can be understood why the police might be more significant than military. Indeed, the practical significance of entity police forces cannot be understated. A police force gives an organized coercive force to each entity; it also means that police forces are unable to pursue suspects across internal boundaries in Bosnia. For the RS, which is routinely described by internationals as a state built on criminal activity, an independent police force is integral to its existence and identity. It is hardly surprising, therefore, that the OHR concentrated on removing this provision and building an integrated, Bosnia-wide police. Indeed, the intensity of international efforts to break the RS's immunity from Bosnian-wide police and judicial practices is an indication of the strength of the RS's ethnic sovereignty. International representatives throughout Bosnia were also confident that reforms, particularly of taxation, would reduce the RS's ability to maintain its own police force.

On the whole, however, the RS activists remained confident that neither an integrated armed forces nor police would work in practice. Some asserted that Bosnian Serbs would not serve in such entities, and others emphasized that these agencies would receive no recognition or cooperation in the RS.[12] As one former RS member of parliament in the Bosnian-wide parliament said in 2005, 'there will be no changes in the police [in the RS]; any will be rejected. No one is that naïve.' Such changes were perceived in the RS as against its constitution, indicative of the view that entity law takes precedence over Bosnian.[13] Indeed, Dodik, once again the RS Prime Minister, declared in August 2006 that the RS would not give up its own police force, (Radio Free Europe 2006a) even though the RS parliament had voted the year before to accept the EU's police reforms.

How police reform proceeds will be a key indicator of the practical tenacity of the ethnic sovereignty of the RS. It may be that the international project succeeds and a formal RS police force is entirely disbanded. Enormous obstacles remain to the integration of society in the RS, let alone in this most sensitive area. In addition, the short history of the RS is one of informalism, particularly in matters of security. Informal security networks are likely to continue to exist, and these will be mono-ethnic by definition. They will continue giving sustenance to the ethnic sovereignty of the RS while obstructing international efforts at undercutting it and reintegrating Bosnia's entities. Effectively, ethnic sovereignty in the RS is being maintained to prevent shared and cooperative governance from emerging.

Cutting the influence of kin states

Under the Dayton Agreement, the entities were given 'the right to establish special parallel relationships with neighbouring states', but this had to be 'consistent with the sovereignty and territorial integrity of Bosnia and Herzegovina'.[14] This potentially ambiguous arrangement has been called a 'concession' that 'purchased' the cooperation of Croatia and Yugoslavia for Dayton (Woodward 2001: 285). How these two practices were reconciled in practice was essential to the functioning of the RS. A weak central BiH authority could not practically override 'special parallel relationships' with, in the case of the RS, Yugoslavia. As with the construction of de facto statehood given to the RS by Dayton, so too did its provisions provide some channels for relations with Belgrade.

The international management of BiH has sought to limit the extent to which both the Croatian and Yugoslav/Serbian-Montenegrin/Serbian states could interfere in Bosnian affairs and support its co-ethnics. The peacemakers had some initial success. Instead of allowing Croatian 'territories' to join with Croatia, or even have their own political-administrative status at the federal level, it was subsumed into what, for example, former High Representative Carl Bildt called a 'minor partnership' in the Muslim-Croat Federation.

In the first years after the war, significant trade occurred between Croatia and the Croatian cantons and Croatian-populated parts of BiH, and this trading relationship was replicated between Serbia and the RS. BiH became unusual among post-communist states for trading more with immediate neighbours than with the EU (Uvalic 2000: 8). While this would seem encouraging for shared governance, these trading relationships were built on ethnic lines and arguably encouraged by international provisions in Dayton. They are the opposite of building multilateral frameworks of cooperation.

The RS is economically fragile, which potentially could make it vulnerable to international pressure to encourage more groundwork for shared governance. By various accounts its unemployment rate was as high as 90 per cent in the late 1990s (Cousens and Cater 2001: 31). The entity has a huge trade deficit (although technically an entity may not have such), and is unable to produce anything of significance. By contrast, some RS economic officials say that the entity is a dumping ground for unwanted foreign goods. That any international economic agreement can only be signed by Bosnian-wide authorities should further limit any sense in the RS that it can develop its economic and trade activities on an ethnic basis. Similarly, international financial institutions such as the IMF will only lend to the central Bosnian authorities. When Dodik explained his call in 1999 that indicted war criminals in the RS and in Yugoslavia should surrender to the ICTY, he did so both on the principle of wrong-doing and that the RS needed outside financial assistance for its economic development (Moore

1999). Recognition of such needs, even and especially by those exercising ethnic sovereignty, provides a key opportunity to international actors to develop shared governance.

As in other areas, the economy raises questions about how the 'right' form of relations can be developed. On the one hand, presumably the development of any (legitimate and legal) economic activity with neighbouring states is to be encouraged, and this also fits with the notion of shared governance. On the other, retaining the integrity of the Bosnian state requires economic relations through Bosnia's central structures. When in July 2006 the RS's Minister of Economy, Energy and Development said the RS was prepared to create a special relationship with Croatia (Radio Free Europe 2006b), this signalled both the RS's determination to have an independent foreign presence, and also the recreation of ties on a non-ethnic and functional basis with neighbouring actors.

As with borders, the psychological dimension of economic welfare may remain strong. It also seems that efforts have occurred in the RS to limit on an ethnic basis what little outside investment has sought to come into the entity: one recent report finds that, despite obvious economic benefits, the RS 'spurns non-Serb investors' (Katan 2005). Furthermore, large areas throughout the post-communist space have been quite capable of living a non-monetary and non-trading existence; while they do not have the conspicuous wealth of the West, and indeed of some other post-communist areas, we should not expect all societies, especially ones attributing high priority to ethnic identity, to conform to Western consumerism.

International political efforts to decouple the entities from their kin states have worked even better than in economic relations.[15] High Representative Westendorp wrote in 1999, perhaps optimistically, that '[t]he destiny of the Bosnian Serbs is no longer controlled by Belgrade. Nor would the great majority of the Serbs who live in Republika Srpska wish it to be' (Westendorp 1999). According to *The Economist*, on the tenth anniversary of Dayton: 'Most Serbs and Croats who wanted to create a Greater Serbia and a Greater Croatia now recognise that Bosnia is here to stay' (*The Economist* 2005). In addition, the imagery and purposes assigned by the kin states to their co-ethnics in Bosnia has changed. One international official said the governments in Zagreb and Belgrade had become 'embarrassed by their country cousins in Bosnia'. One Bosnian Serb said she routinely finds in Belgrade that Serbs now entirely blame Bosnian Serbs for the war and for bringing sanctions against the then Yugoslavia.[16] Perhaps Bosnian Serbs are adopting a pragmatic line out of necessity: as one RS banking official explained in 2005, 'We don't want to be separated from Serbia but we don't want to be their slaves. But we also don't want to be the slaves of the Muslims.'[17]

Both the Croatian and Serbian governments have ministries for their diaspora, but neither uses them to support their co-ethnics in Bosnia. Some Croatian governmental and constitutional provisions might suggest (continuing) irredentism towards Croat-populated areas in BiH, such as including representatives from there in the Croatian parliament in Zagreb and giving Bosnian Croatians dual citizenship. The Croatian Ministry of Diaspora expressly stated, however, that it has no remit for Croatians in Bosnia.[18] This change in policy doubtless dates from the change in Croatian government in January 2000 and the death of Franjo Tudjman, the architect and symbol of Croatian ultra-nationalism. Before them, however, Croatia was instrumental in fostering Croatian political identity in Bosnia. For example, legislation and education curricula for Croatian areas of Bosnia were written in Croatia. In addition, foreign attempts at making the Bosnian–Croatian border a fully fledged international one for economic purposes were limited (Woodward 2001: 285). Now, instead of inciting support for Croatians in Bosnia, the Croatian media generally do not bother to report on events there, and popular interest is minimal.[19]

Domestic regime change in Croatia after 2000 also allowed the country to pursue accession talks with the EU. The EU made clear that cooperation with the ICTY, and through that at least a partial reckoning with Croatia's war crimes in the 1990s, was a prerequisite for accession negotiations. Indeed, the Croatian government was stunned that those talks were delayed by one year in 2004 when indicted General Ante Gotovina had not been surrendered to The Hague. (He was subsequently found in the Canary Islands in December 2005, clearing the way for accession negotiations.) The carrot of EU accession has changed Croatian phraseology towards Bosnia. Instead of Tudjman's references to 1990s Croatia as having the boundaries of its Second World War predecessor – which included territories in Bosnia – the Croatian Ministry of Foreign Affairs and European Integration now stresses its full support for Dayton, for Bosnia's sovereignty, and as a mutually beneficial regional solution that recognizes no ethnicity.[20] Such principles are integral to the success of shared governance. However, Croatia is now the best-case scenario in the region for accepting and promoting these values, and it has reached this point after considerable costs. Unlike the de facto states in the Balkans, or indeed states possessing recognition but lacking full control over its territory (such as Serbia), Croatia enjoys full sovereignty.

The Serbian Ministry of Diaspora, created only in 2004, is overwhelmingly interested in Serbs (or their descendents, and even that is very broadly defined) living in Western Europe and especially North America. Its requirements for citizenship exclude knowledge of Serbian language, and the substantial fee is very high relative to Balkan salaries. When asked about Serbians in Bosnia, ministerial officials acknowledged concern for them and said that Bosnian Serbs may come under their jurisdiction. The Serbian Ministry of Diaspora was much more concerned for the plight of – from the Belgrade government's perspective – an internal diaspora: Serbs in Kosovo. That, ironically, highlights an unspoken reality; that while every pretence is made in Serbia that Kosovo remains part of it, Belgrade exercises no functional authority and its few co-ethnics remaining there are deemed in practice a de facto diaspora. A further feature of limiting the exercise of sovereignty by the entities is international measures to curb engagement in foreign relations.

Foreign relations

Whereas the Kosovar leadership has emulated forms of foreign policy,[21] the RS has been much less successful. The primary expressions of the RS's activity beyond its borders, and without the consent of central Bosnian authority, have again been with Serbia (and its predecessors), foremost the RS's conclusion in 1997 of a defence treaty and a dual citizenship agreement with Yugoslavia (Ramet 2002: 279). Residents of the RS and of Serbia still only need identity cards, rather than passports, to cross each other's border, even though it is technically international.[22] Both of these moves have undercut the integrity of the Bosnian state. RS representatives have tried to engage in foreign relations on other occasions. In October 1999, for example, the Serbian member of the Bosnian joint presidency, Živko Radišić, not only held talks with the Serbian government, but also, when challenged, asserted that he would meet anyone 'if it is in the interests of the Serbian people and the Republika Srpska' (Radio Free Europe 1999a). The assertion was clearly that the RS would not be beholden to Dayton and would instead define and assert the entity's interests abroad on an ethnic basis.

However, as described above, international actors have stridently sought to control the connections between kin states and the entities. According to one former senior RS political leader, Biljana Plavšić was extremely popular among Serbs precisely because she secured a reputation for the RS abroad.[23] Her removal from office by the OHR was similarly explained by international representatives wanting to curb the RS's international standing, and not for suspicion of war crimes (for which she was subsequently convicted). Otherwise, the lack of other foreign policy activity, according to some international officials who have an interest in seeing the RS with no foreign relations, arises simply from the 'incompetence' of the RS, although they also say that they 'stomp' on any efforts by RS officeholders to represent the entity abroad. The RS's 'liaison offices' abroad are not considered by international officials as engaging in foreign policy but as serving to 'globalize' the RS's elite's criminal activity.

By contrast, representatives of the RS still insisted that the entity was entitled to engage in parallel relations with neighbouring states, and that only 'contracts' with other actors need the approval of the central Bosnian authorities.[24] This may be a matter of interpretation. Unlike in Kosovo, international custodians in Bosnia appear to have maintained concerted efforts to limit the RS's international engagement. Lack of resources and personnel may also have created structural limitations. The international presence arising from Dayton has not provided the same administrative infrastructure in the RS as it has in Kosovo for the indigenous ethnic elite to develop and exert 'foreign policy', and other, political-administrative activities. This is hopeful in some respects for shared governance, but the difficulty arises of preventing this from being used to express purely ethnic identity and/or to engage in illicit economic activity.

A final reason for the RS's relative lack of foreign relations is the concerted effort by international custodians to ensure no connection is made between the

fate of the RS and that of Kosovo, though, as the likelihood of Kosovar independence increased during 2006, Dodik warned:

> If Kosovo becomes independent, people in Republika Srpska who agreed to
> participate in Bosnia-Herzegovina despite the fact they have been dissatis-
> fied the whole time will demand the same status for RS as for Kosovo. We
> will ask for the right of confederation of a union of states within the interna-
> tionally recognized borders of Bosnia-Herzegovina.
>
> (Jevremovic 2006)

He also continued his balancing act between international and domestic pressures by cooperating with the ICTY by surrendering an indictee while calling for
an independence referendum in the RS (Pond 2006: 261).

International efforts to disconnect RS claims to the fate of Kosovo are given
by outside reports. For example, the *International Herald Tribune* reported in
2004 from a conference on Bosnia that Serbian Foreign Ministry official Fuad
Sabeta said:

> Nobody wants to mention this, but everyone in Republika Srpska is watch-
> ing what will happen in Kosovo next year. If Kosovo gets independence,
> you can be sure that the Serbs of Bosnia will press for secession and integra-
> tion into Serbia.[25]

By early 2005, the Belgrade government made significant movement towards
a settlement by proposing an ill-defined plan for Kosovo of less than independence but more than autonomy. On 12 September 2006, however, Serbia's parliament voted overwhelmingly to enact a new constitution that called Kosovo an
'integral and historic' part of Serbia. In February 2007, a confirmation of Kosovo's conditional independence was made by the Contact Group, though the
OHR in Sarajevo was unsure that there would not be a secession attempt by the
RS, and there was clear concern about the activities of Dodik.[26]

The influence of the internationals

The most telling area in which the RS's inability to continue to act on a self-
defined ethnic basis is in the overarching powers held by the OHR. An inverse
proportionality can be drawn between the popularity in the RS of an individual
High Representative and the amount of interference exercised in the RS's affairs.
The High Representatives have generally sought to reduce the powers given to
the RS by Dayton, and especially those that RS officials have sought to expand.

OHR interventions have occurred in every aspect of the running of BiH. Two
observers explained the international community's extraordinary powers,
embodied in the OHR: 'outsiders actually set that [i.e., the political] agenda,
impose it, and punish with sanctions those who refuse to implement it' (Knaus
and Martin 2003: 61). Those powers have been deployed particularly in the RS.

Carlos Westerndorp, High Representative in the late 1990s, dismissed RS president Nikola Poplasen in March 1999, in part because he continued to block the installation of Milorad Dodik as Prime Minister, who was acceptable to the international community. Westerndorp (1999) saw Poplasen's efforts to thwart Dodik as tantamount to a 'coup'; many in the RS consequently saw Dodik as a puppet of the West.[27]

Resentment in the RS was foremost against both the office and the personality of Paddy Ashdown. One Bosnian Serb leader condemned the OHR's treatment of the RS as if it were an African colony. Ashdown was attacked personally for his own lack of success in his own country. How, we were asked, did someone who never achieved significant office in the United Kingdom have the right to 'govern' Bosnia?[28] One may conclude that the greater hostility to an individual High Representative, the greater has been his success in undoing some of the RS's de facto sovereignty. That said, some in the RS simply assert Ashdown could 'not impose decisions on RS and we [in the RS] are not responsible for his decisions'.[29]

Nevertheless, an international official asserted that the OHR's interventions so undermined the RS that, having opposed Dayton's terms as limiting the RS's autonomy, later many RS representatives clung to it in desperation. But Dayton still gives the RS its essence, and that arrangement is considered, as noted above, as a de facto state. Secretary of the Bosnian-Croatian party HZD, Vencel Lasić, said: 'Whoever does not see RS behaving like a state is blind.'[30] And when the new OHR introduced plans on 19 October 2007 for changes to governance in Bosnia, Bosnian Serbs in both the central government and RS showed the power of their discontent. The Serb member of the joint presidency resigned, and Dodik threatened to withdraw other Serbian cooperation. While he met with the OHR, he immediately thereafter flew to Belgrade for high-level meetings which also included the Russian deputy foreign minister. Unlike before, the RS now has the support of Moscow to stop centralizing efforts in Bosnia by the rest of the international community (*The Economist* 2007).

Other actions by the international community may be cumulatively changing some popular perceptions in the RS, which in turn may undercut support for its narrowly defined ethnic composition. Among these efforts is accountability for war crimes. In November 1999, Dodik agreed that the ICTY could establish an office in Banja Luka and called that the RS's first act of cooperation with the Tribunal. While he said on that occasion that 'all those who have committed war crimes have to stand trial', he added, 'There is no collective guilt, crimes are individual' (Radio Free Europe 1999b). This move came three weeks after he said that Radovan Karadžić, Slobodan Milošević and Vojislav Sěsělj should also surrender to the Tribunal (Radio Free Europe 1999a). As one Western scholar noted, '[t]hrough the agency of the ICTY, the association with the wartime leadership responsible for the criminal policy of ethnic cleansing has become a serious liability.' The arrest for war crimes of Momčilo Krajišnik, whose posts in the RS included chairing its wartime assembly, caused very little reaction (Akhavan 2001: 14). The issue of the Srebrenica massacre is also emerging in popular discussion,[31] and is seen by some to undermine the continuation of an exclusive Serbian project in the RS. Nevertheless, the decision of some indictees in the RS to surrender themselves to authorities in Belgrade rather than to the ICTY or other international bodies indicates whose authority is recognized.[32]

The RS continues to engage in extensive symbolism to demonstrate its ethnic construction. The RS's capital forewent the use of state emblems of BiH, but instead flies Serbian tricolour flags. Some municipal and entity buildings in Banja Luka, including the City Hall, have bilingual plaques – though not in Bosnian and Serbian, but in Serbian and English. The RS even retains the notion of its own post office, with mail boxes inscribed in Cyrillic with 'Serbian Post'. These public displays of entity identity allowed the RS to escape some of the international community's pressures for conformity.

Perhaps more importantly, the RS is still perceived by many in it and among those that interact with it as having the attributes of statehood. That said, the RS has a fragmented political elite; as suggested above, part of the elite can support Western policies, which include surrendering leading figures to face war crimes charges. This elite is often seen, and consequently despised by others, as Western pawns.[33] But the structures created by the international community through Dayton also allow other RS elites to operate. Most notably, while some in Banja Luka have cooperated with international custodians, other RS officials, such as some of its representatives in the Bosnian presidency, have used those offices to conduct both unilateral and international affairs for the RS. As long as such structures exist and, even more importantly, there is a psychological imperative to believe in a collective identity of the RS, a significant degree of ethnic sovereignty will continue in the RS, and the overall 'shared sovereignty' of Bosnia will be substantially compromised. The tension between shared and ethnic forms of sovereignty has not so far been resolved and, given the situation, this throws significant doubt on the ability of any sovereign framework to provide stability in Bosnia.

Kosovo: from shared sovereignty to shared governance?

Kosovo is by far the most pressing case of sovereignty simulation based upon an ethnic claim in the Balkans, mainly because of the local pressure for a resolution of the final status situation. This was formally held in abeyance after the Rambouillet talks, and also through various ploys used by UNMIK in order to postpone any substantive debate in the context of local and regional opposition, a lack of preparation and, perhaps most importantly, P5 opposition in the Security Council. The 'Standards' framework was the most obvious recent attempt to establish a set of criteria before final status was adjudicated (Standards for Kosovo 2005). Clearly, these processes and relationships have been very useful to the Kosovo Interim Assembly in providing the capacity to claim and simulate sovereignty, and also to intimate that final status has already been decided by some of the peace settlement custodians, notably the United States and United Kingdom (although their diplomats studiously declined to give any formal confirmation of this position). The irony of the 'Standards' process is that it left the sovereignty question open, despite Russian and Serbian objections and a general reluctance of the international community to set a precedent that might promote secessionist entities. The Kosovo question before the declaration of independence was being closely monitored for these reasons. Indeed, as Anglo-American pressure for Kosovar independence began to mount in 2006, Russian president Vladimir Putin stated that if Kosovo gained independence then so should unrecognized entities in the post-Soviet space – implying those supported by his government. Much of Russian official rhetoric since then, and also partly justifying Russia's heavy military intervention in Georgia in August 2008, has been framed in terms of applying another reading of Kosovo's claim to independence and general Western support for that (Fawn 2008). In Kosovo's case, Xhavit Haliti emphasized that final status was raised in an informal agreement at the Rambouillet talks held in early 1999, in advance of NATO's bombing campaign, and implied Kosovar sovereignty would be forthcoming even then.[34] This was seen to be an important aspect of the legitimation of the Kosovo Liberation Army's (KLA) campaign against Serb domination of the region (perhaps culminating in the outcome of the elections of November 2007).

This attempt to legitimate the ethnic sovereignty held by the Kosovar Albanian population, reinforced by the KLA's control of local security, was extended by the emergence of local political figures in institutions established by UNMIK, as well as the development of a police force, and of other social and financial institutions. Early in this peace operation, internationals associated with UNMIK realized that local actors were using the capacity building projects enacted through UNMIK to build a shadow state, and therefore began to focus on not just the existence of the recognizable assets of self-government but also their competency. In so doing, UNMIK became complicit in the development of Kosovo's capacity for independence – as, in normal statebuilding circumstances, one would expect it should. Even the official term 'Provisional Institutions of Self-Government' for the local governance system created by UNMIK was indicative of this process. As he prepared to become SRSG in February 2002, Michael Steiner explained that the UN would be engaged in a 'step-by-step' transfer of authority to the elected interim government (UNMIK 2002).

International versus local competencies: governance and foreign relations

Kosovar officials thus had a set of standards to use as objectives and rewards for their compliance. This set of standards, of course, implied self-determination for local actors, once achieved, though UNMIK sought to deny that this necessarily followed. Most local actors now claim that they have successfully implemented most of the standards, apart from the most problematic one relating to the return of Serb refugees to their properties.[35] Deputy SRSG Bastagli, however, said in March 2005 that, at best, performance on the standards had been very mixed.[36] Consequently, local opinion polls show that Kosovars regard UNMIK poorly because it is perceived as having prevented Kosovar statehood. This gave rise to a tension between the need for local representatives and actors to cooperate fully with UNMIK, while also maintaining pressure on it for statehood. Indeed, as the SSRG indicated, internationals defined the limits within which a solution must occur, delineated between the two principles of no return to the pre-1999 situation and the prevention of partition.[37]

While UNMIK has been instrumental in assisting the development of ethnic sovereignty in Kosovo (as much as multi-ethnicity remains the official aim), it was, as local actors also argue, an obstacle to it.[38] Until recently, it maintained sole competency over domestic security, and continues to do so over talks with Belgrade, foreign policy issues more generally and, to some degree, relations with international financial institutions. The SRSG controlled all communication with Belgrade, though efforts have been made to promote cooperation between committees at social and cultural levels, which could contribute to the groundwork for shared governance. UNMIK, of course, wanted high-level talks between Pristina and Belgrade on the status issue itself, and these first occurred in July 2006.[39]

Before independence, Kosovar representatives and administrators still lacked full control of domestic affairs, and certainly did not enjoy control of their international affairs.[40] UNMIK was largely in control of the latter, which would require a UN Security Council resolution to transfer. Interestingly, however, according to some UN officials many representatives of major powers in Pristina already thought of themselves as 'ambassadors' and acted as such, being engaged in their own battles for representation.[41] UNMIK also controlled any access to IFIs.[42] No Kosovar army was allowed, either. Because the SSRG controlled Kosovo's budget, UNMIK officials argued that the SSRG would know immediately if any conditions were being violated – officially at least.[43]

Despite these limited competencies and UNMIK's institutional control, Kosovar representatives established some informal networks and institutions. Kosovo's House of Representatives had an embryonic committee for international relations, and individual representatives, including the Prime Minister, nurtured relations with key international officials and politicians from the EU and the United States.[44] Kosovar bodies also voted on foreign matters, and this was taken by outside observers as a deliberate attempt to simulate foreign policy. One report claimed that the Kosovar assembly's vote to reject revisions to the Yugoslav–Macedonian border in 2002 was 'best understood as an indicator of pro-independence sentiments among the [Kosovar] Albanians' (United States Institute of Peace 2002: 2). Kosovar leaders also took the opportunity in 2003 to assert the entity's international presence (and to show solidarity with the United States) by offering to send police to Iraq and Afghanistan (*The Economist* 2003: 31; Geshakova 2003).[45]

Economic and trade relations

In economic terms, UNMIK came to serve the development of Kosovo and its international economic outreach. For example, UNMIK oversaw the privatiza-

tion of much of the Kosovar economy, and advertised major industrial and agri-
cultural concerns for foreign tenders in international media. These acts, apart
from the aim of bringing foreign investment to Kosovo, outraged Serbian officials. They assert that no legal reckoning has been concluded regarding the ownership and compensation for such sales, and emphasize that the financing for
those assets came from federal Yugoslav coffers, and thus primarily from Serbia.
Kosovo's ability to function as a de facto state, and indeed to free-ride on the
international custodians, was borne out by the outrage of Serbian officials that
UNMIK's international advertisements for tenders for property in Kosovo made
no mention that Kosovo is part of Serbia and, worse still, that Kosovo appeared
as an entity in its own right.[46]

In addition, some infrastructural improvements overseen by UNMIK not only
gave pre-independence Kosovo direct physical access to the outside world but
were also presented as developing the entity's foreign presence, again without
reference to Belgrade. When the rail link between Kosovo and Macedonia, cut
during the 1999 war, was restored in December 2005, Kosovar Deputy Prime
Minister Adem Salihaj said the reopening was 'not only a technical event, but
also symbolizes an enhanced relationship between Kosovo and FYR Macedonia'
(UNMIK 2005).

The support of the internationals in advancing Kosovo economically gained
further evidence in November 2005. Kosovar Prime Minister Bajram Kosami and
SRSG Jessen-Petersen co-signed a memorandum addressed to the 'International
Donor Community'. While the document anticipated the management of some
donor disengagement, it also made provisions that would 'help us in securing
multi-year pledges of budget support from international bodies'. Nowhere in the
memorandum was reference to the authority of Belgrade made; Kosovar representatives, with UNMIK's assistance, were making economic policy with explicit
reference to and planning for international funding (UNMIK and PISG 2005).

Informal versus international influence

While Kosovars lacked the formal capacity to make decisions in important competencies that define a state, they nevertheless had clear capacity to lobby and
advocate. Kosovar officials and representatives maintained and developed a level
of agency as a precursor to their intended sovereignty. Furthermore, despite
having their direct access to many IOs and IFIs blocked by UNMIK's control of
sovereignty, they already had access to major world actors by virtue of their
presence in Kosovo and in the region. And as we have seen elsewhere, Kosovar
representatives used this representation with IFIs to their advantage and to the
anger of Belgrade. In other words, the very fact of the international presence in
Kosovo provided its representatives with hitherto unimaginable access to and
familiarity on the international stage, and would also prove a contributing factor
to the success of Kosovo's post- independence existence.

Yet, local actors claimed the lack of formal sovereignty was preventing their
independent development and evolution. Indeed, as Fukuyama has argued,

statebuilding projects can lead to internationals actually degrading rather than building local capacity (2004: 53). In Kosovo, many local actors argued that they would be better off having more responsibility rather than less in order to become more fully involved in their own governance. For example, their lack of political status was argued to have impeded their own economic development.[46] Many Kosovars accepted the price for not being administered from Belgrade, however, and were willing to see the SRSG represent them at the UN and control the process of negotiation over final status with Belgrade, despite the obvious problem that any resultant agreements would be more coloured by international interests than Kosovars might like.

However, the then President of the House, Nexhat Daci, argued that UNMIK had little interest in Kosovars developing their own capacity and actively acted to block any such developments.[47] His own personal contacts, and those of others in the government and House with international connections, substituted for the lack of formal recognition, in his view. Indeed, UNMIK had refused his request of cooperation in developing the House's informal foreign relations committee.[48] That said, by 2006 Kosovo's presence in regional cooperation initiatives was being not only advocated by the SRSG but also assisted by him. Jessen-Petersen went with Kosovar president Fatmir Sejdiu to the Heads of State and Government Meeting of the South East European Cooperation Process in Greece in May 2006. While Jessen-Petersen continued after that meeting to represent Kosovo abroad, he declared 'Kosovo is an integral part of this region, irrespective of but also in anticipation of status. It must become a permanent part of regional cooperation in the interests of regional stability' (UNMIK 2006). The meeting also allowed the Kosovar president to meet several heads of state. This was a case of the international representatives both promoting Kosovo's international political identity and facilitating the appearance on the foreign stage of its leadership. By February 2007, the intention of international peacemakers to imbue Kosovo with true foreign policy capability was made in the proposal by the United Nations negotiator for Kosovo, Martti Ahtisaari. His projected constitution stated: 'Kosovo will have the right to negotiate and conclude international agreements, including the right to seek membership in international organizations' (Ahtisaari 2007: 11–17).

Despite the Kosovar Interim Assembly's desire to promote Kosovo's independence of Kosovo, some opportunities for merely de facto recognition had been missed. At the offices of the UN Development Program (UNDP) in Pristina, for example, concern was expressed about difficulties of working with the Kosovar administration, and many projects were being funded and implemented with minimal local government interaction. However, the UNDP was also working on building local government capacity, on the understanding that whether a final solution entailed sovereignty or not, Kosovo would have its own government.[49] Indeed, while large gaps remained in institutional terms, Kosovars have at least taken some control of their own policing and justice system.

A further irony of these nascent claims for sovereignty in Kosovo (and throughout the region) was and is the role EU accession plays.[50] Most actors in the region see the EU as providing both an existential security through the guarantees of the EU framework for political representation and equality, and further hopes for economic development and prosperity. That EU accession involves surrendering sovereignty to Brussels is overlooked. This indicates that sovereignty in the Balkans is actually a route not merely to self-government and resources of statehood, but also to independence from pre-existing regional relations. Sovereignty is understood in juxtaposition to the regional 'other'. EU accession simply reinforces that dilution of local and regional constraints of sovereignty by providing an alternative administrative, political, social, economic and also probably cultural focus. As Daci argued, sovereignty requires multi-nationality, should be multi-confessional, and engender shared resources – though not with Belgrade.[51] Indeed, he ruefully observed that Belgrade had an unfair advantage from its formal sovereignty.

Nevertheless, interviewees both inside and outside Kosovar institutions demonstrated strong conviction that because UNMIK was unaccountable, it resisted a final status agreement which would mean its disbandment. Indeed, UN officials suggested that during the 2005 UNMIK SRSG, Søren Jessen-Petersen had begun to talk of 'status' rather than 'final status', indicating that a transitional situation would probably continue indefinitely.[52] The lack of any such movement in 2006, despite prior predictions, reinforced that interpretation. The pressure remained for the international community to provide progress from the transitional situation before Kosovars withdrew their cooperation from UNMIK. In parallel with its own EU aspirations, the government in Belgrade had been moving towards a compromise on Kosovo (but short of Kosovar independence), asserting that the province could have '95 per cent' autonomy. As Kosovo's declaration of independence became increasingly more likely, Belgrade proposed in 2007 what it called a 'Hong Kong' model for Kosovo – one country but two systems, but obviously denying Kosovo legal sovereignty (Radio Free Europe 2007). Belgrade's modest changes in position were partly due to Kosovar success in arguing for self-determination, as well as to subverting the peacebuilding processes foisted upon them by internationals. While the transfer of institutions to Kosovars might have vindicated any attempts to use shared sovereignty to overcome ethnic sovereignty, indications of shared governance are too few to guarantee that inter-ethnic relations in Kosovo are subsequently sustainable and free of tension.

These moves by Kosovars' representatives helped shape the development of the role of UNMIK and the four pillars after its inception. They had also been instrumental in redefining how UNMIK officials related to emerging Kosovar institutions. As both they and the internationals had planned, as their institutions have developed their agency has similarly increased; the key problem remains that both ethnic communities still do not share their institutions – a matter intensified since Kosovo's independence. Devolution of governance and sovereignty to local actors and institutions may have occurred somewhat faster than internationals desired. Evidence also shows that this has been aimed not just at fulfilling the desired developments directed by internationals, but also at fulfilling local ambitions for statehood. For example, even UNMIK personnel acknowledged that local actors have international contacts in various areas.[53] In some cases, foreign governments were assisting embryonic foreign policy-making capacity by developing relations with Kosovar political figures and bypassing UNMIK. UNMIK also began to ignore some of these activities specifically to allow for the development of foreign policy capacity.[54] It is telling that, of the four pillars, the EU and the OSCE were popular because they were not viewed as interfering with Kosovar claims for sovereignty. Indeed, opinions were expressed that the EU commission might manage the next stage of Kosovo's development, possibly in an OHR-type role, after final status had been decided, and as part of an accession process of an independent Kosovo to the EU.[55]

Proposals for development: shared governance

How can this tension between ethnic sovereignty and shared sovereignty be alleviated? Shared sovereignty is subject to conditionalities imposed by international actors, and allows local actors to manoeuvre for empowerment with other regional actors rather than develop regional cooperation. It is problematic because it encourages relationships between local actors and key international actors, but discourages relationships between local actors. The rewards of building strong vertical relationships are much greater than those of building strong horizontal relationships. Ethnic sovereignty encourages ethnic actors to resist transnationalism and pluralism, and to seek to recreate narrow, ethnically minded

International peacebuilding actors

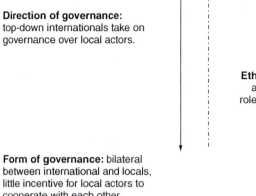

Direction of governance:
top-down internationals take on governance over local actors.

Ethnic sovereignty: leads to local attempts to shape internationals' roles and local outcomes – forming hybrid forms of sovereignty

Form of governance: bilateral between international and locals, little incentive for local actors to cooperate with each other.

Local entity in post-conflict zone

Figure 5.1 Shared sovereignty.

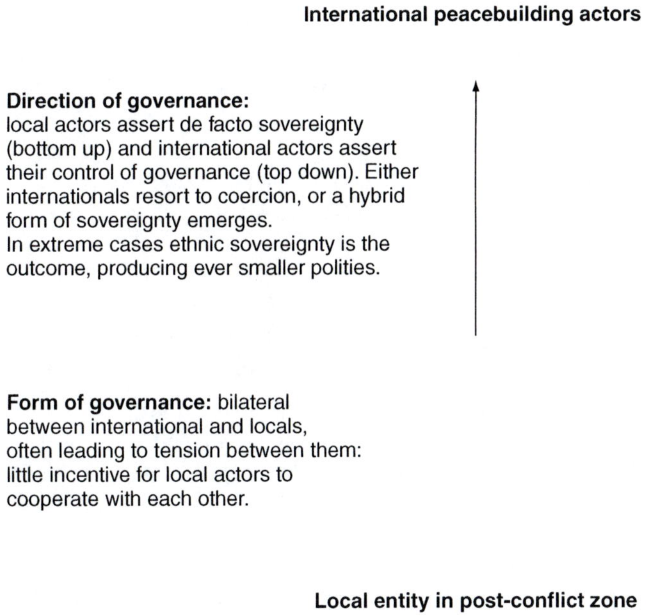

International peacebuilding actors

Direction of governance:
local actors assert de facto sovereignty
(bottom up) and international actors assert
their control of governance (top down). Either
internationals resort to coercion, or a hybrid
form of sovereignty emerges.
In extreme cases ethnic sovereignty is the
outcome, producing ever smaller polities.

Form of governance: bilateral
between international and locals,
often leading to tension between them:
little incentive for local actors to
cooperate with each other.

Local entity in post-conflict zone

Figure 5.2 Ethnic sovereignty.

International peacebuilding actors

Direction of governance:
Local actors assert ethnic sovereignty
within the parameters of negotiations
with international and regional actors,
thus modifying ethnic sovereignty.

Form of governance:
multilateral between international and
locals, and horizontal, being dependent
upon local entities cooperating with each
other.
Hybrid forms of sovereignty emerge,
leading to shared governance.

Local actors also cooperate horizontally

Figure 5.3 Shared governance.

and ethnically homogenous entities though internal censorship and strong vertical relationships with international actors. This often occurs despite the odds against such non-state and unrecognized actors, and at the expense of relationships between actors on the ground. It is a distortion of the neo-institutionalist and liberal arguments about governance and the need for international institutions to anchor a civil peace.

A rebalancing of external involvement with local cooperation is required: sovereignty should be shared vertically, as Krasner suggests, to allow an external guarantee of stability, but also horizontally, between local actors, to allow for regional consensus and consent to develop, as opposed to entities that claim ethnic sovereignty (see Figures 5.1–5.3). It might also be pertinent to point out that liberal forms of sovereignty (as this is the aspiration of the internationals for the Balkans) do not rest merely on the state, but equally on society and on a social contract. A caveat is that the latter must be the priority of any regimes, norms and institutions, and not just in terms of the liberal restriction and guarantee of individual wellbeing, but also in terms of the rights of individuals to define their own peace processes at the micro-level, and in a broad, societal and intersubjective setting. This is made more complex in a collectivist or community-oriented environment. Shared sovereignty and governance that do not allow for this will not attain local legitimacy, and will remain virtual and contested concepts. At best, where reluctance for shared governance remains, ethnic sovereignty would be the best that local actors could achieve – in other words, an unstable stalemate in tension with the international (though contested) norms of the liberal peace framework. The lucrative resources that arise from vertical relationships between local actors and internationals should probably be dependent, however, upon horizontal, regional forms of cooperation emerging quickly.

This means that local cooperation should be institutionalized and promoted in the structures of each entity, and encouraged between them. Local agency should be recognized in both its positive and its negative forms, and any chauvinism expressing itself via international connections with local actors should be discouraged more strongly than has been done. This should not lead to cooperation between mono-ethnic entities across the region, as has been institutionalized by Dayton, but should primarily focus on pluralism and hybridity as a route to cooperation. This, of course, should not be taken as an endorsement of the polarization and binaries introduced by sovereignty in its positivist sense, and should engage with the notion of personal sovereignty, communal identities and the social contract. Ethnic sovereignty, as we have shown, and as international peacemakers largely intend, is clearly to be avoided. Yet shared sovereignty may actually promote ethnic sovereignty because it promotes competition between local entities for the attention of international actors.

Conclusion: shared governance in the Balkans?

International custodians have denied de jure sovereignty to the RS and to Kosovo (status talks and UDI notwithstanding in the case of the latter), but have also contributed to the conditions for de facto sovereignty that lacks incentives for entities to cooperate in the region. This paradoxical situation forms both an under-explored analytical issue in IR and also an important gap in policy that generally discourages local ethnic entities from collaborating or even communicating with each other.

Ethnic sovereignty creates obstacles to the peace settlement, including: (1) a disruption of the official or intended settlement by creating new boundaries and disrupting the intended post-conflict integration type of dependence; (2) an unintended empowerment of some entities; (3) a resulting creation of insecurity for other entities or minorities; and (4) the dependency of some local actors on international custodians. Effectively, this may mean that peace settlements are implicitly being re-negotiated during their implementation, and that shared sovereignty and de jure sovereignty are not all that they seem to be in the Balkans. The question of sovereignty is central to the construction of a liberal state, and it is extremely difficult for a focused peace process to operate where the end goals of strong statehood are undetermined, or not adhered to by component actors. Yet much of the literature on peacebuilding and on peace processes assumes that the end goal will be a liberal state, with some form of unitary, federal or confederal constitution, and that until this is achieved disputants will tend not to think of themselves as sovereign actors. Our findings strongly suggest the opposite. Furthermore, we find that the peace process itself becomes subject to tensions between actors and third parties regarding the exact nature of their status. Neighbouring states also are drawn into their recognition game, along with international actors.

The question in each case – and the gap in theoretical literature – is how these by-products of the liberal peace can be moved towards what we have called shared governance, through a realization of hybrid forms of sovereignty. These are shared by local and international actors, but also predicated upon regional cooperation and a mediation of ethnicity rather than its categorical assertion through state formation processes. This represents our prescription for progress from a sole focus on shared sovereignty, and which we argue is reproducing ethnic sovereignty. In the case of the RS, the Dayton peace was premised on creating mechanisms for shared governance within Bosnia. But outside relations were (arguably by necessity) limited. The RS was allowed special relations with Serbia, but its foreign relations were not to exist of their own accord. The RS's relative weakness and regime changes in both Croatia and Serbia have given international custodians leverage to limit its activities. Nevertheless, the RS has attempted 'cooperation' (which international representatives consider to be criminal activity) with other local actors (and others further afield). This creates the added irony for peacemakers of stopping and undoing such unwanted cooperation while encouraging other cooperation, particularly between entities in Bosnia. Some progress has been made, and remains integral to the construction of any lasting peace. In Kosovo, international custodians advocated not only that Kosovar representatives be involved in direct negotiations (under UN auspices) with Belgrade, but also that Kosovo as an actor be acknowledged and included in regional activities of sovereign states. Kosovar leaders, while frustrated by some limitations imposed on their aspirations of sovereignty by international custodianship, nevertheless used that presence to build a parallel state structure and to exert much more of an international presence instead of simply being the object of international statebuilding.

The above discussion has shown that peacemaking and peacebuilding in the Balkans have so far – as much as international actors may have recognized and even worked against this detrimental problem – reproduced entities that ignore each other, maintain abrasive mutual relationships, simulate their own exclusive and ethnicized sovereignty and representation through their relationship with international actors, and fail therefore to establish a meaningful regional basis for cooperation and development. Anything other than a negative and externally supported peace in the Balkans remains remote. Our prescription of shared governance rather than shared sovereignty underlines how international actors have been drawn into the dispute and have failed to exercise a conditionality that encourages a broader peace, and how such a step forward might be conceptualized intellectually and by the policy community.

Acknowledgements

We are most grateful to the Nuffield Foundation for a generous research grant that facilitated extensive research on ground throughout the Western Balkans.

Notes

1 This chapter focuses on the dynamics leading up to the recent and unilateral declaration of independence by Kosovo on 17 February 2008.
2 For a prescriptive example, see United States Institute of Peace (2002).
3 For more on spoiling and devious objectives, see Newman and Richmond (2006), especially the Introduction and Chapter 3.
4 For more on this line of argument, see Weber (1995).
5 This indicates that intervention is now extremely far reaching, impinging on the human person. For more on this concept, see Foucault (1976).
6 For an early version of this framework, see Richmond (2002).
7 The state as a person of international law should possess the following qualifications: (a) a permanent population, (b) a defined territory, (c) government, and (d) capacity to enter into relations with other states. Article 1 of the Montevideo Convention on Rights and Duties of States, 1933. Available: avalon.law.yale.edu/20th_century/intam03.asp (accessed 17 February 2009). It should also be independent, have a degree of permanence, willingness to observe international law and respect for human rights (Brownlie 1990: 72–79).
8 For example, Croatia's Foreign Ministry was renamed the Ministry of Foreign Affairs and European Integration, to denote both its main aim and the official legitimacy of this aim.
9 This is not to judge the necessity or legitimacy of doing so, simply that it has happened.
10 Lajčàk became Slovak Foreign Minister in January 2009, but in the absence of a replacement has continued (at the time of final revision) in the position of EU Representative.

11 Interview with senior international official, 5 April 2005. These perspectives are reiterated in, Steele (2005).

12 Interviews in Banja Luka. At the same time, one senior international official was confident that a 'Georgian style' revolution would occur in the RS and remove the existing, self-interested powers, and usher in new legality and anti-corruption campaigns.

13 Interview with Petar Kuhić, Professor at the Faculty of Law, Banja Luka University, and member of the Parliament of BiH, and former Deputy Prime Minister and Minister for Local Administration of the RS, 6 April 2005.

14 See Annex 4, Article III: Responsibilities of and Relations Between the Institutions of Bosnia and Herzegovina and the Entities. Available: www.daytonproject.org/PDFs/060219_State_Entity_Competencies_English_FINAL.pdf (Accessed 17 February 2009).

15 An international official's perspective was that the only significant activity in the RS was the handling of stolen cars from Western Europe.

16 Anecdotal evidence from discussions in Banja Luka in early April 2005.

17 Personal Interview in Banja Luka, 6 April 2005.

18 Communications with authors.

19 Interview with a leading Croatian media analyst, Zagreb, 8 April 2005.

20 Interviews at the Croatian Ministry of Foreign Affairs and European Integration, 8 April 2005.

21 This chapter takes the term 'foreign policy' in its conventional understanding as expressly being the activity of recognized international actors. Because the RS is not empowered to have 'foreign policy' of its own, we use the term 'foreign relations', but we are obviously examining the extent to which de facto foreign policy is being attempted.

22 Indeed, citizens of former Yugoslav republics can often travel across international borders with minimal identification, which ironically suggests that in this way a degree of cross-border openness already exists.

23 Interview, Banja Luka, 7 April 2005.

24 Interview with Kuhić.

25 But Serbian ambassador Nedeljko Despotovic retorted; 'I don't agree. There is no link between Kosovo and Bosnia. Republika Srpska will continue to function with the state of Bosnia-Herzegovina' (Cohen 2004). Interviews within the OHR in February 2007 also confirmed this view.

26 Personal interviews with OHR Diplomatic Personnel, 1 February 2007.

27 This view was repeated while in the RS in April 2005.

28 Interview with the former co-president of BiH, Sarajevo, 4 April 2005.

29 Interview, Banja Luka, 7 April 2005.

30 Interview, Sarajevo, 5 April 2005.

31 By way of anecdotal evidence, Serbs in Banja Luka generally say that they were aware of 'Srebrenica', although they did not call it a 'massacre'. Further, they noted that they, and more of their acquaintances, acknowledged its occurrence where even five years ago they would not have.

32 Interview with Miljenko Dereta, Belgrade, 30 March 2005.

33 Among the examples is the striking case of OHR Carlos Westendorp having NATO troops find and stop a moderate MP on the highway and return him to parliament for a vote when the opposition SDS were absent, thinking a vote could not therefore occur, allowing controversial and Western-backed legislation to squeak through. See Kelly (1998: A21).

34 Interview with Xhavit Haliti, 24 March 2005, Pristina.

35 Interview with Haliti.

36 Interview with Francesco Bastagli, Deputy SSRG for Kosovo, Pillar 2, Pristina, 26 March 2005.

37 Interview with Bastagli.

38 Interview with Haliti. He argued that Kosovo was a 'school' in which its administrators were being taught by the internationals.
39 Interview with senior UNMIK official, Kosovo, 23 March 2005.
40 Interview with Haliti.
41 Interview with senior UNMIK official, Pristina, 23 March 2005.
42 Interview with Professor Dr. Nexhat Daci, President of the Assembly of Kosovo, Personal, Pristina, 23 March 2005.
43 Interview with senior UNMIK official.
44 Interview with senior UNMIK official. For example, members of the government and the president had visited various EU states, including a trip to the German parliament, sponsored by the EU. A lack of funds has meant these activities have been more limited than desired.
45 The Kosovar offer was arguably made also to counter Belgrade's similar offer. See Fawn (2006).
46 Interview with Sasha Mart, Serbian Foreign Ministry, April 2005.
47 Interview with Haliti. Indeed, it has been argued that Kosovo is simply a colony of UNMIK, rather than a 'trust'.
48 Interview with Daci.
49 Personal Interview with official source, UNDP, Pristina, 24 March 2005.
50 For example, in the case of Albania, the priority is EU accession first and support for Kosovo's independence second. Interview with P. Milo, Member of Parliament, Ministry of Foreign Affairs, Tirana, 28 March 2005.
51 Interview with Daci.
52 Interview with UNMIK official.
53 Interview with UNMIK official. He confirmed that the Kosovar Prime Minister has an informal presence in many major capitals.
54 Interview with UNMIK official.
55 Interview with UNMIK official.

References

Ahtisaari, M. (2007) 'Comprehensive Proposal for the Kosovo Status Settlement'. Available: www.assembly-kosova.org/common/docs/Comprehensive%20-Proposal%20.pdf (accessed 12 February 2009).

Akhavan, P. (2001) 'Beyond Impunity: Can International Criminal Justice Prevent Future Atrocities?', *American Journal of International Law*, 95/7: 7–31.

Annan, K. (1999) 'Two Concepts of Sovereignty', *The Economist*, 18 September.

Belloni, R. (2001) 'Civil Society and Peacebuilding in Bosnia and Herzegovina', *Journal of Peace Research*, 38/2: 163–a80.

Brownlie, I. (1990) *Principles of Public International Law*, Oxford: Clarendon Press.

Cohen, R. (2004) 'Globalist: The Serbian question, still on Europe's plate', *International Herald Tribune*, 12 October.

Cousens, E. M. and Cater, C. K. (2001) *Towards Peace in Bosnia: Implementing the Dayton Peace Accords*, Boulder, CO: Lynne Rienner.

Diez, T. (2005) 'The EU and the Transformation of Conflict Constitutional Systems', in T. Giegerich (ed.) *The EU Accession of Cyprus*, Baden-Baden: Nomos.

Diez, T., Albert, M. and Stetter, S. (2008) *The European Union and Border Conflicts: Assessing the Impact of Integration and Association*, Cambridge: Cambridge University Press.

Dillon, M. (2003) 'Culture, Governance and Global Biopolitics', in F. Debrix and C. Weber (eds) *Rituals of Mediation*, Minneapolis, MN: University of Minnesota Press.

Duffield, M. (2001) *Global Governance and the New Wars*, London: Zed Books.

European Commission (2007) 'Communication from the commission to the council and the European parliament: enlargement strategy and main challenges 2007–2008', 6 November. Available: ec.europa.eu/enlargement/pdf/key_documents/2007/nov/strategy_paper_en.pdf (accessed 12 February 2009).

Fawn, R. (2006) 'Central and Eastern Europe: Independent Actors or Supplicant States?', in R. Fawn and R. Hinnebusch (eds) *The Iraq War*, Boulder, CO: Lynne Rienner.

Fawn, R. (2008) 'The Kosovo – and Montenegro – Effect', *International Affairs*, 84/2: 269–294.

Foucault, M. (1976) *The Birth of the Clinic*, London: Routledge.

Fukuyama, F. (2004) *State Building: Governance and Order in the Twenty First Century*, London: Profile.

Geshakova, J. (2003) 'Serbia and Montenegro: Belgrade offers Washington Soldiers for Afghanistan', Radio Free Europe radio liberty. Available: www.rferl.org/content/article/1104587.html (accessed 14 February 2009).

High Level Panel on Threats, Challenges, and Change (2004) 'A More Secure World: our shared responsibility'. Available: www.un.org/secureworld (accessed 15 February 2009).

International Commission on Intervention and State Sovereignty (2001) *The Responsibility to Protect*, Ottawa: International Development Research Centre.

James, A. (2000) 'The Concept of Sovereignty Revisited', in A. Schnabel and R. Thakur (eds) *Kosovo and the Challenge of Humanitarian Intervention: Selective Indignation, Collective Action and International Citizenship*, Tokyo: United Nations University Press.

Jevremovic, J. (2006) 'Kosovo would Raise Repuplika Srpska', Glas Javosti, September 19. Available: www.kosovo.net/news/archive/2006/September_19/4.html (accessed 15 February 2009).

Katan, G. (2005) 'Republik Srpska spurns non-Serb investors'. Online. Balkan Crisis Report, 28 October. Available: www.iwpr.net/?p_bcr&s_f&o_256842&apc_state_henpbcr (accessed 12 February 2009).

Kelly, M. (1998) 'A Chance to Change History', *The Washington Post*, 21 January.

Knaus, G. and Martin, F. (2003) 'Lesson from Bosnia: The Travails of the European Raj', *Journal of Democracy*, 14/3: 60–74.

Krasner, S. (2004) 'Sharing Sovereignty: New Institutions for Collapsed and Failing States', *International Security*, 29/2: 85–120.

Krasner, S. (2005) 'The Case for Shared Sovereignty', *Journal of Democracy*, 16/1: 69–83.

Lipschutz, R. D. (2002) 'The Clash of Governmentalities: The Fall of the UN Republic and America's Reach for Imperium', Paper presented at 'Exploring Imperium', University of Sussex, 11 December.

MacGrew, A. (1997) *The Transformation of Global Democracy*, Cambridge: Polity.

Mandelbaum, M. (2002) *The Ideas that Conquered the World*. New York, NY: Public Affairs.

Meier, V. (1999) *A History of its Demise*, translated by S. Ramet, New York, NY: Routledge.

Mitchell, C. (1992) 'External Peacemaking Initiatives and Intra-national Conflict', in M. Midlarsky (ed.) *The Internationalisation of Communal Strife*, London: Routledge.

Moore, P. (1999) 'Bosnian Serb Prime Minister says "send Karadzic and Milošević to the Hague" ', RFE/RL Balkan Report 3:39, 15 October.

Neufeld, M. (1993) 'Interpretation and the "Science" of International Relations', *Review of International Studies*, 19/1: 39–61.

Newman, E. and Richmond, O. P. (2006) *Challenges to Peacebuilding*, Tokyo: United Nations University Press.

Owen, D. (1996) *Balkan Odyssey*, London: Indigo.

Paris, R. (2002) 'International Peacebuilding and the "Mission Civilisatrice"', *Review of International Studies*, 28/4: 637–656.

Paris, R. (2004) *At War's End*, Cambridge: Cambridge University Press.

Pond, E. (2006) *Endgame in the Balkans*, Washington, DC: Brookings.

Radio Free Europe (1999a) 'Bosnian Serb Leader Defends Talks with Milošević', Radio Free Europe newsline, 13 October. Available: www.rferl.org/content/Article/1142012.html (accessed 12 February 2009).

Radio Free Europe (1999b) 'Dodik says War Crimes Tribunal can Open Office in Banja Luka', Radio Free Europe newsline, 4 November. Available: www.rferl.org/content/Article/1142027.html (accessed 22 February 2009).

Radio Free Europe (2006a) 'Bosnian Serb Premier Wants to Keep Entity's Police Force', Radio Free Europe newsline, 16 August. Available: www.rferl.org/content/Article/1143696.html (accessed 23 February 2009).

Radio Free Europe (2006b) 'Bosnian Serbs Reportedly Ready to Reach Special Agreement with Croatia', Radio Free Europe newsline, 12 July. Available: www.rferl.org/content/Article/1143671.html (accessed 23 February 2009).

Radio Free Europe (2007) 'Serbia Proposes Hong Kong Model for Kosova', Radio Free Europe newsline, 6 November. Available: www.rferl.org/content/Article/1143988.html (accessed 24 February 2009).

Ramet, S. P. (2002) *Balkan Babel: The Disntegration of Yugoslavia from the Death of Tito to the Fall of Milošević*, Boulder, CO: Westview Press.

Richmond, O. P. (2002) States of Sovereignty, Sovereign States, and Ethnic Claims for International Status', *Review of International Studies*, 28/2: 381–402.

Richmond, O. P. (2004) 'UN Peace Operations and the Dilemmas of the Peacebuilding Consensus', *International Peacekeeping*, 10/4: 83–101.

Richmond, O. P. (2005) *The Transformation of Peace*, London: Palgrave.

Shaw, M. (2002) 'Exploring Imperia: Western-global Power Amidst the Wars of Quasi-imperial States', Paper presented at 'Exploring Imperium', University of Sussex, 11 December. Available: www.theglobalsite.ac.uk (accessed 28 February 2009).

Standards for Kosovo (2005) UNMIK. Available: www.unmikonline.org/standards/priorities.htm (accessed 23 February 2009).

Steele, J. (2005) 'Today's Bosnia: A Dependent, Stifled, Apartheid Regime', *Guardian*, 11 November.

The Economist (1996) 'Bosnia: Carving Smoothly', *The Economist*, 2 March.

The Economist (2003) 'Cuddling Up to the Americans', *The Economist*, 23 August.

The Economist (2005) 'Bosnia, Rebuilt but Still Divid(ed.)', *The Economist*, 23 November.

The Economist (2007) 'Bosnian Politics: Cracking Up', *The Economist*, 27 October.

United States Institute of Peace (2002) 'Kosovo Final Status: Options and Cross-border Requirements', Special report 91, July. Available: www.usip.org/pubs/specialreports/sr91.pdf (accessed 14 February 2009).

UNMIK (2002) 'Gradual Transfer of Power to Kosovo Authorities Key Goal, New UN Mission Chief Says', UNMIK news, 8 February. Available: www.unmikonline.org/archives/news02_02full.htm#0802 (accessed 14 February 2009).

UNMIK (2005) 'PDSRSG Larry Rossin inaugurates Pristina-Skopje passenger railway service', UNMIK press release, UNMIK/PR/1470, 20 December. Available: www.unmikonline.org/DPI/PressRelease.nsf/0/6EBFFD99FDE0FD55C12570-DE002A35C2/$FILE/pr1470.pdf (accessed 14 February 2009).

UNMIK (2006) 'SRSG: Kosovo must become a permanent part of regional cooperation', UNMIK press release, UNMIK/PR/1547, 4 May 2006. Available: www.unmikonline.org/dpi/pressrelease.nsf/0/6094094E1D5646FAC125716C003808A2/$FILE/pr1547.pdf (accessed 14 February 2009).

UNMIK and PISG (2005) 'Letter between UNMIK and PISG to International Donor Community', 2 November. Available: www.unmikonline.org/archives/EUinKosovo/upload/Letter%20of%20Intent%20Kosovo%20Memorandum%20of%20Economic%20and%20Financial%20Policies.pdf (accessed 17 February 2009).

Uvalic, M. (2000) 'Regional cooperation in southeastern Europe', Working paper 17/01, University of Pergugia. Available: www.one-europe.ac.uk/pdf/wp17.pdf. (accessed 17 February 2009).

Vulliamy, E. (2005) 'Farewell, Sarajevo', *Guardian*, 2 November.

Weber, C. (1995) *Simulating Sovereignty*, Cambridge: Cambridge University Press.

Westendorp, C. (1999) 'Bosnian Serbs can help to guarantee the peace', *International Herald Tribune*, 15 March.

Woodward, S. L. (2001) 'Compromised Sovereignty to Create Sovereignty: is Dayton Bosnia a futile exercise or an emerging model?', in S. Krasner (ed.) *Problematic Sovereignty: contested rules and political possibilities*, New York, NY: Columbia University Press.

6 Policing the state of exception in Kosovo

Barry J. Ryan

Introduction

It is over ten years since the United Nations Interim Administration Mission in Kosovo (UNMIK) Civilian Police (CIVPOL) contingent began recruiting and training men and women to form the Kosovo Police Service (KPS). For this entire period the KPS has existed in a subservient position to the real providers of security in Kosovo – the Kosovo Protection Force (KFOR), UNMIK and the European Union. In passing UN Security Council Resolution 1244 the international community afforded itself executive authority over the territory of Kosovo, granting itself the monopoly over the use of force. In so doing, an assemblage of police officers from over forty-two different states assumed the power and practice of law enforcement in Kosovo. This power derives from the assumption by the UN of sovereign authority over the area (Decker 2006: 504). Backed by the military capacity of KFOR, the largest deployment of international police officers ever has, together with the KPS, successfully maintained the sovereign authority of the international community for over a decade. They have accomplished this by maintaining Kosovo in a state of exception, whereby the maintenance of order is given priority over the rule of law. It is within the international community's tendency to position security as an elemental feature of liberal democracy in Kosovo that we find the structural causes of the KPS's failure to be accepted as a legitimate and objective law enforcement institution; one that would have the capacity to police the multi-ethnic state devised by the international community.

This chapter forms a critique of policing practices in Kosovo. As policing is essentially a political activity dedicated to maintaining the socioeconomic order of a state through the threat or usage of violent force, any understanding of the problematic position in which the KPS has found itself necessarily needs to define the order which it has been tasked to maintain. This leads us to explore the contested nature of Kosovo's (domestic) sovereignty – the competing claims on Kosovo made by the Republic of Serbia, the Kosovo Assembly and the international community. It compels us to accept that sovereignty is the most profound and prevalent issue behind all juridico-political problems in Kosovo, and that the loyalty of the KPS is caught between mutually exclusive visions of Kosovo's future. Moreover, it raises the issue as to the nature of Kosovo's democracy and the improbability that its long history of exclusionary policing based on a politically malleable and easily revoked rule of law will end.

This chapter illustrates that in Kosovo there has always been a minority contesting the territory's sovereignty, and this minority has always lived beyond the protection of the rule of law. It will draw on Carl Schmitt's understanding of sovereignty and upon Giorgio Agamben's notion of *homo sacer* to situate the KPS between the international community's sovereign authority and the will of ethnic Albanians to rule to the territory.

Thus, I argue that the international community's statebuilding plan is ahistorical. It constitutes an attempt to end both the history of Kosovo and the European tradition of nation-state building in which the emphasis has always been placed on the importance of identity-based homogenizing institutions that evoke national loyalty. This tension between traditional nation-state building and the post-national multi-ethnic state envisaged by the UN and the EU manifests itself in the role of the KPS. Financed by, and under the legal authority of, the international community, the KPS is at the same time subject to the moral authority of the majoritarian ethnic Albanian national will. The KPS is caught between the actions of the international regime, the standards it has set out, and the status of self-determination that is being sought for by ethnic Albanians. Its task is to enforce a liberal democratic multi-ethnic constitutional order that does not exist. It is a force trapped between history and an attempt to end history.

Sovereignty and Kosovo

There are many meanings to the concept of sovereignty (Suganami 2007), but in the early 1920s Carl Schmitt defined sovereignty in terms of 'political community'. The history of nation-state projects in Europe serves as testimony to the idea that communities either assimilate to a common national identity or remain exterior to the national order. Benedict Anderson's (1991) study of identity categories in South-East Asia highlighted the simplification and relative arbitrariness of ethnic categories in a nation-building context. While Anderson would disagree with Schmitt's primordial pre-political conception of community, he would nevertheless conclude, as Ger Duijzings (2000: 23) has, that unambiguous delineations of ethnic identity with clear criteria for inclusion and exclusion appear to be central to any modern nation-building process. Roger Brubaker's study of nation-building, for example, in France and Germany is indicative. France, he writes, constituted nationhood in terms of political unity as a 'striving for cultural unity' (1992: 184), and thus follow assimilationist immigration policies. Germany, on the other hand had a more closed primal concept of nation – a pre-political understanding that its people were already a nation that needed a state. One cannot simply comply with the German sense of nation by assimilating – one is either German or one is not. It is this Germanic understanding of sovereignty as a primal concept that we find in the writings of Schmitt; 'the concept of the state presupposes the concept of the political' (Schmitt 1976: 37). The creation of a state is a method of reversing Clausewitz's maxim – the state is the continuation of war through politics. Schmitt understood sovereignty to be a political concept concerning the conflict between insiders and outsiders – friend and enemy. A sovereign community is one in which a community governs itself and accords itself the legal right to exclude those with antithetical moral or political values. Moreover, it would seem that sovereignty for Schmitt rests with the group with the greatest will to power – 'the grouping is always political which orients itself towards this most extreme possibility of war … this grouping is therefore always the decisive human grouping' (Schmitt, cited by Suganami 2007: 517).

Slavoj Zizek (1999) has pointed out that the sovereign ruler compels us to respect the very laws he or she is above. By being the one who can decide the difference between friend and enemy, the sovereign reserves the power to declare a state of emergency, to suspend the rule of law so as to impose his order. He is therefore not subject to his own law, which he can interpret as his needs demand. For Schmitt, the sovereign is the one who defines the homogeneity of the 'people' or the nation, and who ultimately decides which group will enjoy equal rights and which group shall not (Mouffe 1999). The sovereign ruler is therefore, 'he who decides upon the exception' (Schmitt: 2006: 5). As Hidemi Suganami has pointed out, this idea of the sovereign was followed closely by Hans Morgenthau when he observed:

> that authority within the state is sovereign which in case of dissension among the different law making factors has the responsibility for making the final binding decision and which in a crisis of law enforcement, such as revolution or civil war, has the ultimate responsibility for enforcing the laws of the land.
>
> (cited by Suganami 2007: 517)

Girogio Agamben (1995, 2003) takes up this point when he argues that the sovereign power's ability to suspend the law and institute violence in order to re-establish the *status quo* means that the sovereign is both inside and outside the law. The legal constitution of a state is therefore valid only when the sovereign deems it to be. Any struggle over a territory might therefore be seen in terms of a contest over the ability to decide the threshold of exception. Agamben further draws out this understanding in order to propose that the power granted to the sovereign to make this decision means that sovereignty is more than simply political, and that in fact it refers to a power over life itself. Exploring this avenue through Foucaultian biopolitics, he points out the historical existence of *homo sacer*; a human whose politico-legal identity falls beyond the limits of the community – those who are excluded from the sovereign community and for whom the state of exception is normality. *Homo sacer*, according to Agamben, is constantly faced with violence, and exists in an eternal state of exception beyond the boundaries of legal protection. In Kosovo, it might be argued that the title of *homo sacer* has shifted between its communities, depending upon which political grouping occupied the sovereign seat. Seen as such, sovereignty, tied to a rigid notion of ethnic political community, becomes a matter of life or death. For Michael Dillon (2009), the liberal way of rule is guided by a need to establish sovereignty over this power over life itself. War is waged on humans paradoxically to remove the scourge of war from the human. Having been defined as ethnically based, the conflict in Kosovo has produced a liberal war-like strategy to eradicate the ethnic factor. Kosovo therefore represents a radical experiment to further the evolution of liberalism which identifies ethnic categories as an impediment to perpetual peace.

Historically, as agents in the process of European nation-state building, the police had a quite clear function to maintain an ethno-political order and to separate the included from the excluded. Numerous studies into the inherent racism of police forces around the world together point to the complicity of policing in exclusionary practices of nation-building. In fact, liberal attempts to reform police forces in Australia, the UK and the US (among others) have manifestly failed to eradicate the traces of this complicity (Chan 2000). Places such as Kosovo or East Timor, which have long been exposed to extra-juridical police violence in the name of a sovereign authority's order, therefore provide liberalism with a raw opportunity to construct a more effectively policed jurisdiction. This justifies the continuation of the state of exception and requires the international community to establish itself firmly as the sovereign authority.

Consequently, in order to form any analysis of policing in Kosovo, we first need to establish the nature of the region's sovereignty. The UN granted itself the ability to decide the exception in Kosovo by passing Resolution 1244. The sovereign ruler of Kosovo in this sense is the Special Representative of the Secretary General (SRSG), who has authority over UNMIK. More pertinent to Schmitt's idea of sovereignty is the power accorded to the SRSG to make and revoke all appointments within the UNMIK structure. As Vojislav Kostunica observed in 2000, 'Kosovo is not under our sovereignty, but under that of the international community' (cited in Dragovic-Sovo 2002: 258). The SRSG was additionally granted the ultimate power over Kosovo by being granted the 'final authority of interpretation of Resolution 1244' (Secretary General 199: para 4). Moreover, as Alexandra Gheciu (2005: 127) points out, the SRSG retained the position as final authority over the Interim Administrative Council – which consisted of UNMIK, ethnic Albanian leaders and a Serb leader – providing veto power over any bill submitted to his office. Even the Constitutional Framework – which passes wide powers of self-government to Kosovo – reserves the ultimate for the SRSG, thus, as Irene Bernabeu observes, entitling 'the SRSG to override any decision or law emanating from elected institutions'. In fact, the twenty-four powers reserved for the SRSG in the 2001 Constitutional Framework largely relate to the ability of the Representative to intervene and suspend the rule of law if he or she deems it necessary.[1] With a large NATO army, a well-armed international police force and an indigenous police force, the SRSG had ample resources to secure this sovereign position. By the Standards for Status process initiated in 2003 he gained more power, in that he established a right to decide not only the nature of Kosovo's future, but also who would be next in line for the throne. Before we explore the manner by which this power was exercised, however, it worthwhile reminding ourselves of the fate of previous regimes that wielded such power over the inhabitants of Kosovo.

The history of sovereign contests

Kosovo has always been a territory explained in terms of a violent contest fought on the basis of ethnicity. Located between competing expressions of nationalism, Kosovo was a chaotic place. In the last days of the Ottoman Empire, Kosovo witnessed violent uprisings between Albanians and the Turks. Ethnic rivalry was compounded by the expulsion after the 1878 Berlin Congress of Muslims to Kosovo, and Christians from Kosovo to Serbia proper. This has been recognised as the moment when the division between Albanian and Serb was first constructed into a concrete political division (Duijzings 2000). Consequently, the Second Balkan War at the start of the twentieth century was indicative of rival ethnic groups contesting land as a source of nationhood – according to Stevan Pavlowitch (2002: 84), the war was fought not simply to acquire territory, but between rival populations of antagonistic ethnic groups. Ceded to Serbia from the Ottoman Empire in 1913 through the Treaty of Bucharest, the legend of Kosovo as the symbolic source of Serb identity was cast. It did not matter that few in the region at the time considered themselves Serb; nor did it matter that the war had resulted in a hostile Muslim Albanian population. Sovereign authority over the sacred territory of Kosovo had been won, and the region was incorporated into the wider Serb nation-building process. Ominously, Pavlowitch observes that the ethnic Albanians who stayed in the region 'resisted Serbia's authority whenever and however they could' (ibid.: 85).

Mostly illiterate and unfavourably treated in land reform, ethnic Albanians obviously fared badly as a minority in the Royal Kingdom of Yugoslavia established after the First World War. However, that is not to say that Serbs living in Kosovo fared much better. The theme of Kosovo throughout the twentieth century has been a history of economic neglect. Being a border zone, peripheral to the centre and inhabited by political groupings antagonistic to Serb hegemony, Kosovo was (and remains) an economically backward region. Michel Roux has called it the 'Third World within Europe', comparing its economy in the late 1980s to that of Honduras and the Ivory Coast (1992: 238). Tito assigned Kosovo a role that effectively made it a colony after the Second World War. The wealth of raw materials extracted from the mines at Trepica, for instance, was spent modernizing the northern half of Yugoslavia. Julie Mertus (1999: 23–29) has pointed out that Kosovo as a province had the lowest levels of infrastructural development and exhibited the highest rates of unemployment, inflation, food shortages, housing crises and poverty in Yugoslavia.

Economic dependency was made all the more suffocating by Aleksander Rankovic's security policies. For Rankovic, who controlled the police in Yugoslavia, the province constituted a security threat to the unity of Yugoslavia. The state of emergency that pertained to Yugoslavia until 1948 as Tito consolidated power over Stalinist elements persisted in Kosovo until the mid-1960s. Kosovo was a police 'state' controlled by Rankovic and his secret police. The firmness of Rankovic's grip on the lives of Kosovo's inhabitants was only realised after his purge from the party in 1966. Moreover, Rankovic's patriotic enthusiasm to secure Kosovo was debunked when evidence of the extent of his involvement in illicit activities came to light (Crampton 2002: 128). Interestingly, in interviews with Kosovo Serbs who recalled the time, Mertus records a Serb who argues that under Rankovic 'everything was fine and there was order' (cited in Mertus 1999: 128), and that it was only after Rankovic was purged that life became intolerable as the ethnic Albanians grew more assertive. This perception was given credence by the emotive reaction of Kosovo Serbs to his death in 1983. Consequently, ethnic Albanians were in the ascendency in the Kosovo Communist Party from 1966, and the fortunes of Serbs in Kosovo altered dramatically. The 1974 Constitution arguably gave Kosovo more independence than it presently enjoys – it had its own government, the right to fly the Albanian flag and to pursue independent foreign relations, and, through a policy of positive discrimination, Albanians were given preferential treatment in public appointments (Dragovic-Sovo 2002:116). Nevertheless, the purge of Rankovic did not lift the state of exception in Kosovo. As the police altered from being under Rankovic's control to becoming an ethnically Albanian force, the contest for sovereignty continued. As ethnic tensions increased, the ethnic Albanian police force fought a two front war – one that targeted Albanian nationalists, and a more silent one that discriminated against Serbs living in the virtually independent province. One Albanian interviewee recorded by Mertus speaks about the omnipresence of the 'Orwellian' secret police in the 1970s and 1980s. His extra-juridical arrest in 1978 was typical: kidnapped by twenty-four secret police officers in broad daylight and interrogated at a hunters' lodge. In fact, the interviewee was quite fortunate, as Mertus cites an article written in *Der Speigel* in 1978 alleging that, under interrogation, 'Albanians were beaten into insanity, had their arms and legs broken under torture, were forced to conduct prolonged hunger strikes and were shot inside solitary cells' (cited in Mertus 1999: 21). In the meantime, Serbs were emigrating *en masse* from the region. The situation eventually became intolerable for Belgrade after demonstrations in 1981 by ethnic Albanians seeking republic status within Yugoslavia. A massive crackdown on dissent ensued. By 1982 a more aggressive form of protest was evident, as arrests were recorded for crimes such as hijacking police vehicles and for the issuance of threats of armed uprising if demands for a separate republic were not met. Dragovic-Sovo cites a study that neatly encapsulates the reversible fortunes of ethnic communities in Kosovo between 1945 and 1989:

> The [League of Communists] party represented the vehicle of ethnic domination in all parts of communist Yugoslavia, which meant in Kosovo – as elsewhere – the ethnic group which controlled the Party apparatus at a particular time (Serbs from 1945 to 1966, Albanians from 1966 to 1988, and Serbs again from 1989) discriminated against members of the other ethnic

community, using all instances of power: legal system, media, security apparatus and education.

(Dragovic-Sovo 2002: 121)

It is no coincidence that Milošević, in a suburb of Pristina on 24 April 1987, made a point of asserting his authority over the ethnic Albanian police officers who were using what were evidently normally brutal methods to control a gathered crowd of 15,000 angry and insecure Serbs. Ordering the police officers back from the crowd and telling his audience that 'Nobody has the right to beat you' was a politically symbolic gesture in a sphere where ethnic Albanians were seen to be maintaining an order that excluded Serbs. Milošević, in effect, was declaring to the Serbs that the exceptional methods being used by ethnic Albanian officers on Serbs would end – that Serbs would not be the political grouping excluded from the law. Milošević was asserting his right to decide upon the exception. Milošević dismissed the ethnic Albanian police force and, having imposed an official state of emergency in 1989, replaced it with a compliant Serb force. Having been disbanded after the fall of Rankovic, the militia – a special paramilitary police unit – was revived to ensure compliance with the 470 special measures, or decrees, introduced to Kosovo between 1990 and 1992 (Clark 2000: 71). Ethnic Albanians suddenly found that their status reversed to that of *homo sacer*.

Kosovo as terra sacer

One must therefore understand that Kosovo has existed in a de facto state of exception since 1913 (or perhaps from even earlier). The territory existed in an excluded economic, political and legal sphere from the rest of Yugoslavia. Indeed, as Agamben (2003) found sacredness to be associated with condition of *homo sacer*, Kosovo has similar attachments of sacredness to be found in its category as the Jerusalem for Serbs, the site of the nation's birth. So, excluded economically, Kosovo was included by way of its sacred status.

But just as Kosovo was a *terra sacer* to Serbs, one could equally argue that the international community assigned a similar status to the entire Federal Republic of Yugoslavia (FRY). Excluded economically through sanctions for a decade, excluded politically through the revocation of its membership of the OSCE but *included* in the largely symbolic ceremony that was the Rambouillet conference, the FRY shares many attributes of the *homo sacer*. In this sense, the violence (bombing) over the FRY was an extra-juridical act perpetrated by a community upon an outsider that enabled the international community to wrest from the FRY its capacity to decide the state of exception.[2] And just as Milošević had dismissed ethnic Albanian officers and introduced emergency measures in 1989, in 1999 the international community disbanded Milošević's security structures and installed an international police force backed by a strong military component, and a compliant indigenous police force whose function was to uphold order in what has been termed a 'legal anarchy' (Rausch 2002: 13).

Thus, the passage of Resolution 1244 should be viewed as affording the UN, or the SRSG, the capacity to continue the state of exception in Kosovo (see Yannis 2004). From early in its tenure, particular emphasis was placed on the mission's goal to restore public security. Liberal democracy and the rule of law was the end goal – but the means of attaining these ends were not to be in any way democratic. It is henceforth that the abyss alluded to by Schmitt between the ahistorical normative liberal order pronounced by the international community and the actuality of conditions begins to open (Zizek 1999). Gheciu is but one observer who has pointed out 'a tension between the norms around which the international administration defined its role and its actual governance of Kosovo' (2005: 122). Bernabeu, too, has shown in her study of security sector reforms (SSR) in Kosovo that 'the Constitutional Framework for Kosovo, which clearly laid the foundations for a democratic system in the province, made an exception regarding the security sector, which remained within the authority of the SRSG' (2007: 77). Remarkably, the nature of powers granted to UNMIK is not considered by either author as exceptional. Ominously, Gheciu's paper in fact argues that the international administration and the institutions of self-government in Kosovo have recently come to share a normative framework.

UNMIK and the state of exception

For the first two months after the Serb forces had withdrawn, Kosovo was policed by KFOR soldiers and was, therefore, under de facto martial law. More accurately, Kosovo was effectively under no law. Vesna Peric-Zimonjic (1999) described Kosovo as a place with 'Four Governments, six armies and no law'. Local judiciary structures remained dysfunctional for up to eight months after the arrival of KFOR, resulting in detainees being held for up to six months while they awaited they awaited a judge to hear their case (Rausch 2002: 28). As the prison at Istok had been bombed by NATO, many of these detainees were held in tents. Moreover, when eventually these detainees did make it into the courtroom there was confusion as to which law was to be applied – legislation dating from before the 1989 declaration of emergency, or the legislation that was in effect on 24 March 1999? To solve this conflict, UNMIK Resolution 1999/24 decreed that law dating from 1989 would be applicable but that UNMIK regulations concerning the protection of human rights took precedence. These human rights standards were certainly not applied, however, to those who were subject to 'executive detentions' by UNMIK under the authority of the SRSG when it bypassed the justice system in the name of public security (Bernabeu 2007: 77). As Collette Rausch comments, the new regulation caused more confusion and effectively 'allowed the police and judiciary to pick and choose the laws they wished to apply' (2002: 16). Systemic violation of the Criminal Police Code lasted until 2001 (Decker 2006: 506).

More interesting to this study is the manner by which exceptional laws became the liberal way of ruling Kosovo. For instance, under Yugoslav law a prisoner had to be brought before a magistrate within twenty-four hours of his or her arrest. In exceptional cases, however, where the judge could not be found, this period was extendable to seventy-two hours. As Christopher Decker observes, 'while the 72 hour rule was supposed to be the exception, it became the rule' (2006: 506). In 2004, when the Provisional Criminal Code of Kosovo was drafted, this seventy-two hour rule slipped into the legislation (under Article 14(2)) so that detainees in Kosovo became subject to holding periods originally set aside for exceptional circumstances. A more serious and structural lack in the rule of law concerns the police's use of force – a matter that goes to the heart of Kosovo's exceptional status.

The executive authority that was granted to police officers of CIVPOL refers to their mandate to protect and serve the United Nations sovereignty over the region of Kosovo. Between 2000 and 2008 there were approximately 1400 international officers in CIVPOL operating in Kosovo at any one time. CIVPOL was recruited from approximately forty-two countries with varying standards on the use of deadly force. This variation on standards was not addressed by UNMIK, whose procedures are quite vague on the use of force. Thus, it would seem that there was some discretion afforded to CIVPOL officers during events when the use of firearms was warranted. Moreover, according to UNMIK Regulation 2000/47, 'UNMIK personnel shall be immune from any form of arrest or detention.' Numerous cases emerged between 2000 and 2008 that illustrated that UNMIK CIVPOL members were above the law. In 2002 there were two such incidents – one where an officer was alleged to have beaten and raped an ethnic Albanian girl, and another where an Austrian officer allegedly beat and threatened to kill a man in his custody. However, the most indicative example occurred in 2007, when an internal investigation found insufficient evidence in the case of two Romanian CIVPOL officers accused of excessive force leading to the death of two ethnic Albanian protestors in Pristina in February 2007. The leader of the protestors on the day, Albin Kurti, was incidentally arrested and placed under house arrest in a sentence reminiscent of more authoritarian regimes; Kurti had been imprisoned for similar offences during the Milošević era (Amnesty International 2008). Film footage gathered by the Balkan Investigative Reporting Unit showed Romanian officers repeatedly firing rubber bullets into a crowd of protestors who were seen to be running away from the international police (Xharra and Gashi 2007). That the Romanian officers in question were part of a police paramilitary unit leads us to another aspect of policing in the state of exception: the civil military response to domestic security.

The international policing response to public security in Kosovo has been led by 'police with military status'; heavily armed gendarmerie units that blur the distinction between law enforcement and military policing. It should be remembered that military forces within Kosovo are not subject to civil authority. Military police from the Romanian *Politia Militaria* and the Slovenian Military Police can be found alongside inter alia Italian *carabinieri* and French *gendarmerie* (Hansen 2002). The close cooperation between UNMIK, CIVPOL and KFOR, with soldiers used as a force multiplier for police units in Kosovo, continues a long tradition of governance in Kosovo. The use of joint police–military patrolling – military back-up for police – and the use of military facilities for law enforcement purposes characteristic of the UNMIK administration, was also evident during the 1989–1999 period. Commentators such as John Cockell (2002), for instance, write about the success of the strategy, arguing that police–military cooperative relations should move to 'coordinated unity of effort'. Nevertheless, there is no doubt that this martial style of security will harden the police culture in institutions shaped by the international community. As Eric Scheye (2002) has pointed out, the manner by which executive authority in Kosovo is practised and the transition of those powers to local officials is operationally and conceptually intertwined. For the members of the Kosovo Police Service, being trained and monitored in such an environment makes it inevitable that civilian policing standards are going to be viewed largely as a theoretical construct. This was bluntly illustrated by the KPS's behaviour during sectarian rioting in March 2004, only weeks after UNMIK declared the transition of policing authority to the Kosovo Police Service.

Policing to post-national standards

Yasemin Nuhoglu Soysal's (1994) study into the institutionalization of universal human rights in European states finds evidence that individual human rights have begun to transcend the identity-based rights found in the nation-state model. 'Post national citizenship', it is claimed, 'confers upon every person the right and duty of a participation in the authority structures and public life of a polity, regardless of their cultural ties to that community' (Soysal 1994: 3). If this liberal tendency away from the traditional nation-state model is indeed observable, it constitutes a radically different project from more traditional attempts to define the boundaries of a state by reference to its nationality. It moves from Yossi Shain's idea that 'within the nation state, the idea that political loyalty should be directed toward the nation is intimately linked to the relationship between the national community and the state's power' (1989: 6). By grafting international declarations, charters and conventions dealing with human and group rights onto the Constitutional Framework document[3] (2001) (and by including further protections for group rights), UNMIK was explicitly rejecting this traditional nation-state model. The need to accommodate Serbs and other minorities into a type of final status whereby ethnic Albanians would not be able to impose their national identity upon Kosovo motivated the UN to insist on a normative post-nation-state model. Throughout, the KPS has been seen by the international administration as the independent variable in this experiment. Based on the liberal precept that the rule of law is the foundation of order and stability, establishing and developing an multi-ethnic police force in Kosovo was a 'political project', aiming to change power relationships in society (Dwan 2002: 126). The police, from the outset, were at the vanguard of this project.

It is illustrative, therefore, that Bernard Kouchner, as SRSG, told the first batch of 173 KPS recruits who graduated in October 1999, 'With you lies the real possibility of a break from the past' (cited in Gray 1999). The police force was designed to reflect the multi-ethnic character of the province, and by 2006 comprised 7,203 officers; 84 per cent were categorised as being ethnic Albanian, 10 per cent as Serbian and 6 percent as belonging to 'other' ethnic groups. Ethnicity was foremost in the minds of state-builders. The same considerations for proportionality was not implemented in relation to gender; 86 per cent of the KPS were male (UNMIK 2006: 5). Over 50 per cent of the KPS were former fighters in the Kosovo Liberation Army (Yannis 2004). These 7,203 officers, together with the 1,300 CIVPOL officers (and 16,300 KFOR) in charge of law enforcement, represent a higher ratio of CIVPOL and national police to the total population than in statebuilding operations in Afghanistan and Iraq (Wilson 2006: 160). The training for these officers gradually evolved from a highly accelerated course lasting four weeks towards the less accelerated twenty-week course in place by 2006 (Decker 2006: 508). Training includes modules that deliver the rudimentary elements of community policing, and human rights is a constituent aspect of the entire course. In fact, as Decker (2006) reveals, human rights policing is learned during on-the-job situations with UNMIK police and paramilitary police officers – many of who hail from police forces with abysmal human rights records.

By June 2003 the international community felt confident enough to launch tentative 'mixed patrols', composing twenty Serb and ten ethnic Albanian police, into Mitrovica, the interface town in northern Kosovo. Accompanied by UNMIK officers, KFOR of course was also alerted to the exercise. Various other attempts at 'normalisation' were made. Within two weeks, UNMIK disingenuously declared that the transfer of authority to the KPS was complete. On 6 November, UNMIK decided that the bridge in Mitrovica, the focal point of inter-ethnic violence, was no longer to be protected by KFOR and that 'Kosovo's new police would take control' (ICG 2002: 12). Later that year, policing became subject to its own section in the Standards for Status 'contract' introduced by UNMIK on 10 December 2003. The Standards required for final status talks in the area of the rule of law sought a

> sound legal framework and effective law enforcement compliant with European standards. Police, judicial and penal systems act impartially and fully respect human rights. There is equal access to justice and no one is above the law: there is no impunity for violations. There are strong measures in place to fight ethnically-motivated crime, as well as economic and financial crime.
>
> (Standards for Kosovo 2003)

What follows from this overarching standard is a list of attributes that describe the liberal democratic ideal of how a police force should operate in a post-national state. However worthy the aims, the distance which the KPS (and the PISG (Provisional Institutions of Self-Government) would have to travel to reach these standards is immediately evident. What must be deduced, therefore, is that these standards are basically unattainable in a contested territory which is under a de facto state of emergency. Rather than marking out the actual destination of policing in Kosovo, the standards delineate the boundaries of policing. They serve to contain the KPS within the post-national statebuilding project, and act as a mechanism to prevent nationalist elements from utilising the potential of the police. Moreover, they keep policing very much in the hands of the international community.

To be sure, by connecting standards to the issue of final status, the international community seemed to assume that there was universal agreement on the nature of final status. It was never certain, however, that final status – interpreted by the UN as a multi-ethnic, inclusive arrangement – was the same final status as interpreted by ethnic Albanians. Little research is available on the political strength of ethnic Albanians who view as credible the idea of creating a Kosovo that contains dissenting non-Albanian elements. There is certainly, however, a strong historical strain of nationalism to be found among ex-leaders of the Kosovo Liberation Army who occupy senior posts in Kosovo's Assembly. One commentator, attached to the Office of the Prime Minister in Kosovo, attested to this when he pointed out that the vast majority of ethnic Albanians do not want a multi-ethnic final status (Welch 2006). Ethnic Albanian leaders must be acutely aware of the difficulties posed to an independent Kosovo inhabited by a relatively large number of Serbs who actively dispute the legitimacy of the government. When this minority is supported financially by a hostile neighbouring state (the Republic of Serbia), ethnic Albanian leaders in building legitimacy for national institutions will find themselves with the same dilemmas faced by their Serb predecessors. This dilemma concerns 'national' security, and necessarily constitutes a policing problem. As a policing problem, minority dissent will doubtlessly be viewed as an exceptional situation, which will require exceptional powers to maintain order. As Bernabeu warns, 'in a selective democracy, the security sector may become an arena of oppression' (2007: 80). Thus, even if the KPS manages to attain the arguably unachievable standards set out by the international community, these standards will always be set aside when the ethnic Albanian government has to confront the 'Serb problem'. Serbs living in an independent Kosovo will, therefore, be deemed *homo sacer*, and not subject to the same rights as ethnic Albanians living in Kosovo. There is little distinction between the means by which the international community aim to eradicate the ethnic factor through force and the means by which sectarian ethnic Albanians will respond to ethnic Serb dissent. Furthermore, as the violence perpetrated on the Roma and Ashkali populations in March 2004 illustrated, it may not only be the Serbs who will constitute the 'other' in an independent Kosovo.

In March 2004, nine months after UNMIK had declared that it had passed authority for policing to a newly trained corps of local police managers, sectarian violence, which began in Mitrovica, spread rapidly throughout Kosovo. In south Mitrovica, the KPS were left stranded among rioters by French KFOR troops who refused to assist them (Welch 2006: 232). In thirty-three other sites throughout Kosovo, ethnic Albanian mobs attacked Serbs and other minority groups. It was the first true test of how the KPS might function without international support.

Had the KPS simply failed to control the rioting it would have easily been attributable to the scale of violence, the lack of military support and the quality of training received. In the wake of the violence, however, it was found that members of the KPS had acquiesced in it and, worse, that they had actively participated. The International Crisis Group reported that there were at least two instances in which KPS officers had thrown petrol bombs (ICG 2004: 20). UNMIK stated that about 100 KPS officers were under investigation for crimes ranging from failure to act, failure to prevent use of excessive force, and direct involvement in the riots (BBC Monitoring 2004a). Furthermore, members of the Ashkali and Roma communities also made grave accusations against members of the KPS, claiming that police officers had physically and verbally abused them and helped protestors to torch their homes (BBC Monitoring 2004b). The March 2004 riots lifted the lid on ethnic Albanian society; the intolerance and ethnic hatred revealed by the International Crisis Group when they looked inside tragically confirms Schmitt's thesis that sovereignty is structured around a friend–enemy distinction. In its report, the ICG cites a Kosova-Albanian boy who said 'Once the Serbs are gone, and then the Bosniaks, the Ashkalis and the Turks, we will look for enemies. We need to hunt for enemies' (ICG 2004: 32). Their analysis of the March 2004 riots concludes, 'Kosovo Albanian society contains insufficient checks and barriers to prevent it from gradually expelling all foreign bodies within its midst or in its path' (ibid.: 32). It is certain that the minority communities in Kosovo similarly concluded that the KPS is neither a check nor a barrier to such a possibility.

Community policing in Kosovo

The events of March 2004 are illustrative of the abyss separating UNMIK's normative liberal order and the actual social reality in Kosovo. The international community suddenly realised that large segments of ethnic Albanian society were not committed to UNMIK's post-national statebuilding project (Gardner 2008: 545). For minorities, the violence exposed how vulnerable they were in a multi-ethnic society governed and policed by an antagonistic majority community. This vulnerability was made all the more concrete when a survey by the South Eastern and Eastern Europe Clearinghouse for the Control of Small Arms and Light Weapons revealed that there were more than 317,000 guns held illegally by citizens and armed groups in Kosovo. In other words, neither the international community nor the PISG actually fully controlled the monopoly of violence. The same survey revealed that only 28 per cent of the poll said that they trusted the KPS. Those who felt most secure in the region tended to live in mono-ethnic environments (BBC Monitoring 2007). This was further confirmed by an OSCE survey, undertaken in 2007, which found that neither community trusts each other's police officers (OSCE 2008: 7). Cross-community policing is impossible in such an environment. Too subservient to UNMIK to remain an independent variable in their post-national statebuilding experiment, the KPS and Kosovo simultaneously fragmented along ethnic lines. The OSCE points blame at the Kosovo Assembly, which it claims, quite ironically, is attempting to assert its influence over the KPS: 'The police institutions of Kosovo are often subject to political interference. This appears to be a consequence of the general political culture in Kosovo, which often does not respect institutional independence' (OSCE 2008: 8).

Hence, when one speaks about community–police relations in Kosovo it is with reference to one community policing itself against another community, each laying claim to the right to decide the exception, and contesting the international community's sovereignty. While community policing is usually associated with policing multicultural environments, in Kosovo it is emphatically a movement against multiculturalism.

Paul Virillo's argument, 'the political power of the state is *polis*, police, that is, management of the public ways', is quite pertinent to Kosovo (1986: 12). More often than not, community policing in Kosovo manifests in roadblocks set up by Serbs as they attempt to assert control over who can enter 'their' territory. Interpreted in this light, there are thus numerous examples of community policing to be found in Kosovo. For instance, one might consider the mainly ex-Serb police 'bridge watchers' formed to protect the entrance to the 'Serb side' of Mitrovica to be a form of neighbourhood watch (International Crisis Group 2002: 3). Outside the town of Mitrovica in northern Kosovo, Serb police regularly patrol the roads, requesting identification and harassing ethnic Albanian travellers.[4] The political power of the Kosovo state institutions does not penetrate Serb areas, where Serb control effectively dissolves the border between Serbia proper and Kosovo. This increases their power as a political community vis-à-vis ethnic Albanians by erasing any jurisdictional division between this territory and Serbia proper. Following the declaration of independence made by Kosovo's Assembly in February 2008, all ethnic Albanian officers were pulled out of northern Kosovo and replaced with 290 ethnic Serb officers who broke off all contact with the KPS management structure. Local elections were held in the region in May 2008, and a Kosovo Serb Assembly was convened without interference from UNMIK. The Serb Ministry of Interior has also established a presence in the region (ICG 2008). Clashes that have occurred since between KFOR and Serbs attempting to occupy municipal buildings and courthouses in north Kosovo and in Serb enclaves in southern Kosovo should therefore be seen as the beginning of a new conflict over the sovereignty of Kosovo.

It remains to be seen what the European Union mission to Kosovo will contribute. Inauspiciously, its strategy seems to deviate little from the original dogmatic intention. The blueprints for a multi-ethnic police force and the insistence that the rule of law alone has the ability to unite antagonistic political communities remain. Furthermore, EULEX will inherit from UNMIK the power to decide the state of exception, maintaining a strong paramilitary police unit which will intervene when 'Kosovo authorities fail to prevent violence against non-majority communities or where there is political interference undermining the rule of law' (EULEX 2008). Thus, it would appear that a normative experiment will continue to be violently imposed on Kosovo. The European Union's post-national project will continue from where UNMIK has failed. The international community would seem to have mired itself in the very history it claimed it could end.

Conclusion

This chapter argues that Kosovo is a site of experimentation for the international community. It is a project that could only emanate from a liberal internationalist self-belief that history can be defeated by the strategic application of violence which ostensibly rests upon the rule of law. Ethnicity was seen as the enemy of peace and progress in Kosovo, and thus a post-national state which would eradicate the ethnic 'problem' was imposed. At variance not only with the history of nation-state building, but also with the political views of Kosovo's inhabitants, from the outset the project required exceptional security measures. As a security operation, the police were placed at the vanguard of policies that strove to bring political homogeneity to the deeply divided population. Over the past decade, thousands of NATO soldiers have acted as a force multiplier to a massive body of local and international police, who in turn act as a force multiplier to a concert of NGOs and international organisations. One need not look further than Kosovo to argue that the liberal way of rule is an extension of the liberal way of war.

Nonetheless, the liberal blueprints to end the tragic history of Kosovo are unlikely to result in a post-national state wherein peace is maintained by a neutral consensus-oriented police force. On the contrary, what we witness is that the authoritarian aspects of liberalism adapt remarkably quickly to the historical condition of exceptionalism in Kosovo. In other words, the reliance on security as a mode of rule suggests quite strongly that security is a central mode of liberal governance. It is predicted, therefore, that the KPS is destined to be as politically subservient to the whims of the Kosovo Assembly and the national spirit as CIVPOL is politically bound to the dictates of the SRSG. When these deductions are placed alongside the empirical conditions of policing in Kosovo – a predominantly ethnic Albanian police force comprising a high percentage of individuals from a majority group that had until recently been an oppressed minority – the future of a multicultural inclusive democracy taking root in Kosovo seems bleak. Inhabitants of the region have retreated into the security of their ethnic categories, and the friend/enemy distinction is more visible than ever in the region's political map. Had he lived to see contemporary statebuilding practices, Schmitt might have pointed out that by studying the plight of Kosovo we are compelled to examine how each of us is caught in the contradictions of liberal democracy, which paradoxically requires extraordinary security to create what it considers to be political freedom (Ryan 2009). Perhaps Agamben has a point, then, when he observes that we are all *homines sacer*: each of us conferred as sacred through individual human rights and a rule of law that, in the name of a greater good, precludes our political opinions and, if needs be, our lives (1998: 115).

Notes

1 See Chapter 8 of the *Constitutional Framework* document available at www.unmikon-line.org/pub/misc/FrameworkPocket_ENG_Dec2002.pdf (accessed 24 June 2009)
2 For instance, *The Economist* argued that 'the war against Kosovo was a startling new departure – but one that is likely to prove the exception, not the rule' (*The Economist* 1999: 16).
3 See Chapters 3 and 4 of the Constitutional Framework (2001).
4 See, for instance, the ethnic Albanian newspaper *Koha Ditore* (2008), which reported on 6 June 2008 that civilian clothes officers with Serb Ministry of Interior identity cards were stopping cars and requesting documents.

Bibliography

Agamben, G. (1995) *Homo Sacer; Sovereign Power and Bare Life*, Stanford, CA: Stanford University Press.

Agamben, G. (2003) *State of Exception*, Chicago, IL: Chicago University Press.

Amnesty International (2008) 'Albin Kurti – a politically motivated prosecution?' Amnesty International Report. Available: www.amnesty.org/en/library/asset/EUR70/014/2007/en/EUR700142007en.html (accessed 22 October 2008).

Anderson, B. (1991) *Imagined Communities; Reflections on the Origin and Spread of Nationalism*, London: Verso.

BBC Monitoring (2004a) 'Several Local Police Officers under Investigation for Involvement in March Riots', BBC Monitoring International Reports Section: Europe, 28 July. Available: http://docs..newsbank.com (accessed 22 August 2008).

BBC Monitoring (2004b) 'Ashkali Community Accuses Kosovo Police of Violence during March Riots', BBC Monitoring International Reports Section: Europe, 30 April. Available: http://docs..newsbank.com (accessed 22 August 2008).

BBC Monitoring (2007) 'Kosovo – Armed to the Teeth – Illegal Firearms', BBC Monitoring International Reports Section: Europe, 3 August. Available: http://docs..newsbank.com (accessed 10 August 2008).

Bernabeu, I. (2007) 'Laying the Foundations of Democracy? Reconsidering Security Sector Reform under UN Auspices in Kosovo', *Security Dialogue*, 38(1): 71–92.

Brubaker, R. (1992) *Citizenship and Nationhood in France and Germany*, Boston, MA: Harvard University Press.

Chan, J. (2000) *Changing Police Culture*, Cambridge: Cambridge University Press.

Clark, H. (2000) *Civil Resistance in Kosovo*, London: Pluto Press.

Cockell, J. G. (2002) 'Civil–Military Responses to Security Challenges in Peace Operations: Ten Lessons from Kosovo', *Global Governance*, 8/4: 483–502.

Constitutional Framework (2001) 'Constitutional Framework for Provisional Self Government', UNMIK/REG/2001/9, 15 May. Available: www.unmikonline.org/const-framework.htm#1 (accessed 29 October 2008).

Crampton, R. J. (2002) *The Balkans Since the Second World War*, London: Longman.

Decker, C. (2006) 'Enforcing Human Rights: The Role of the UN Civilian Police in Kosovo', *International Peacekeeping*, 13/4: 502–516.

Dillon, M. (2009) 'The Liberal Way of War: Killing to Make Life Live', Oxford: Routledge.

Dragovic-Sovo, J. (2002) '*Saviours of the Nation'; Serbia's Intellectual Opposition and the Revival of Nationalism*, London: Hurst and Co.

Duijzings, G. (2000) *Religion and the Politics of Identity in Kosovo*, London: Hurst and Co.

Dwan, R. (2002) 'Conclusions', in R. Dwan (ed.) *Executive Policing; Enforcing the Law in Peace Operations*, SIPRI Research Report, Oxford: Oxford University Press.

EULEX (2008) 'EULEX Kosovo Police Component', Available: www.eulex-kosovo. eu/?id=9 (accessed 31 May 2008).

Gardner, A. M. (2008) 'Democratic Governance and Non-State Actors', *Review of International Studies*, 34: 531–552.

Gheciu, A. (2005) 'International Norms, Power and the Politics of International Administration: The Kosovo Case', *Geopolitics*, 10: 121–146.

Gray, A. (1999) 'Kosovo Police Cadets Prepare for Life on the Beat', *Reuters America Inc.* October 16. Available: *http://docs.newsbank.com* (accessed September 19 2008).

Hansen, A. S. (2002) 'Civil–Military Cooperation: The Military, Paramilitaries and Civilian Police in Executive Policing', in R. Dwan (ed.) *Executive Policing; Enforcing the Law in Peace Operations*, SIPRI Research Report, Oxford: Oxford University Press.

International Crisis Group (2002) 'UNMIKs Kosovo Albatross: Tackling Division in Mitrovica', Balkans Report no. 131, 3 June. Available: www.crisisgroup.org/library/ documents/report_archive/A400672_03062002.pdf (accessed 5 October 2008).

International Crisis Group (2004) 'Collapse in Kosovo', Balkans Report no. 155, 22 April. Available: www.crisisgroup.org/home/index.cfm?id=2627&l=1 (accessed 30 October 2008).

Koha Ditore (2008) 'Serb MUP members Patrol Northern Streets', *Koha Ditore*, 6 June.

Matveeva, A. and Paes, W. C. (2003) *The Kosovo Serbs: An Ethnic Minority Between Collaboration and Defiance*, London: Saferworld.

Mertus, J. (1999) *Kosovo: How Myths and Truths Started a War*, Berkeley, CA: University of California Press.

Mouffe, C. (1999) 'Carl Schmitt and the Paradox of Liberal Democracy', in C. Mouffe (ed.) *The Challenge of Carl Schmitt*, London: Verso Publications.

OSCE (2008) 'Human Rights, Ethnic Relations and Democracy in Kosovo (Summer 2007–Summer 2008)', Organization for Security and Cooperation in Europe. Available: www.osce.org/documents/mik/2008/09/32879_en.pdf (accessed 31 October 2008).

Pavlowitch, S. K. (2002) *Serbia: The History of an Idea*, New York, NY: New York University Press.

Peric-Zimonjic, V. (1999) 'Four Governments, Six Armies and No Law', *Inter Press Service*, 14 July.

Rausch, C. (2002) 'The Assumption of Authority in Kosovo and East Timor: Legal and Practical Implications', in R. Dwan (ed.) *Executive Policing; Enforcing the Law in Peace Operations*, SIPRI Research Report, Oxford: Oxford University Press.

Roux, M. (1992) *Les Albanais en Yugoslavie. Minorite nationale territoire et development*, Paris: Editiions de la Maison des Science L'Homme.

Ryan, B. J. (2009) 'The EU's Emergent Security-first Agenda: Securing Albania and Montenegro', *Security Dialogue*, 40/3: 311–331.

Scheye, E. (2002) 'Transitions to Local Authority', in R. Dwan (ed.) *Executive Policing; Enforcing the Law in Peace Operations*, SIPRI Research Report, Oxford: Oxford University Press.

Schmitt, C. (1976) *The Concept of the Political*, translated by George Schwab, New Brunswick, NJ: Rutgers University Press.

Schmitt, C. (2006) *Political Theology: Four Chapters on the Concept of Sovereignty*, Chicago, IL: University of Chicago Press.

Secretary General (1999) 'Report of the Secretary General on the United Nations Interim Administration in Kosovo', S/1999/779, 12 July. Available: www.un.org/Docs/sc/reports/1999/sgrep99.htm (accessed 24 June 2009).

Shain, Y. (1989) *The Frontier of Loyalty: Political Exiles in the Age of the Nation-State*, Middletown, CT: Wesleyan University Press.

Soysal, Y. N. (1994) *Limits of Citizenship, Migrants and Postnational Membership in Europe*, Chicago, IL: University of Chicago Press.

Standards for Kosovo (2003) 'Standards for Kosovo: Leaflet', 10 December. Available HTT: www.unmikonline.org/standards/docs/leaflet_stand_eng.pdf (accessed 28 June 2009).

Suganami, H. (2007) 'Understanding Sovereignty through Kelsen/Schmitt', *Review of International Studies*, 33: 511–530.

The Economist (1999) 'Leader: Sorting out Kosovo', *The Economist*, 19 July.

UNMIK (2006) 'Kosovo in October 2006'. Available: www.euinkosovo.org/upload/Fact%20Sheet%20October%202006.pdf (accessed 5 October 2008).

Virillo, P. (1986) *Speed and Politics*, New York, NY: Semiotext[e].

Welch, A. C. (2006) 'Achieving Human Security after Intra-state Conflict: The lessons of Kosovo', *Journal of Contemporary European Studies*, 14/2: 221–239.

Wilson, J. (2006) 'Law and Order in an Emerging Democracy: Lessons from the Reconstruction of Kosovo's Police and Justice Systems', *Annals of the American Academy*, 605: 152–177.

Xharra, J and Gashi, K. (2007) 'Investigation: Romanian Police Blamed for Kosovo Protest Carnage', BIRN, 23 February. Available: www.birn.eu.com/en/71/10/2346 (accessed June 27 2009).

Yannis, A. (2004) 'The UN as Government in Kosovo', *Global Governance*, 10: 67–81.

Zizek, S. (1999) 'Carl Schmitt in the Age of Post-Politics', in C. Mouffe (ed.) *The Challenge of Carl Schmitt*, London: Verso Publications.

7 Explaining the international administration's failures in the security and justice areas

*Giovanna Bono**

Introduction

Experts and policymakers disagree vigorously in their evaluation of the international administration's record in Kosovo. There is, however, a certain consensus that one of its key weaknesses lies in the failure to establish a fair and equitable security and justice system. Thus, for example, the European Commission – the body that until 2008 funded the majority of activities of the international administration in Kosovo – pointed out that in 2007, eight years after the end of the war, there were still serious challenges in the protection of minorities because their freedom of movement remained restricted due to security concerns (European Commission 2007: 21). The legislative framework to tackle organized crime was incomplete; for example, there were no witness protection programmes and no anti-Mafia laws in place. In addition, despite knowledge of the widespread practice of human trafficking, the courts were not issuing sentences for these crimes (ibid.: 47). There were still more than some 250,000 refugees and internally displaced persons (IDPs) who were expected to return to their homes in Kosovo (ibid.: 21).[1]

The failures in these areas provide one of the official reasons why some states decided to support the unilateral declaration of independence proclaimed by the Kosovar Assembly on 17 February 2007, on the condition that Kosovo Albanians and Kosovo Serbs accepted a continuous international oversight of the security and justice sectors. In fact, between 2005 and 2008 a group of states planned and negotiated a transfer of responsibilities from UNMIK to the International Civilian Office (ICO) and to an EU rule of law mission, known as EULEX Kosovo, and to Kosovar institutions, believing that only by doing so could they resolve the challenges present in the security and justice systems.

This chapter evaluates competing explanations put forward for the international administration's failure in the security and justice sector in light of events that occurred between 2007 and early 2009. The dominant explanation for the failure is that the international administration did not address the final status of Kosovo earlier in its engagement. In contrast, alternative sets of explanations assert that the failures are due to a combination of factors: the lack of capacity; the unwillingness of the international community to act and coordinate its activities during the early years of its engagement; the existence of a bias on the part of certain states towards the Kosovo Albanians; and the nature of the strategies pursued by local actors, in particular the Kosovo Albanians who ingeniously co-opted the international community into building institutions that served their own national aspirations, while the Kosovo Serbs adopted an overall stance of resistance vis-à-vis the international administration.

The first part of this chapter outlines these competing explanations and then assesses whether the events from 2007 to early 2009 complement these explanations. It is argued that, given the way in which the negotiations on status issues were conducted and the deterioration in the security and justice areas that occurred in 2008, the status issues cannot be considered a rational explanation for the international administration's failures. The way in which the status issue was resolved has highlighted the bias of certain states in favor of the Kosovo Albanians. Moreover, the events of 2008 have modified the dynamics of interaction between the local actors and international players because the Kosovo Albanians have found a new ally in the work of the ICO, and this has facilitated the consolidation of the Kosovo Albanians over important security institutions such as the Kosovo Security Force and the Kosovo Police Force.

In contrast to alternative explanations provided for the period 1999–2007, it cannot be asserted that there was a lack of strategy on the part of the international community, because some members of the Contact Group[2] did have a clear policy of pushing for 'supervised' Kosovo independence. However, their policies backfired because of the level of resistance organized by the Kosovo Serbs, Serbia, Russia, and other UN and EU member states which feared the consequences of such recognition. Moreover, in contrast to the 1999–2007 period, there have been more serious open divisions within the four international missions present in Kosovo (UNMIK, ICO, EULEX and KFOR), and the strategies of the Kosovo Serbs are today not only shaped by resistance but also influenced by wider international dynamics. Overall, past and new complex dynamics are coming together in a way that indicates that a successful reform of the security and justice sector will be difficult to achieve: Kosovo could be a 'failed state' in the making.

Explanations for the failures: 1999–2007

Why did the international administration not succeed in quickly reforming the security and justice sector in Kosovo between 1999 and 2007? There are four competing explanations, which can be summarized as follows: first, the combination of a lack of strategy and bias amongst sections of the international community during the early stages of engagement; second, the impact of the policy of 'institution building', privileged by the international administration; third, specific local players' strategies, in particular the 'policy of co-option' that the Kosovo Albanians successfully managed to develop vis-à-vis the international administration; and fourth, the simple and dominant explanation that the failure was due to the inability of the international administration to address the question of final status earlier on in its engagement. The following sections examine each explanation in more detail.

The international community's lack of strategy and the influence of biased actors

At the end of the NATO bombing campaign against the Federal Republic of Yugoslavia on 10 June 1999, the UN was given the central role in the governance of the province through UN Security Council Resolution 1244. UNMIK exercised full executive and legislative authority over all aspects of governance of the province of Kosovo. It dealt with policing and judicial affairs, under the first two of its 'four pillars' structure. In addition, under Resolution 1244, the NATO-led KFOR was responsible for the overall security situation and had a role in the disarmament, demobilization and re-integration of the Kosovo Liberation Army (KLA) and the transformation of the KLA into the Kosovo Protection Corps (KPC). KFOR also had a number of functions that ranged from providing border security to guaranteeing the safe return of refugees and displaced persons.

Despite the substantial powers given to KFOR and UNMIK in 1999, there was a security vacuum in the aftermath of NATO's intervention. Serbian military and police forces had withdrawn, and many civilians had fled. UNMIK was unable to take over the security tasks. As Andreas Heinemann-Grüder and Igor Grebenschikov explain, it took UNMIK three years to form special units against organized crime, and when it did so UNMIK's law enforcement was subject to political interference (2007: 37). In addition, there are suggestions that KFOR was unwilling or unable to act because of a turf war with UNMIK over the nature of its responsibilities.[3]

As a consequence, whereas during 1998 and 1999 the Kosovo Albanians suffered many casualties and were subject to extensive human rights abuses by Serbian police officers, in late 1999 and early 2000 there was a round, of what some have described as 'reverse ethnic cleansing' (Gil-Robles 2002; Leurdijk and Zandee 2001: 117). This time, the Kosovo Serbs were the victims. It is estimated that 230,000 Kosovo Serbs took refuge outside of Kosovo, an estimated 271 Serbs were killed and 650 went missing (Bernabeu 2007: 74).

The delay in the deployment of UNMIK and the failure of KFOR to act meant that local institutions representing the Kosovo Albanian and Kosovo Serb communities took root and began to organize parallel security and justice structures. As an International Crisis Group report explained:

> In the second half of 1999, the new Kosovo Protection Corps appeared part of a broad KLA front that would dominate Kosovo's institutions. Unelected, the KLA had control of all municipal administrations except the three Serb-majority ones north of the Ibar. Its leader, Thaci, headed a provisional central government.... The NATO-KLA demilitarization agreement declared that the 'international community should take due and full account' of the KLA's

contribution during the recent crisis, and consider including KLA members in the administration and police.

(International Crisis Group 2006: 17).

Indeed, KFOR failed to take decisive action in relation to the decommissioning process of the KLA. There is some evidence to suggest that, despite the fact that after 2001 KFOR took stricter control over the KPC, they remained free to act autonomously, with the support of key sections in KFOR. In fact, the process of demobilizing the KLA did not work well, and the KLA became the core element of the Kosovo Protection Corps (KPC). Of the estimated 20,000 KLA fighters, roughly half returned to their own previous positions. Some 5,000 ex-KLA fighters ended up in the KPC and some 2,500 in the Kosovo Police Service (Heinemann-Grüder and Grebenschikov 2007: 34–35).[4]

The failure of the decommissioning process became apparent in 2001, when elements of the KPC provided substantial support to the National Liberation Army in Macedonia, which was engaged in seeking to violently overthrow the government. The KPC was also accused of involvement in criminal activities, including illegal policing, killings, and terrorist attacks against Serbs (International Crisis Group 2006: 20–21). Further evidence of the lack of decommissioning was the behaviour of the Kosovo Police Service (KPS) during the riots of March 2004. The KPS was unable to quell the riots, and some of its members actively participated in them (Heinemann-Grüder and Grebenschikov 2007: 42; Human Rights Watch 2006, 2008: 10).

The inability of the international community to take responsibility in its early years of engagement in Kosovo and the failure to develop a coherent strategy has also been documented in studies of the reform of the justice system. As in the case of the police and military, the judiciary dissolved in 1999 and UNMIK did not act sufficiently quickly to replace it. This led the KLA to form the 'Provisional Government of Kosova', to appoint mayors and establish parallel government structures. Moreover, UNMIK took an ambivalent position towards clarifying which law should be applicable. It first stated that the applicable law was that of 24 March 1999 because it had strong human rights provisions, but the Kosovo Albanian judges refused to apply Serb law from the 1990s. They wanted the application of the law in place in 1989, before the revocation of Kosovo's independence. UNMIK initially gave in to the demands of the Kosovo Albanians. Then, noting the emergence of a strong bias on the part of Kosovo Albanians against the Kosovo Serbs in criminal proceeding, the international administration sought to remedy the situation by appointing international judges and prosecutors (Zaum 2007: 144–147). However, it is believed that the approach adopted, and the failure to impose a generic penal code and a code of criminal procedures with modern human rights guarantee prior to 2004, strongly contributed to the recurring weakness of the legal system in Kosovo (OSCE Mission in Kosovo 2006: 27–28).

'Institution building' and the policy of 'co-option'

Another explanation for the failures of the international administration has to do with the strategy developed in order to integrate the parallel judicial and security institutions that had come into existence in 1999 and the differences in strategies pursued by the Kosovo Serbs and the Kosovo Albanians vis-à-vis the international administration.

Jason Franks and Oliver P. Richmond argue that after 1999, the overall strategy of the international community came to be based on the policy of 'building of institutions' (2008: 81–103). Indeed, between 2000 and 2004 the international community put a lot of resources and effort into establishing the Provisional Institution of Self-Governance (PISG). Although these institutions – which included the elected Kosovo Assembly, the President of Kosovo and the government – did not have overall control over the security and justice sectors, which remained a reserve power of UNMIK, it created the basis for the development of independent political institutions that were 'captured' by the Kosovo Albanian majority with the explicit aim of building an independent state.

Franks and Richmond maintain that the international administration's strong support for the process of building political institutions was problematic, given that the issue of the actual geography of the disputed entity was not resolved. By pursuing such a strategy, the international administration gave implicit support to the creation of a new entity. In their analysis, the Kosovo Albanian leadership 'co-opted' the international community to their agenda; they went along with the ideas and proclaimed the values of the international community (rule of law, democracy, market economy) in order to ensure the creation of an independent state and obtain the necessary know-how and resources for so doing. In fact, the Kosovo Albanian leadership, while at times strongly criticizing the action of UNMIK, put a lot of effort into cooperating with the activities of UNMIK in the PISG, whereas most of the Kosovo Serbs refused to engage with them.

Jens Narten provides a detailed account of this process, and his work is based on the observation that local actors are far from powerless in peacebuilding processes (2008). While reviewing the literature, he states that local actors can take three types of positions vis-à-vis the external peacebuilders' strategies. First, the local elites can accept the peacebuilders' strategies; second, they can demand modification and force external peacebuilders to change the content and deliver a program more consistent with local interests; and third, they can take a more confrontational position. In the first case, there is 'cooperative peacebuilding', in the second 'captured peacebuilding', and in the third 'confrontational peacebuilding' (ibid.: 370). In his detailed review of the strategies pursued by the Kosovo Albanians and Kosovo Serbs during 1999–2007, Narten shows that the Kosovo Albanians engaged more consistently in a policy of co-opted peacebuilding, whereas the Serbs, with some variations, opted more for a policy of confrontational peacebuilding for a number of reasons, including the failure of the international community to protect them in 1999 and again during the March riots of 2004, when 19 people were killed, 900 injured and 3,600 Serbs were displaced, and when over 800 historical, cultural and religious building of Serb origin were destroyed (ibid.: 376–385).

Dominant explanation: the failure to initially resolve the status issue

In contrast to these explanations, there is one dominant explanation for the international administration's failure in Kosovo: the international administration did not address the final status issue sufficiently early. This account emerged in both diplomatic and academic circles after the riots of March 2004. Kai Eide, the Special Envoy appointed by the UN Secretary General to review the situation in Kosovo following the March riots, officially reflected this view in his report submitted to the UN (United Nations Security Council 2005). His main conclusion was that while the strategy of the international community to introduce standards – that is, a set of benchmarks for Kosovo institutions and society that should be achieved before addressing Kosovo's final status – had not been fully implemented, it was crucial to move to the next phase of the political process by creating the conditions for negotiations on the status issue to begin. As Kai Eide explained:

> addressing the question of the future of status should not be delayed any longer. The risks that would follow from a continue 'wait and see' policy – in terms of increasing political, economic and social frustration – could soon be far greater than the risks related to a future status process.
>
> (United Nations Security Council 2005: 7)

The status negotiations did in fact become the key concern of the international community towards Kosovo, and this line of reasoning was evoked by many officials and media reports for the decisions that were taken by sections of international community so as to support Kosovo's unilateral declaration of independence.

Re-evaluating explanations in light of developments: 2007–2009

Taking into account the way in which the negotiations were conducted and the events that have occurred between 2007 and the early part of 2009, to what extent can it be argued that the resolution of the final status issue was the key factor that explains the past failures of the international administration? Can it be argued that other factors previously identified were also valid? Or are there new dynamics that are likely to complicate or facilitate the process of meeting the challenges of the security and justice sectors in Kosovo?

The 'early status' explanation

It is beyond the scope of this chapter to elaborate in detail the position of the various parties during the final status negotiations or to provide a detailed overview of the evolution of events (see Antonenko 2007; Weller 2008a, 2008b). Instead, here I focus on examining some of the key features of the negotiations. It is argued that despite the concerns that the international community had about the security and justice situation in Kosovo, there was always a willingness, particularly on the part of the United Kingdom, France, Italy, Germany and the United States, to ensure that the Kosovo Albanians could declare independence from Serbia even if Belgrade would not consent to it, and even if there was insufficient support among UN members.[5]

The negotiations on the status of Kosovo began in November 2005, when the then UN Secretary General Kofi Annan appointed Martti Ahtisaari as Special Envoy for the future status of the Kosovo process. At the same time, the Contact Group countries released a set of 'Guiding Principles' for the resolution of the Kosovo's status.[6] The Contact Group affirmed that the UN Security Council should endorse the final decision on the status of Kosovo.

The talks began in February 2006, and during that year, while progress was made on a number of important issues, such as decentralization, both parties remained deeply divided on the question of status, with Belgrade offering wide-ranging autonomy and Kosovo calling for independence. On 2 February 2007 the Contact Group put forward a draft settlement to the parties, and it received a very negative reaction from Serbia. The proposal involved the concept of 'supervised independence', and argued that the 'international supervisory structures provided the foundations for a future independent Kosovo' (Weller 2008a; 671–679).

The Ahtisaari Plan, also known as the Comprehensive Proposal for the Kosovo Status Settlement, was presented at the UN on 26 March 2007 (Ahtisaari 2007). It included very important provisions for the security and justice sectors. Let us look at this proposal in more detail.

The Ahtisaari Plan's provisions in the security and justice sectors

The Ahtisaari Plan, a text of what was to be an international agreement, consisted of a main body with fourteen articles that formed its key principles, and twelve annexes. Although the text did not mention independence, it did provide for Kosovo to seek membership of international organizations and to make international agreements. The ten principles were focused on the importance of a multiethnic society, open market economy, the renunciation of territorial claims, the right to negotiate and conclude international agreements, and the powers of supervision of the international community. A number of articles and annexes dealt very specifically with the security and justice sectors, and went under the titles 'Security Sector', 'International Civilian Presence' and 'International Support'. They described the 'reconfiguration' – that is, the restructuring, of the international community's presence in Kosovo. They stressed that the international community should retain substantial powers of control over the justice and security areas. The international presence was to consist of three principle components:

1 An International Civilian Representative (ICR), double-hatted as the EU Special Representative, was to be appointed by an International Steering Group (ISG) comprising key international stakeholders. The ICR was to be the ultimate supervisory authority over the implementation of the Settlement, and was to have specific powers conferred upon him to allow him to take actions necessary to oversee and ensure successful implementation of the Settlement. These included the authority to annul decisions or laws adopted by Kosovo authorities, and to sanction or remove public officials whose actions were determined by the ICR to be inconsistent with the letter and the spirit of the Settlement. In addition, it was argued that the ICR would have the power to appoint international judges and prosecutors, and assume powers in the area of the judiciary, police, customs and correctional services (Ahtisaari 2007: Annex D).

2 A European Security and Defence Policy (ESDP) mission was to be deployed, which would monitor, mentor and advise on all areas related to the rule of law (ibid.: Annex X).

3 A NATO-led International Military Presence (IMP) would provide a safe and secure environment in conjunction with the ICR and the support of Kosovo's institutions (ibid.: Article 13, Annex XI).

With the exception of the tasks allocated to these bodies, the Ahtisaari Plan argued that in the security sector area 'Kosovo shall have authority over law enforcement, security, justice, public safety, intelligence, civil emergency response and border control over its territory' (ibid.: Article 9.1). It then specified that the roles of the ICR and the IMP would be of supervision in that area (ibid.: Article 9.2). A new professional and multi-ethnic Kosovo Security Force (KSF) would be established within one year, and would have a maximum of 2,500 active members and 800 reserve members (ibid.: Article 5, Annex VIII). The Settlement stipulated that the current Kosovo Protection Corps (KPC) was to be disbanded within one year (ibid.: Articles 9.4, 9.5, 9.6; Annex VIII, Article 6). It stated that 'all organizations not authorized by law to conduct activities in Kosovo in the security sector shall cease to operate' (ibid.: Article 9.7).

When the Security Council began private consultations on the Ahtisaari proposal on 3 April 2007, some states attempted to put forward preliminary drafts for a new UN resolution to replace Resolution 1244. One draft resolution was circulated in early May 2007 and, according to US officials, the new resolution was to lay the groundwork for Kosovo's independence and provide mandates for new international missions in Kosovo under a Chapter VII authorization. Russia, in a competing draft, called for further negotiations between the parties, leading to an impasse regarding the process of drafting a resolution in the UNSC that would have allowed authorization for Kosovo to be given independence and end the application of UNSC 1244. Then, in July 2007, Belgium, France, Germany, Italy and the UK put forward a new resolution that made the case for giving Kosovo the right to independence (Weller 2008b: 1224–1225).

Thus, although in July 2007 the Contact Group officially renewed efforts to find a negotiated solution, the mood in some European capitals and in the United States was to push for the recognition of the Ahtisaari Plan and for Kosovo's independence, even if Serbia objected to it. The German government, for example, decided to recognize the independence of Kosovo, even without the approval of Belgrade, in the autumn of 2007 (*Der Tagesspiegel* 2007). Thus, in close synchronization with Brussels and Western capitals, on 17 February 2008, the Kosovo Assembly declared independence. The following day the United States, France and the United Kingdom formally recognized Kosovo's independence. A majority but not all of the EU's twenty-seven member states then supported it – Spain, Cyprus, Romania, Slovakia and Greece expressed strong reservations.

The decision on the final status issue, far from being a factor that facilitated the resolution of the challenges in the security and justice area, has contributed to the worsening of the security and justice situation during 2008 and the early part of 2009. In fact, the outcome of the final status negotiations has been to drastically sharpen the divisions among the local players and the international community.

In response to the declaration of independence, Serbia announced that the declaration was null and void and requested that all Kosovo Serb employees withdraw from Kosovo institutions. Kosovo Serbs living in the North of Mitrovica followed the demands from Belgrade and withdrew their participation in the Kosovo Police Service (KPS) and in judicial structures, as well as simultaneously strengthening their own parallel structures. A similar phenomenon occurred in the Kosovo Serb enclaves to the south of the River Ibar, but the extent of the responses to Belgrade's demand varied. Although Serbia did not suspend the delivery of electricity power to the province and did not impose an economic blockade, as some Serb government officials had threatened, the unilateral declaration of independence led to a confrontation on 17 March 2008 when KFOR entered a court that had been taken over by Kosovo Serb protesters, in order to regain control. The clash resulted in the death of a UNMIK officer and sixty-four UNMIK, twenty-four KFOR and roughly seventy Serb injuries. In the summer and autumn of 2008, Kosovo Albanians' dissatisfaction with the process of 'transferring' responsibilities from UNMIK to Kosovo Albanian institutions led to protests, and an armed Kosovo Albanian group placed a bomb in front of the ICO office and threatened further violent actions.

If the failure to address the status issue earlier on in the engagement cannot provide a valid explanation for the weak record of the international administration in the security and justice sectors, what about the 'alternative explanations' previously mentioned?

Lack of strategy and bias

In contrast to the 1999–2004 period, it is difficult to sustain the claim that there was a lack of strategy on the part of the international community because, as previously argued, a group of member states worked towards a particular resolution of the status issue through the concept of 'supervised independence' and the planning of the transfer of 'responsibilities' from UNMIK to the EU and ICO over a number of years. The implementation of the strategy was hindered by the reaction of a number of players. On the part of the supporters of Kosovo independence, there was an underestimation of the humiliation felt by the Russian government, for which the Kosovo issue had become connected to a perceived Western strategy to isolate and 'threaten' Russia by enlarging NATO in its backyard and by installing a missile defence shield in Eastern Europe. Moreover, the strategy to recognize Kosovo was not paralleled by sufficient efforts to persuade most UN states, particularly European ones such as Spain, Romania, Greece and the Slovak Republic, which have substantial ethnic minorities in their own territories.

The events of 2008 and 2009 have thus brought to the surface the bias of some states in favour of the Kosovo Albanians, and this has become institutionalized in the work of the International Civilian Office (ICO), which has contributed to the deepening of divisions among the international missions present in Kosovo. Let us look at these issues in some details.

The International Civilian Office

The ICO was established ostensibly with the role of implementing the Ahtisaari Plan. On 28 February 2008, a group of European countries and US representatives convened a meeting of an International Steering Group (ISG) on Kosovo in Vienna. At that meeting, the ISG formally appointed Dutch diplomat and EU Special Representative Pieter Feith to be the International Civilian Representative for Kosovo.[7] The decision to double-hat him seemed to have been part of a US-led strategy to influence, if not more directly control, the EU financial and security engagement in Kosovo. On the financial side, the EU agreed to pay more than two billion euros for the period 2007–2011,[8] and to send more than 2,000 police officers, judges and administrators, while allowing US police and administration officers to be part of the mission. The ICO's overall aim was to take on some of UNMIK's tasks in a wide range of policy areas, including security and justice.

Given that the Ahtisaari Plan was not approved by the UN and that the establishment of the ICO took place outside the UN framework (the ICR's appointment has not been endorsed by the UN), the demands of the ICO to take over the tasks of UNMIK in the security and justice sectors have proved extremely controversial vis-à-vis not only the UN, as will be discussed below, but also the Kosovo Serbs, Serbia, and other states that remained concerned about the legality of the international missions in Kosovo.

Nevertheless, the activities of the ICO have been crucial in contributing to the consolidation of the Kosovo Albanian's control over resources, institutions and know-how. The ICO has in fact very quickly established its own presence. Until May 2009, the ICO seemed to be 'unwilling' to exercise strong executive functions in the security and justice sectors and to be more disposed towards working on formulating a strategy that seeks to foster a 'single economic, political and security space'. This can be seen in the approach taken towards the competing demands of the Kosovo Serbs and the Kosovo Albanians on controversial subjects such as the transformation of the Kosovo Protection Corps into the Kosovo Security Force and a new interpretation of the Kosovo Police Force's role.

The transformation of the KPC into the KSF

The question of supervision and disbanding of the KPC and the establishment of a KSF was of crucial importance, since, as previously mentioned, there was strong evidence to suggest that certain elements of the Kosovo Liberation Army had remained active in the KPC (International Crisis Group 2006: 14). The Kosovo Albanians wanted a quick transformation of the KPC into the KSF, seeing the KSF as their future army. In June 2008, the self-proclaimed Kosovo government passed a number of laws covering justice and security. One of these states: 'The mission of the Kosovo Security Force is to support the Government of the Republic of Kosovo.' Most importantly, the law on 'the establishment of the Kosovo Security Council' states that it is up to the Commander of the Kosovo Security Force, together with the Director of the Intelligence Agency and other political figures, to take the key decisions.

This law was therefore in open contradiction to the Ahtissari Plan, which gave the International Military Presence and the ICR a vital role in security. Indeed, it should be stressed that apart from a section at the end of the 'Kosovo Constitution' that mentions such 'supervisory powers' on the part of the ICO and NATO, most of the laws enacted by the Kosovo self-proclaimed government since February 2008 in the area of security do not make any explicit reference to the provisions in the Ahtisaari Plan. Rather, they stress the independence and autonomy of the Kosovo state in this area.

Given UNMIK's residual powers and the continued existence of UNSC 1244, the UNSR argued that it needed to be consulted over the decision to disband the KPC. The Kosovo Albanians, however, strongly contested this role, and preferred to work together with the ICO. To put it simply, the Kosovo Albanians perceived the ICO as a close ally, and their strategy did pay off. In fact, although the international community did put some effort into decommissioning former KLA fighters during the summer and autumn of 2008, there was resistance from some KPC elements, who refused to be 'pensioned' off but rather wanted to remain active in the KSF. Mr Feith, the EUSR/ICO, openly argued that concessions should be made regarding the demands of the KPC to retain most of its officers, because if it this was not done there was the fear that such elements would branch out on their own and pose an internal threat (Feith 2009). By so doing, the ICO/EUSR accommodated the demands of the KPC's hardliners. Indeed, subsequent to the statement made, there were violent protests by residual elements of the KPC. The response of KFOR and the ICO was to decide to give in to these demands by allowing former KLA members who had not originally been selected to be part of the KPC to become part of the force, even if only for training purposes (BBC 2009a, 2009b).

Until May 2009, the ICO's task seems, therefore, not to have been about implementing the principles and articles of the Ahtisaari Plan, which has no real legal basis, but rather to slowly contribute to the consolidation of the Kosovo Albanians's control over the disputed territory. This is evident in the fact that Mr Feith argued that the Kosovo Police Force should be given the task to take over KFOR's role in providing security for a great number of Serbian sites and monasteries that had been attacked in the riots of March 2004 and which, under the Ahtisaari Plan, were to be protected by KFOR (Feith 2009).

Divisions among the international missions

In contrast to the period 1999–2004, today there is much more open competition between the international presence in Kosovo. There are in fact four international missions with overlapping competencies in the security and justice areas: UNMIK, KFOR, ICO and EULEX Kosovo. Although the ICO wanted to take over most of the tasks of UNMIK, and also control the activities of EULEX Kosovo and more directly liaise with KFOR, this did not happen according to plan because of the lack of recognition of Kosovo's independence by the majority of UN members, and divisions within the EU and NATO.

In fact, the UN had to take a 'status neutral' approach, and the UN Secretary General had to call for UNMIK to maintain a residual presence in Kosovo for some time (United Nations Security Council 2008). During the summer and autumn of 2008, UNMIK engaged in negotiations to seek a political resolution to some of the key outstanding issues, including in the justice and security areas. This resulted in the decision by the UN Secretary General, taken in November 2008, with the support of the Serbia, to agree to a six-point plan (ibid.). As part of this new agreement, Belgrade lifted, at least in the diplomatic realm, its original opposition to the deployment of EULEX Kosovo, although it continued to insist that EULEX Kosovo should report to the UNSC and remain neutral on the status issue. In contrast, the Kosovo Albanians strongly opposed this agreement.

The lack of recognition by most UN member states, along with the divisions among EU member states, also had an impact on the deployment of EULEX Kosovo. Between 2008 and 2009, this EU rule-of-law mission had difficulties in establishing a strong working relationship with the ICO, KFOR and UNMIK. Officially EULEX was given a broad mandate, ranging from the maintenance and promotion of the rule of law, public order and security, to ensuring that cases of war crimes, terrorism and organized crime are investigated and prosecuted. EULEX was supposed to implement its mandate through monitoring, mentoring and advising, while retaining certain executive tasks (European Council 2008). Despite the fact that the EU had a team of people working towards the deployment in Kosovo since 2006, by mid-June 2008 EULEX had deployed only 300 of its envisaged 2,000 personnel (International Crisis Group

2008). Although on 14 December 2007 the European Council confirmed the political decision to send an ESDP rule-of-law mission to Kosovo, it decided to protract the discussions on the modalities because of divisions over whether the ESDP mission should be sent with or without a new UN Security Council Resolution. Some countries did not want to deploy until the international legal situation became clearer; there was also a lack of personnel due to the simultaneous demands put on the EU member states to deploy in Georgia and in sub-Saharan Africa. Most importantly, there were difficult negotiations between NATO, UNMIK and the ICO over the extent to which the EULEX should take over some of the most controversial criminal files and the 'riot components' of KFOR, which involved negotiations over personnel and security agreements between the different organizations.

Although EULEX's tasks are defined in its mandate, how they will be implemented on the ground remains an open question at the time of writing. Some European states would like EULEX to work together with the ICO in ensuring that all UNMIK functions are transferred to either the Kosovo Albanians or the ICO so as to consolidate the boundaries of the newly created state, even if it means coming into open confrontation with the Kosovo Serbs in the North of Mitrovica. Others take a more cautious approach. There are also divergent attitudes over the extent to which EULEX should implement the 'executive functions' vis-à-vis the Kosovo Albanians by ensuring, for example, that international judges take on the most sensitive criminal cases which will deal with prominent political Kosovo Albanian figures. Another divisive issue is the pace of the downsizing of KFOR, which has already begun and which could have important consequences on the security situation (BBC 2009c).

The strategies of local actors

In the new circumstances created by the unilateral independence of Kosovo, the strategies of the local actors have changed substantially. As previously mentioned, the Kosovo Albanians have found strong support in the activities of the ICO. Ultimately, they want UNMIK to leave as quickly as possible; the ICO and EULEX Kosovo to help them consolidate control over security and economic institutions in the contested territory; and then for both EULEX and ICO to relinquish all of their residual powers to Albanian Kosovo institutions. In contrast, the Kosovo Serbs at first reacted with total defiance to the ICO and EULEX, and then changed their strategy to partial cooperation with EULEX and UNMIK. However, they are suspicious of the two international missions' long-term aims. In fact, the UN six-point plan agreement does not seem to have resolved key outstanding issues related to the chain of command of the Kosovo Police Service and the nature of the deployment of EULEX Kosovo in the north of Mitrovica.

Ultimately, there are some clear divisions within the Kosovo Serb community. The majority at present want to work towards maintaining a closer union with Belgrade, while a minority are prepared to negotiate a more solid local compromise with the Kosovo Albanian authorities, with the support of UNMIK and, potentially, EULEX Kosovo, but not the ICO. The position of Belgrade vis-à-vis the strategies of the EU towards its membership will have an impact on the pattern of competition and cooperation among Kosovo Serbs and Kosovo Albanians. However, the willingness of the Kosovo Albanians to treat the Kosovo Serbs and other minorities as equal citizens remains to be proven. In fact, as a Commission report published in 2008 pointed out, despite the introduction of laws to protect the religious and cultural heritage of minorities, attacks against religious and cultural sites have taken place. The living conditions of minorities have not improved, and there are some 20,000 IDPs in Kosovo (European Commission 2008a: 23). The issue of IDPs and refugees remains a problem: apart from the 20,000 IDPs in Kosovo, 206,000 inhabitants of Kosovo are displaced in Serbia, and some 16,000 in Montenegro (ibid.: 24). The potential for violent attacks on Kosovo Serbs and other minorities remains real. In fact, although KFOR is downsizing its presence, Western secret services are examining riot scenarios so as to be prepared to react to them. These scenarios are based on the model of the March 2004 riots, but start from the assumption that the riots might be located, against Kosovo Serbs, in the North of Mitrovica (BBC 2009d). Moreover, in light of divisions among EU member states, along with the repercussions of the economic crisis on EU enlargement policies, it is unlikely that Serbia will be admitted into the EU club very easily over the coming years. The willingness of Russia to facilitate a compromise between Belgrade and Pristina over the future of Kosovo in exchange for a Western change of policies towards the enlargement of NATO in its backyard, particularly in Georgia, could have an influence on the relationship between Pristina and Belgrade.

Conclusions

Did the international administration in Kosovo fail to reform the justice and security sector because of an inability to address the final status issue early or did it fail because of other reasons? This chapter has argued that the inability to address the final status issue cannot account for the lack of success. Rather, some of the alternative explanations that have been offered, which cover the 1999–2007 period, provide a better account for subsequent developments. The events between 2007 and the early parts of 2009 have brought to the surface the bias of some states towards the Kosovo Albanians, and this has now been institutionalized in the work of the ICO. In contrast to the early years of engagement, however, when there was a lack of strategy on the part of the international administration, this time there were concerted efforts on the part of a group of states to impose a particular solution on the parties involved, which backfired because of local and international resistance. This has substantially intensified a pattern of divisions among international players, which was already present in the earlier period. Moreover, the international missions in Kosovo and their restructuring to deal with the security and justice sectors are subject to more complex international dynamics than ever before. This is because the international missions' deployments and restructuring have been linked to the issue of Serbia's membership to the EU in exchange for its consent to consolidation of Kosovo's statehood. At the same time, Russia has made a connection between the recognition of the independence of Kosovo and its decision to recognize the independence of Abkazia and South Ossetia following the war with Georgia in 2008, as well as the issue of NATO enlargement. Given the interconnections between these complex diplomatic subjects and the likelihood of resistance by local players to the imposition of an executive style of external policing or heavy-handed sentencing in war-crimes cases, there is a serious likelihood that Kosovo might become a failed state.

Notes

* Giovanna Bono's views are entirely her own, and do not represent her current institute or other institutions with which she has previously been associated.
1 This figure includes persons who sought refuge in Serbia and in Montenegro.
2 The Contact Group led the negotiations, and was composed of France, Germany, Italy, the Russian Federation, the UK and the United States.
3 Personal interview with a former member of KFOR (Brussels, February 2008).
4 The International Crisis Group report has a slightly different estimate: 'The KPC and KPS each include about 2,000 who claim to be former KLA fighters in their ranks.... Roughly 25 per cent of the 7,000 KPS and 70 per cent of the 3,052 active KPC personnel were once rebel fighters' (2006; 3)
5 For example, in an internal 2005 document the Commission had linked the EU's responsibilities in the post-status Kosovo negotiations with the outcome of the status negotiations, and had urged contingency planning for a possible ESDP mission (European Parliament 2007)
6 The principles included the requirement that there is no return to the situation prior to 1999, that there is no change in Kosovo's borders (that is, no partition of Kosovo), and no union of Kosovo with any neighbouring state.
7 The governments of Serbia and Russia protested at the creation of the steering group as illegal.
8 The sum is calculated taking into account monies provided under the following programmes: Macro-Financial Assistance, CARDS, Stability Instrument, ECHO, EIDHR, Pilot actions, UNMIK, ICO, EULEX, and IPA (European Commission 2008b).

References

Ahtisaari, A. (2007) 'Report of the Special Envoy of the Secretary-General on Kosovo's future status', S/2007/168. Available: www.unosek.org (accessed 23 June 2009).

Antonenko, O. (2007) 'Russia and the Deadlock over Kosovo', *Survival,* 49/3: 91–106.

BBC (2009a) 'Kosovo Security Force Minister, Disbanded Members Reach Agreement and End Protest', *BBC Monitoring European,* 24 February.

BBC (2009b) 'Kosovo Security Force not be Corps Successor – KFOR Commander', *BBC Monitoring European,* 25 February.

BBC (2009c) 'NATO Reportedly to 'Drastically' Reduce KFOR in Kosovo – Serbian Paper', *BBC Monitoring European,* 3 March.

BBC (2009d) 'Western Services' Planning Northern Kosovo's "Operation Storm" – Serbian Daily', BBC *Monitoring European,* 12 May.

Bernabeu, I. (2007) 'Laying the Foundations of Democracy? Reconsidering Security Sector Reform under UN auspices in Kosovo', *Security Dialogue*, 38/71: 71–92.

Der Tagesspiegel (2007) 'Plan Berlin das Kosovo anzuerkennen?' *Der Tagesspiegel*, 24 October.

Eide, K. (2005) 'A Comprehensive Review of the Situation in Kosovo. Report on Behalf of the UN Secretary-General, Submitted to the President of the UN Security Council', S/2005/635, 7 October 2005.

European Commission (2007) 'Commission Staff Working Document: Kosovo under UNSCR 1244 Progress Report 2007', COM(2007)663. 6 November. Available: ec.europa.eu/enlargement/pdf/key_documents/2007/nov/kosovo_progress_reports_ en.pdf (accessed 15 June 2009).

European Commission (2008a) 'Commission Staff Working Document: Kosovo (Under 1244/99) 2008 progress report accompanying the Communication from the Commission to the EP and the Council: Enlargement and Main Challenges 2008–2009'. COM(2008) 674, 5 November.

European Commission (2008b) *Who's is Who in Kosovo*? European Commission. Pristina: Commission Office in Pristina.

European Council (2008) 'Council Joint Action 2008/123/CFSP of 4 February 2008 appointing a European Union Special Representative in Kosovo', 4 February.

European Parliament (2007) 'The EU Presence in a Post-status Kosovo: Challenges and Opportunities', Policy Department External Policies, Commissioned Study. Brussels: European Parliament.

Feith, P. (2009) 'Official recording of the appearance of Mr Feith in front of the Foreign Affairs Committee of the EP on 11 February 2009'. Available: www.europarl.europa. eu/wps-europarl-internet/frd/vod/player?eventId=20090211-1500-COMMITTEE-AFE T&language=en&byLeftMenu=researchcommittee (accessed 4 April 2009).

Franks, J. and Richmond, O. P. (2008) 'Co-opting Liberal Peacebuilding: Untying the Gordian Knot in Kosovo', *Cooperation and Conflict*, 43/81: 81–103.

Gil-Robles, A. (2002) 'Kosovo: The Human Rights Situation and the Fate of Persons Displaced from Their Homes', Council of Europe, October.

Heinemann-Grüder, A. and Grebenschikov, I. (2007) 'Security Governance by Internationals: The Case of Kosovo', in M. Brzoska and D. Law (eds) *Security Sector Reconstruction and Reform in Peace Support Operations*, New York, NY: Routledge.

Human Rights Watch (2006) 'Not on the Agenda: The Continuing Failure to Address Accountability in Kosovo Post-March 2004', *Human Rights Watch Report*. 18(4D), May.

Human Rights Watch (2008) 'Kosovo Criminal Justice Scorecard', *Human Rights Watch Report*, 20 2(D), March.

International Crisis Group (2006) 'An Army for Kosovo?', *Europe Report* No. 174, 28 July.

International Crisis Group (2008) 'Kosovo's Fragile Transition', *Europe Report* No. 196, 25 September.

Leurdijk, D. and Zandee, D. (2001) *Kosovo: From Crisis to Crisis*, Aldershot: Ashgate.

Narten, J. (2008) 'Post-conflict Peacebuilding and Local Ownership: Dynamics of External–Local Interaction in Kosovo under United Nations Administration', *Journal of Intervention and Statebuilding*, 2/3: 369–390.

OSCE Mission in Kosovo (2006) 'Kosovo Review of the Criminal Justice System 1999–2005', Department of Human Rights and Rule of Law, Pristina, OSCE.

United Nations Security Council (2005) 'Letter dated 7 October 2005 from the Secretary General to the President of the Security Council', S/2005/635, 7 October.

United Nations Security Council (2008) 'Report of the Secretary-General on the United Nations Interim Administration Mission in Kosovo', S/2008/354, 12 June.

Weller, M. (2008a) 'The Vienna Negotiations on the Final Status for Kosovo', *International Affairs*, 84/4: 659–681.

Weller, M. (2008b) 'Kosovo's Final Status', *International Affairs*, 84/6: 1223–1243.

Zaum, D. (2007) *The Sovereignty Paradox: The Norms and Politics of International Statebuilding*, Oxford: Oxford University Press.

8 Kosovo: the final frontier?

From transitional administration to transitional statehood

James Gow

Introduction

The coordinated declaration of independence by the Kosovo authorities on 17 February 2008 was an exception founded on an exception. A territory that had been subject to international humanitarian action that was, for many, regarded as being an unlawful action, exceptionally justified by a particular situation (Serbian forces' ethnic cleansing action against the majority ethnic Albanian population in the province), had been placed under UN mandated transitional administration following that exceptional action (Henkin 1999; House of Commons Foreign Affairs Select Committee 2000; Lowe 2000). Transitional administration was also an exceptional situation: unlike other cases of international intervention and statebuilding (except the mission in East Timor for which Kosovo was a precedent, although it was also qualitatively and legally distinct), international actors took complete responsibility for the exercise of sovereign rights, leaving Belgrade with only an implicit, formal say over the quality and status of Kosovo's borders (Matheson 2001; Ruffert 2001; Wilde 2001; Caplan 2005; Gow 2007). The exception of transitional administration gave way not, as might have been supposed in some quarters, to a fully formed outcome, but to a transitional state – one that was far from having the qualities of complete statehood, despite a claim to being independent and being backed by important and powerful Western actors (Ker-Lindsay 2009).

It was, at best, a work in progress. That work in progress was caught in a murky limbo, recognized by some states as sovereign and having independent international personality but not recognized by the vast majority of others, and blocked from membership of the UN and other international bodies because of the objections of many states – and certain powerful ones, such as Russia, in particular. Those backing the coordinated declaration of independence claimed that the Kosovo case was 'unique'. However, the reality is that, while all cases are unique in their specific detail, none is, in principle or practice (Roberts 2006). Thus, the attempt to create a 'final frontier' in the context of Yugoslavia's dissolution and war not only failed to be complete and satisfactory in that context initially, but it was almost immediately a precedent for dangerous developments elsewhere, as events in Georgia in the summer of 2008 demonstrated (Gow

2007; King 2008). This is a principal argument in the present analysis that traces the incubatory framework of the international transitional administration in Kosovo against a background of international diplomacy and questions concerning status and statehood.

UNMIK's opportunities missed

UNMIK – the UN Mission in Kosovo – was created by UN Security Council 1244 (1999), which marked the end of armed hostilities in Kosovo in 1999. UNMIK was wholly responsible for civilian affairs, while KFOR, the NATO-led military presence, provided security. UNMIK was the first case in which the international community took complete control of a territory, placing all formal and administrative authority in the hands of the transitional administration (Caplan 2005). Legally a part of Serbia (and also, at that time, the Federal Republic of Yugoslavia, which also included Montenegro), the southern province had been the source of tension and low-level conflict between the ethnic Albanian majority in the province and the Serbian authorities for over a decade, which became outright armed conflict in the late 1990s (Judah 2000). As with other parts of the former Yugoslav region, the conflict was marked by 'ethnic cleansing', which prompted major international action (Bellamy 2002; Gow 2003). This included seventy-eight days of air bombardment against Serbian forces between March and June 1999 (Daalder and O'Hanlon 2000; Arkin 2001; Gow 2003).

It was in these circumstances, against the background of Belgrade's record of gross abuses of human rights, that the UN Security Council authorized arrangements in which Belgrade's sovereign rights would be suspended and all authority would be exercised by UNMIK. Although SCR 1244 envisaged a limited official Serbian presence, this never materialized (Gow 2007). However, Serbia maintained an interest in the ethnic Serb community in Kosovo and in historic and religious sites, as well as a few other areas, regarding which Belgrade maintained relations with UNMIK (Ker-Lindsay 2009).

With KFOR primarily responsible for security, UNMIK's mission was to provide interim government, while preparing Kosovo for substantial self-governance. This mission was conducted in concert with the OSCE, responsible for democratic institutions, and the EU Pillar, responsible for economic development. UNMIK had overall authority as well as primary responsibility in areas such as policing. A Special Representative of the Secretary General (SRSG) had 'reserve' powers, under the terms of UNMIK's creation, to take binding decisions (Caplan 2005). With responsibility for all aspects of civilian administration and the rule of law, UNMIK was a large and expensive undertaking – reaching almost $240 million in 2005–2006, reducing to $210 million in 2007–2008 (UNMIK 2008: 2). Cost was coupled with pressure and impatience from the ethnic Albanian majority, on one side, and Washington, which wanted to end the mission, on the other. As a result, Washington pushed diplomatically to engineer arrangements by which Kosovo would gain provisional, supervised independence from Serbia – with or without Serbian agreement – and the EU would take over responsibility for civilian administration and justice, ending UNMIK and the US contribution to it. However, this proved not to be possible in face of Russian opposition to passing a UN Security Council Resolution that would allow this, among other factors. Consequently, the United States and a majority of EU states pursued a messy diplomatic path in which there was a coordinated declaration of independence by the Pristina government and recognition by those countries (Ischinger 2008).

The EU mission to Kosovo was agreed by all EU countries in relation to the existing Resolution 1244 just before the declaration of independence, as part of the coordination. Two days before Kosovo declared independence, the EU approved EULEX, a major policing and security mission. However, approval itself only came with a sleight-of-hand manoeuvre whereby a deadline for objections to the mission to be expressed by midnight Friday 15 February was quietly set, rather than a formal agreement being made by ministers meeting face-to-face and where disagreements would emerge again. The date for this silent decision was clearly set to be adopted technically while there was no contest regarding Kosovo's actual status and the UN mandate was clear, which would not be the case once the expected declaration of independence had been made on Sunday 17 February. There was a clear sense of disingenuousness in this approach, but the compromise permitted the EU to act collectively, despite reservations in some quarters, leaving each member state to pursue its own policy regarding recognition of Kosovo.

As UNMIK moved towards reconfiguration, an assessment of its record indicated uneven progress and underachievement. UNMIK's uneven and underachieving record was largely a product of leadership by various SRSGs. Bernard Kouchner (who became France's Foreign Minister in 2007), SRSG during the first year and a half of UNMIK, may have wasted the most propitious conditions ever for a UN operation, especially a transitional administration. With full authority available, unlike almost all other missions, and with an unusually welcoming local population, the chance to shape Kosovo was missed, as Kouchner argued that it was hard for the mission to start its work properly while Kosovo's final status – and so the goal towards which UNMIK had to work – was not defined. This was a wholly mistaken position, evident in the approach of his German successor, Michael Steiner, who rightly argued that whatever the final status of Kosovo, the condition and quality of government and law and order would need to be the same. He established a strong policy of 'Standards before Status'. However, following violent protests coordinated by elements in the ethnic Albanian provisional government in 2004, his Norwegian successor, Soren Jessen-Petersen, reversed that position with the work towards final status – tacitly understood to mean independence – starting. The next SRSG, German Joachim Ruecker, attempted to work with the moves towards final status, including the provision for 'supervised independence' developed by Finnish diplomat Martti Ahtisaari (discussed below), while upholding a balanced approach with ethnic Serb communities and gaining their confidence. Unhappy with arrangements as the EU prepared to move into Kosovo with Security Council authority or Belgrade's agreement, and Pristina having declared independence, his resignation was rejected by UN Secretary General Ban Ki Moon, as he sought to maintain his authority with the Serb communities amid a political and diplomatic mess. Lamberto Zannier replaced Ruecker in the summer of 2008, coming into an office confronted with managing the aftermath of Kosovo's messy coordinated declaration of independence and the botched attempts to arrange for the EU to replace UNMIK (see below.)

The 'Final Status' proposal put forward by Ahtisaari, the UN Special Envoy for Kosovo, the 'Ahtisaari Plan', envisaged 'supervised independence' for Kosovo, meaning that for a period of five years the EU would be involved in the governance and administration of Kosovo to ensure that resources were in place, international standards were observed and there would be provision for security (UN Security Council 2007a). This would all be under the authority of a Chapter VII UN Security Council Resolution that made its provisions binding and accorded full authority to the EU countries for implementing the proposal. This was based on the model that reduced the UN and NATO roles in Bosnia, although there were significant differences between the cases of Bosnia and Kosovo themselves, and in the less extensive powers the EU would have in Kosovo.

International diplomatic manoeuvring and Kosovo's status

International diplomacy surrounding Kosovo was riven with tensions from the NATO action onwards (Bellamy 2002). UNMIK's creation in June 1999 represented a rapprochement between NATO countries and Russia, following deep divisions over NATO's use of force over Kosovo without Security Council authorization. For much of UNMIK's mission, despite fluctuating relationships in other respects, common positions were maintained – including in the early stages of developing the Ahtisaari Plan. However, Russia became aware that Western intentions in creating EU supervision to replace UNMIK were less focused on cooperative management of the situation in Kosovo and more concerned with obtaining a new Security Council Resolution that would remove the effect of Resolution 1244 and create an ambiguous position in which independence could be declared and recognized without the complicating factor of that resolution. Russia, however, had consistently (and credibly) argued that Resolution 1244 defined Kosovo's status under formal Serbian sovereignty in a way that made it binding in international law.

Russia backed Serbia's position and claims to sovereignty, and consistently rejected moves in the Security Council that could undermine this, including blocking formal approval of UNMIK's reconfiguration, although if SRSG Zannier had been able to agree terms for this with Belgrade in 2008 it was likely that Russia would not have obstructed a resolution. In the meantime, Russia had begun to supply humanitarian assistance and mine-clearance teams to Serbia to help it to support the ethnic Serb communities in Kosovo and remove unexploded munitions remaining from NATO's 1999 air action; both moves were intended to symbolize Serbia's sovereign rights and to up the diplomatic stakes regarding UNMIK, its relationship with Belgrade and its status. It is evident that, along with the wasted potential of the mission, UNMIK also became the focus for turning success in rebuilding relations between Russia and the West into friction.

US Secretary of State Condoleezza Rice visited Moscow in mid-May 2007 in an attempt to persuade Russia not to veto the proposed UN Security Council Resolution on Kosovo. Washington and London were introducing a draft UN Security Council Resolution to endorse the Ahtisaari Proposal,[1] as discussed above. If Moscow had been persuaded to support a new UN Security Council resolution on Kosovo, this would have eased the way to Kosovo's independence from Serbia before the end of June 2007 without Serbia's agreement. However, Moscow was not ready to accede to Western schemes to avoid Belgrade's agreement on any change in Kosovo's status.

Russia introduced a counter-draft in the Security Council to that of the United States and United Kingdom; this offered a model of 'monitored' or 'supervised' autonomy (rather than 'supervised independence') and called for further discussions involving Belgrade and requiring its agreement. Before this, Russia was also responsible for arranging a visit by diplomats from each of the current Security Council delegations to Serbia and Kosovo at the end of April, following which the South African Permanent Representative complained that the situation on the ground in Kosovo was 'grossly' different from the picture painted in official reports by the UN Administration in Kosovo (Mappes-Niediek 2007). That visit was led by the President of the UN Security Council and Belgium's Permanent Representative, Jan Verbeke, and noted the idea of 'supervised autonomy', which briefly entered discussion in the Security Council, as well as suggesting that there was considerable work still to be done, despite clear expectations among the majority population (UN Security Council 2007b).

After that visit, it appeared that the United States and the United Kingdom would have problems mustering a nine out of fifteen votes majority in the Security Council plus no permanent member's using its right to veto a resolution (the P5 – the United States, the United Kingdom, China, Russia and France): the United States and the United Kingdom were joined by France, Belgium and Italy; Slovakia and Russia rejected the proposal; South Africa, Congo, Ghana, Indonesia and China were less ardently opposed; and the remaining countries – Peru, Panama and Qatar – remained undecided. However, on 11 May the new US Permanent Representative to the UN asserted that there would be majority support for the resolution. In response, on 12 May Russia's Permanent Representative to the United Nations in New York, Vitaliy Churkin, said that it was becoming 'more and more likely' that Russia would use its veto to block the US–UK proposal if necessary (Reuters 2007). American officials, as part of a very forceful approach, had already begun to indicate US preparedness to bypass a Russian veto and act unilaterally to recognize Kosovo as an independent international personality, come what may, asserting that Kosovo would be independent, in its view, with the only question over how 'messy' the process involved would be.

Sovereignty, Resolution 1244, and precedent versus the 'uniqueness' of Kosovo

At the heart of the dispute between Russia and the West is the legal and political concept of sovereignty, the basic principle of international society, embedded, inter alia, in the UN Charter (Fowler and Bunck 1995; Jackson 1999; Krasner 1999; Gow 2005). Russia, China (which could also veto any resolution, but preferred to avoid this) and most of the non-permanent members of the Security Council were highly protective of sovereignty and of the concomitant principles of non-interference in internal affairs and preserving the territorial integrity of states against changes without agreement or resulting from use of force. In addition, five EU member states were strongly opposed to the US–UK-led process.[2] Despite a strong desire for common EU policy, it was clear that one or more of these could veto aspects of the proposed EU administration, fostering instability. Ahtisaari and Washington were at pains to stress that Belgrade's record of ethnic cleansing in the 1990s, the NATO presence, and the period of international administration separating the province from the reach of any central government factually made Kosovo a unique case. On that basis, they argued that endorsing Ahtisaari's proposal would not be a precedent for other cases around the world, where territories might declare themselves to be independent, although it would, exceptionally, be a radical departure (Ischinger 2008).

There were three scenarios, therefore, regarding diplomatic management of the status question. The first of these entailed a new Security Council Resolution resulting in Kosovo's effective and formal independence – a process of 'coordinated independence' (Ischinger 2008). The main objective of the US–UK-led process of endorsing the Ahtisaari Proposal under a Chapter VII binding UN Security Council Resolution was to end UN SCR 1244 and to remove the formal and binding statement in international law on sovereignty embedded in that resolution. The Ahtisaari Proposal envisaged the creation of institutions appropriate to an independent state, including the capacity to enter into independent international relationships and to join international organizations, including international financial institutions such as the IMF and the World Bank. A new Security Council resolution to endorse the 'final status' proposal by ending Resolution 1244 would remove any formal statement on sovereignty, a crucial international legal issue, creating an ambiguous grey area in which different interpretations could be present – crucially, including interpretations supporting coordinated independence.

By setting out something with the characteristics of an independent state, this was a device that would create a situation in which, according to US and UK intentions, Kosovo would declare independence, acknowledging the need to accept 'supervised' status. Washington and EU capitals would then recognize Pristina's independence, expected to come during June, with outgoing UK Prime Minister Tony Blair hoping to celebrate this at his last EU summit in Germany at the end of June. However, some EU member states were strongly opposed, and rejected diplomatic recognition. As a result, this scheme did not materialize as those promoting it intended. Instead, there would be an even messier position, as Washington, London and Brussels pressed on, despite the failure to achieve a resolution that, even if achieved, would have created a messy enough situation.

Emphasis moved to the other scenarios. Compromise options were pursued as an alternative. Germany, although it was not a member of the Council, proposed seeking an alternative Security Council resolution which would defer the 'status' question, ensure continuing authority for the NATO presence in Kosovo and guarantee the proposed EU role. However, while not addressed explicitly as an issue, any new resolution would replace UN SCR 1244, and thus the absence of the formal inclusion of a new statement on sovereignty would also create a position of ambiguity in which Pristina could declare independence and states around Europe and the world could choose diplomatically to recognize that declaration, albeit without the support of those elements in the Proposal which described the institutions of an independent state. A compromise proposal of this kind, also making reference to the sovereignty question but ending the continuing effect of Resolution 1244, even if against US policy, might not have been vetoed by America if it had been for a set period to be renewed or changed, in contrast to the indefinite character of 1244. However, no alternatives emerged in practice.

Because of the failure to endorse the Ahtisaari Proposal with a new Security Council Resolution or to find a compromise outcome, the United States indicated that if, as was being planned and coordinated, Kosovo declared independence without a new Security Council Resolution, then Washington would proceed to recognize Pristina diplomatically. Washington also expected that EU member states would do likewise. However, it was not initially certain that all (or even any) of the EU's member states would grant recognition in these circumstances, although some would consider their options. Germany's Chancellor, Angela Merkel, had spoken out against 'unilateral' actions and emphasized the need for action to be orderly and collective, based on Security Council authority. This appeared to imply that while Germany supported the West European EU members in the Security Council in seeking a new resolution, neither it nor other EU countries committed to positions on the rule of law could easily move to diplomatic recognition that contravened the binding effect of Resolution 1244 in international law. While previous US administrations would almost certainly have taken the same position, the Bush administration established a reputation and record for action not necessarily embedded in conventional interpretations of international law. There would therefore be a very awkward and messy period with some states recognizing Kosovo's independence and others not doing so, thus straining international relations and adding to security risks, given the lack of a coherent international position. This was, in the end, what transpired.

The Kosovo final status proposal was hotly contested, particularly between Russia and the West. Washington expected, as in past cases, to secure Moscow's acquiescence, even if some compromise was required. Events, however, resulted in a situation where Kosovo declared itself independent and Washington, as well as other states, granted it recognition, even if some delay occurred as part of a compromise. This opened the way for international financial assistance and the

EU mission; it was believed and hoped that all of this would result in economic growth for Kosovo. It impacted negatively on Serbia and its relations with the EU, however.

It was clear that any way out of the impasse into which impatience in Washington, London, Brussels and other European capitals had forced the handling of Kosovo would require a change in international relationships with Belgrade. In April 2008, Serbia signed a Stabilisation and Association Agreement (SAA) with the European Union, taking EU policy in the Western Balkans a step further. The SAA signing was a major achievement for both the EU and Serbian President Boris Tadić and his political allies – and reinforced Tadić, as he, against expectations, prevailed in elections in Serbia. However, this was not easily achieved. The EU had hoped to sign the SAA months earlier, either before or immediately after Kosovo's declaration of independence in February; in part as an implied quid pro quo to ease the pain of the Kosovo question and to ease the way for the EU police and security mission being deployed as part of 'supervised' independence under the Ahtisaari Plan. However, while the SAA and further development in the relationship was needed by both Belgrade and Brussels, the reality was that Tadić and the Belgrade authorities had been forced to make it clear that Kosovo and EU integration were separate matters, not to be linked. Thus, the SAA and improving relations made little real difference in terms of Kosovo.

The need to change relations with Belgrade for the better also led the EU to relax, as far as possible, its demands on cooperation with the International Criminal Tribunal for the former Yugoslavia. For many years, the EU and its member states had set full cooperation as a condition for the SAA. This was difficult for democratic forces in Serbia, who were not well placed to counter Military Security Service protection to the few remaining – but prominent – war crimes suspects. Following recognition of Kosovo by eighteen of the twenty-seven EU members, even the democrats in Belgrade shifted to a position where the war crimes suspects were 'not a priority' for Serbia, judging that recognition of Kosovo, in their view, was a breach of an internationally legally binding UN Security Council Resolution, which removed their obligation to cooperate under a similar resolution concerning the Tribunal. One of the main EU proponents of a hard line on cooperation, the United Kingdom, immediately softened its stance in the light of this position. However, the long-time proponent of the hard line, the Netherlands, maintained its stand, and was joined by Germany and Belgium, following violent attacks on their Belgrade embassies in the wake of Kosovo's recognition. However, the EU and its member states were really looking to soften their position, as the United Kingdom had done, without losing face. The reality was that, as Belgrade still showed strong cooperation, it was increasingly seen as such (rather than not enough) as the list of wanted men was reduced to just two: General Ratko Mladic and Croatian Serb political leader Goran Hadzic. In this context, the type of diplomatic easing of conditions that had emerged in the context of Croatia's record on cooperation and relationship with the EU was inevitable (Gow 2007).

The EU efforts to mollify Serbia over Kosovo had little purchase, though the mutual relationship remained strategically important for both. In practice, Serbia adopted a position of reasoned principle, ruling out any resort to force under the then government (a realist appraisal of the situation), but seeking to maintain links with the Serbian communities in Kosovo, despite Pristina's declaration of independence. Belgrade also took every opportunity to reassert its principled claim for sovereign rights. Thus, there was an ambiguous situation in which significant security risks inhered.

UNMIK and the aftermath of the Kosovo declaration of independence

Violent unrest involving the death of a United Nations policeman followed Pristina's coordinated declaration of independence. One month after the Kosovo government declared independence from Serbia, inter-communal tensions began to boil over. Parts of northern Kosovo, with a focus on the town of Mitrovica, witnessed increasingly violent incidents, culminating in the death of the UN policeman. While there were symbolic protests initially, and the general approach taken by both the Serbian authorities in Belgrade and local Serbs in Kosovo was to avoid violence, poor management of situations by the UN administration in Kosovo and NATO-led troops of KFOR led to escalation.

The main spark was an attempt by fifty-three court officials to return to work in the Mitrovica courthouse. These were employees of the old Serbian judicial administration, who had been sacked in 1999 after UNMIK, the UN transitional authority in Kosovo, took over. The attempt was entirely peaceful, although clearly planned and coordinated to test the combined forces of UNMIK, KFOR and the government in the Kosovo capital, Pristina. The move to make a particular issue of this, at this stage, was clearly in response to Kosovo's declaration of independence, intended as a non-violent means of symbolically marking Serbia's claim to jurisdiction in the area. After days of protesting outside the courthouse to claim back their old jobs, on the morning of 14 March the protesters used ambulances to drive through the closed gate to the court building, while UNMIK and KFOR stood back (B92 2008a). A group that involved judges, officials and clerks (including a large number of women) proceeded to occupy the building, but made a point of not entering offices or touching any documents – something that they stressed in public statements. This was an example of how the former employees sought to test the combined capacities of UNMIK, KFOR and the government by emphasizing the justice of their case and not once verbally calling into question the authority of any of these authorities, even though their demand to get back their jobs was in itself a silent challenge.

The Pristina government largely kept out of the question – both wisely and because it could afford to hide behind others. UN Special Representative Joachim Ruecker appeared to take the action as a provocation and challenge to the authorities, considerably exaggerating the issue in statements condemning the use of force and violence, where driving through closed gates with the ambulances (while UNMIK police stood aside, not trying to stop them) was the only part of the scenario that could at all be described as forceful. Ruecker rejected Belgrade's 'interference' rather than defusing the situation diplomatically and seeking a way out by accepting the protesters' requests to meet them or suggesting that a way might be found for them to apply for jobs (their old ones or new ones under a 'modernization' scheme). Instead, his deputy Larry Rossin ordered French KFOR and UNMIK police to enter the building and arrest the Serb protesters. This happened at 0530 hours on 17 March, with the Serbs offering no resistance to arrest. The timing of this action, on the fourth anniversary of violent action by ethnic Albanians that resulted in 4,000 Serbs being driven from their homes, contributed to the tension, suggesting bad judgement on the part of UNMIK – or even, as Serbia's Minister for Kosovo Slobodan Samardzic suggested, deliberate ill intent, seeking to provoke wider armed hostilities (B92 2008b).

However, as UNMIK police attempted to transfer the prisoners a large crowd gathered, mobilized around a group who permanently agitated in the vicinity of the bridge over the River Ibar connecting northern (Serbian) and southern (Albanian) Mitrovica. Augmented by large numbers of other Serbs, the crowd blocked the passage of police vehicles and, as violence emerged with some of the crowd throwing stones and explosive devices, including hand grenades, two police vehicles were destroyed and twenty of the prisoners were released (the remainder were eventually taken to Pristina and cautioned). The UNMIK action was counterproductive, from clearly flagged US police seen manhandling handcuffed female protesters on television, to the use of automatic weapons in response to the rebellious crowd. In terms of the situation, the response played into the hands of nationalist Serbian propaganda, with recognized moderates such as President Boris Tadić condemning the 'excessive' use of force and warning that it could lead to escalation, while the Radicals' leader Tomislav Nikolic ominously warned that Serbia could not remain 'dumb' in face of the situation in Kosovo much longer. Belgrade called on the UN to undertake an official inquiry.

Prospects of partition

The initial effect of these events was to embed a de facto boundary along the River Ibar. As a result of the violence, a de facto border ran through the town of Mitrovica, effectively separating the area to the north from the remainder of Kosovo. This inevitably prompted thoughts in some quarters about the partition of Kosovo.

Following the incident, only a small US military KFOR presence and a small UNMIK police contingent remained north of that line nominally marking Kosovo's northern border. However, neither of these elements was operating border control normally – vehicles were not stopped, documentation was not checked and customs control was not exercised. At the same time, French KFOR strengthened positions along the Ibar, establishing additional checkpoints and exercising firm control. This, in effect, appeared to partition Kosovo along the

River Ibar, making northern Kosovo something close to a no-go area for either the international presence or the Kosovo government as UNMIK police withdrew from the area, transferring security responsibility to KFOR. KFOR, though, refrained from undertaking policing roles, remaining in reserve for major incidents. Bob Galuci, the US diplomat in charge of UNMIK in the region, noted that Serbs had not attacked Albanians in the course of these events and had also cooperated with UNMIK locally, including in the evacuation of UNMIK civilians. Galuci was reported to have resigned because he disagreed with Pristina's approach to the region, but this was not confirmed, while other reports said that the Pristina headquarters had rejected it. Meanwhile, following talks with local Serbs led by a Russian representative of UNMIK, agreement was reached to allow UNMIK police to return to control police stations. A symbolic victory for the Serbian side was the explicit reference in the agreement to implementing the terms of UN Security Council Resolution 1244, which Serbia argued had been breached by the Pristina declaration of independence.

Kosovo – the final frontier?

The effective (if perhaps temporary) partition of Kosovo reignited discussion of the old question of partition, with the likelihood that some in the EU, NATO and the UN discussed such partition and the impossibility of resisting it should Belgrade and the local Serbs seek this. Those who supported partition believed that severing the ethnically Serb-dominated northern part of Kosovo and allowing it to remain part of Serbia could achieve two things.

First, the major challenges (if not impossibility) of extending the EU's mission into the northwest part of the territory would be avoided. EULEX, the EU's rule-of-law mission agreed just before the declaration of independence to supervise Kosovo's development, was not welcome in Serb-dominated areas. This mission was not recognized by Belgrade or by local Serbs, who regarded it as unlawful and proposed its disestablishment. The EU preference was to bypass the UN, while replacing UNMIK and, in any case, operating irrespective of the UN. Belgrade, by contrast, insisted on maintaining UNMIK and UN primacy under the terms of Resolution 1244. The Serbian side refused to cooperate with EULEX in anyway. Therefore, initial plans to deploy EULEX, including in the Serb-dominated northern areas, at an early stage were stalled. Those in Brussels murmuring about partition might have been particularly motivated by these realities on the ground.

Second, some in international circles believed that if there were an agreement to partition Kosovo, with part of it remaining with Serbia, this would 'lance the boil' of Serb passion regarding the issue. Partition, it was thought, would allow Serbia and the Serbs more easily to come to terms with the loss of Kosovo, giving the sense that the Serbs had not been completely overridden as victims.[3]

There were three main factors that militated very strongly against partition, however. The first of these was that the Ahtisaari Proposal and the constitution that went with this very strongly and explicitly underlined the territorial integrity of Kosovo, and that nothing should be allowed to partition it. While this could be seen as an ironic, if not hypocritical, position in the context of paving the way for Kosovo to be partitioned from Serbia, it created a formal position from which it would be very difficult for those backing Kosovo's independence to retreat. This was already clear in statements made by US officials, reinforcing the US position that there could be no question of partition, in response to reports that some in Europe were thinking in these terms.

The second major hindrance to thinking on partition was that any move towards further partition would have precedent effect. While Kosovo's declaration of independence already put this issue on the agenda, any new steps that would mean designating completely new borders based on ethnic political communities would provoke difficulties around the world (one factor in China's crackdown in Tibet could well be the Kosovo's declaration of independence) but, most acutely and immediately, in the region. Partition of Kosovo would remove the restraint that prevented Bosnian Serb leaders from declaring independence (because of an agreed Serb position – see below). More significantly, it would fuel demands for, and open the way politically and logically to demands from, ethnic Albanians in northwest Macedonia to separate from Macedonia (and possibly to unite with their kin community in Kosovo). This was opposed internationally, with NATO and the EU working to stabilize Macedonia. This would become an unsustainable position if Kosovo were to be partitioned.

Finally, an agreement on partition seemed unlikely because it would run counter to Serbia's policy of maintaining the high ground of legality and principle on which it was backed by Russia and China in particular. Since the declaration of independence by Pristina, Belgrade's position had been to exercise restraint, avoid violence, and seek every opportunity to reinforce its claims over Kosovo by emphasizing issues of sovereignty. In line with this, the Serb leaders in Bosnia were cautious not to claim Kosovo as a precedent for them to declare independence, instead upholding the principles of sovereignty and territorial integrity. This position of principle would go immediately if there were partition of Kosovo, putting pressure on Bosnia's statehood. Agreement to allow UNMIK to return to northern Kosovo emphasized the continuing presence of Serbian legal bodies there (though not criminal ones). In addition, when in the past Serb nationalists had raised the question of partition, their thinking had always included the Serbian Church's historic holy sites – none of which could be found within the region where elements of de facto partition began to emerge.

Although events drove the issue of partitioning Kosovo onto the agenda, there were very strong factors blocking moves in that direction – even if it were judged to be desirable. If there were Serbian agreement to a partition, also agreed by Pristina, then, despite firm US opposition, it was always likely that an agreement of this kind would be endorsed internationally. However, that prospect was not at all likely in the short term, given the strong factors militating against it. Yet, despite the good reasons not to develop ideas of partition, it seemed likely to remain on some agendas. In the meantime, with partition not a realistic option, the pressure would be on to find ways in which to accommodate EULEX and UNMIK and to allow for an effective international presence north of the River Ibar.

International disarray in Kosovo

There was tension over the deployment of the EU rule-of-law mission, EULEX, not only with the Belgrade authorities but also with the UN mission. Western plans had envisaged that UNMIK would be wound up 120 days after Kosovo had declared independence. It was to be replaced by an EU supervising authority, envisaged in the Ahtisaari Plan, starting with the rule-of-law mission, EULEX. Instead, however, UNMIK had to be reconfigured, rather than ended, as had been foreseen in the 2007 plans to hand over administrative responsibility fully to the EU. In June, UN Secretary General Ban Ki Moon submitted a proposal for UNMIK's reconfiguration to the UN Security Council. Russia rejected Ban's proposal. However, providing UNMIK remained present in Kosovo with ultimate authority, Resolution 1244 did not exclude its responsibilities being devolved to others. The SRSG, Lamberto Zannier, though, appeared to have wanted the reconfiguration to proceed on the basis of discussion with Belgrade, if possible, even though President Boris Tadić opposed any reconfiguration not endorsed by the Security Council (as did others, including Russian diplomats, who suggested that specific authority was needed for anything other than UNMIK to carry our policing roles in Kosovo).

Difficulties and divisions within the EU gave an additional dimension to the lack of coherence regarding the situation, especially on the ground in Kosovo, where significant tensions emerged with UNMIK. Both Belgrade and local Serbs made clear that they would continue to work with the UN mission, which they regard as legitimate, but would only work with EULEX if it were formally acknowledged as being subordinate to UNMIK under Security Council Resolution 1244. Added to this, Belgrade's decision to assert its formal sovereignty by including Kosovo in parliamentary elections in May 2008 added to tensions.

Among international actors, senior military and diplomatic figures in Kosovo expressed sharply divergent views about cooperation between the UN and the EU. In an increasingly tense security situation, it was strongly rumoured that UNMIK Chief Joachim Ruecker was about to resign because of tensions over the EULEX deployment when he went to New York to present his report on the situation at the Security Council in closed session in mid-April. This followed an earlier attempt by his junior working with Serb communities in Kosovo to resign in the wake of Kosovo's declaration of independence. He did not, but he was replaced by Zannier within months. These troubles within UNMIK reflected tensions in Kosovo and with EULEX. There were sharp differences between the international missions.

On 29 April 2008, Ruecker publicly judged that the proposed transfer to EULEX, scheduled for June, was 'far from certain', and the UN mission's responsibility would continue 'as long as Resolution 1244 exists' (B92 2008c). This followed the strong words by his military advisor, General Raul Cunha, a

week before that the EU and international position on Kosovo was highly ques-
tionable, saying that 'we are either liars or hypocrites', in terms of Kosovo's
uniqueness, and that although the mission was said to be about creating peace
and stability it was heading in the 'direction of instability' and it would be necessary to continue the UN mission in the northern Serb majority areas of Kosovo
(Cunha 2008). As a compromise, current Slovenia's EU presidency suggested
that EULEX should be seen as supporting UMMIK and 'strengthening the EU
Pillar' under it. However, EULEX chief General Yves de Kermabon had already
rejected this position, publicly declaring that he rejected any power-sharing
arrangement (B92 2008d).

Given UNMIK's mission to build civilian arrangements for self-government,
its work in education, training and the holding of local and Kosovo-wide elections, resulting in a provisional government, were positive achievements. This
gave scope to supporters of Kosovo's independence to argue that circumstances
had changed enough for independence to be possible. However, it was evident
that many problems remained, including significant issues concerning corrup-
tion, organized crime linked to the authorities, rule of law and adequate judicial
provision, as noted in scathing international reports, even as Kosovo sought
independence (The European Commission 2007).

On one level, the serious deficiencies evident in March 2008 and identified by
Cunha were why the EU mission intended to replace UNMIK, EULEX, was
necessary – but also why its presence was part of the problem and why retention
of UNMIK was required. Deployment of EULEX was not straightforward, given
UNMIK's continuing role. Relations between the missions were fraught.
Working out a division of responsibilities became a key issue for SRSG Zannier
and others. Zannier made it clear that UNMIK's mission should continue to
apply to the whole of Kosovo rather than just the northern Serb-majority areas,
which had been suggested by some observers and which would have embedded
a de facto division within Kosovo. It was clear that despite the opportunity available the UN mission had not managed to deal with either standards or status
fully, and that these issues would inevitably continue to generate friction for
some time, including between UNMIK and the EU mission, as it eventually
deployed. This was particularly the case because the latter, in practice, supported
independence for Kosovo, while the UN mission remained officially neutral on
the question.

UNMIK's reconfiguration was set to proceed with a reduced presence and
reduced scope, while EULEX would build up over the coming months.
UNMIK's record of opportunities missed at great expense could not be overcome, but it was possible it might be mitigated. This depended largely on the
international diplomatic context being shaped positively, however, and, in particular, arrangements meeting with Russian approval. Anything else meant a
further phase of uncertainty, mixed signals and fudging. Therefore, the EU took
enhanced responsibilities, in effect, under the UNMIK 'umbrella', ensuring that
international involvement in Kosovo remained formally in line with the terms of
Resolution 1244. UNMIK itself was to be significantly reduced in size. In part,

UNMIK had to remain because Belgrade only recognized UNMIK as having authority under Resolution 1244, and the ethnic Serb communities in northern Kosovo would only deal with the UN. In part, it was because Russia backed Serbian positions on non-recognition of, and UN authority in, Kosovo.

Conclusion: the final frontier? Beyond Kosovo's 'unique' situation – new transitions of statehood

UNMIK represented the best opportunity ever for the successful transformation of a territory under international transitional administration. The population was welcoming to the NATO-led KFOR-underpinned security, and the UN mission had full authority. These were such propitious circumstances as might never appear again. They were the opportunity to make Kosovo a viable polity, irrespective of its final status. The reality was always that Kosovo needed to be a functioning political community with adequate levels of governance, security, justice and administration, ideally as an emerging liberal democracy under the international tutelage of the UN, the EU and others providing exceptional beneficial support. This was clearly a long-term project, but it held great prospects for success, given the starting conditions. Yet because of shortcomings, as argued above, and attempts unnecessarily to shortcut processes of transitional administration, that opportunity was blown away. Instead, the unseemly and ultimately inexplicable hurry to finish the period of Yugoslav dissolution and conflict resulted in something other than the final frontier desired: a messy proliferation of transitional states in even murkier circumstances than there had been previously.

This is because, despite the wishful protestations of Western diplomats that Kosovo was 'unique', it was not and never could be in any politically meaningful sense. Events in Georgia, in August 2008 and afterwards, confirmed this. Following five days of major armed hostilities in August 2008, fighting in Georgia died down following EU mediation led by France. French Foreign Minister Bernard Kouchner, followed by President Nicolas Sarkozy, shuttled from Moscow to Tblisi to agree five principles on which the ceasefire was based: the complete withdrawal of Georgian forces from the breakaway regions; a return to positions prior to 6 August for Russian forces; the continuing presence of Russian 'peace' forces, deployed under agreements in the early 1990s; an increased international monitoring and security presence; and a UN Security Council Resolution to underpin arrangements.

Since the early 1990s, Russia had had no immediate desire to separate the de facto states of South Ossetia and Abkhazia from Georgia. Rather, it had sought to compromise Georgia's independence through support for these regions, using them as a pretext to ensure a Russian military presence, formally monitored by UN and OSCE missions (which were therefore seen as providing legitimacy for operations that are neither by the UN nor by the OSCE). This situation incubated separatism in the territories, always with Russian backing (Lynch 2004). This included support for the development and training of armed forces, as well as active support, at times, to those forces. Between Kosovo's declaration of independence and the events in August, Russia spent several months preparing to exploit the Kosovo precedent. It supported South Ossetian forces, assisting with training and the preparation of small-scale provocative operations against Georgian forces, firing onto Georgian territory, while mobilizing its own armed forces ready to intervene. The Russians sought to provoke Georgia, which responded as expected, preparing to launch military operations in response.

Russia's action left the United States, NATO and the West, generally, exposed. While factors such as Iraq and Afghanistan – including but not restricted to the major military deployments involved – contributed to Western weakness, Kosovo was the cornerstone of it in terms of legitimacy. The US-led approach to Kosovo's independence was a significant factor in shaping events in Georgia. Russia formally upheld the key principle of international law and politics – sovereignty and territorial integrity – regarding Kosovo, blocking formal UN Security Council endorsement of de facto arrangements driven by the United States and Western countries to 'unfreeze' the conflict there and separate Kosovo from Serbia. At the same time, Western action on Kosovo in February was the signal for Russia to take the initiative on the 'frozen conflicts' in Georgia. Yet the Russians did not need to change their approach to the matters of principle. Although there appeared to have been a Russian role in provoking Georgia's military action accompanied by the incursion of armed forces in a murky situation, it was clear that Georgian forces were prepared for significant action, thereby breaching agreements under which Russia's 'peace operation' in South Ossetia had been deployed. In addition, Georgian forces attacked and killed both Russian military personnel and South Ossetians, whom Russia had made citizens. Moscow could, therefore also claim to be acting in self-defence in international law (citizenship was a device purely to be able to invoke this right).

Thus, while the West had ceded the high ground of principle over Kosovo, Russia engineered a situation in which it could complete the de facto separation of territories from Georgia following the Kosovo model, yet continue to proclaim its adherence to principle and international law. At this point, the only option for the West to counter Russia was to backtrack on Kosovo. That was, in effect, impossible, although adjustments over UNMIK and EULEX had to be made. The shift from transitional administration to transitional state did little to alter the challenges UNMIK, EULEX and others would face in seeking to develop Kosovo politically and economically. These were the same challenges already evident. However, they would now be challenges where the complete authority to confront them would be absent. Instead, a territory under transitional administration, with the potential to be a success whatever the final status of its border, had become an entity with blurring around its borders and blurring within them regarding political and legal authority, making it a newly proclaimed but rapidly failing polity with, at best, a 'tenuous' character (Heathershaw and Lambach 2008). Worse than this, the supposed conditions that had made it unique – de facto separation over several years, under international protection because of past commission of atrocities and gross abuses of human rights – were not changed in the case of Kosovo, while they became a precedent for other cases. Aside from the claims made in the case of the Georgian territories, the same incubating, isolating, protecting features could be said to apply to Iraqi Kurdistan or to territories elsewhere. A rush to end the clearest and most opportune transitional administration of all and to create one final frontier in the Yugoslav context set a new phase of transitional statehood spinning with no real controls and not a single final frontier as an outcome – just several final frontier questions for the future, and security challenges to go with them.

Notes

1 The full text of the draft resolution is available at: www.b92.net/eng/ insight/strategies. php?yyyy_2007&mm_05&nav_id_41258&version_print (accessed 16 December 2008).
2 In discussions with the author, several senior diplomats made clear that Cyprus, Greece, Romania, Spain and Slovakia were adamantly opposed to recognizing Kosovo's independence in the absence of agreement with Belgrade or a Chapter VII mandatory UN Security Council Resolution.
3 This view was clearly and strongly expressed by senior diplomats in discussion with the author; one of these senior figures said that independence was 'a fact' and that Serbia just needed 'to get over it'.

References

Arkin, W. M. (2001) 'Operation Allied Force: The Most Precise Application of Air Power in History', in A. J. Bacevich, J. Andrew and E. A. Cohen (eds) *War over Kosovo: Politics and Strategy in a Global Age*, New York, NY: Columbia University Press.

B92 (2008a) 'Ruecker to Belgrade: Stop Attacking Kosovo', B92 News 14 March. Available: www.b92.net/eng/news/politics-article.php?yyyy_2008&mm_03&dd_14&nav_id_48443 (accessed 17 February 2009).

B92 (2008b) 'UNMIK Out, Serbs Released; Over 100 Injured', B92 News 17 March. Available: www.b92.net/eng/news/politics-article.php?mm_3&dd_17&yyyy_2008 (accessed February 2009).

B92 (2008c) 'Ruecker: Transfer to EULEX 'Far from Certain' ', B92 News, [online] 29 April. Available: www.b92.net/eng/news/politics-article.php?yyyy_2008&mm_04&dd_29&nav_id_49831 (accessed February 2009).

B92 (2008d) 'EULEX rules out Power Sharing', B92 News [online], 27 April. Available: www.b92.net/eng/news/politics-article.php?yyyy_2008&mm_04&dd_27&nav_id_49787 (accessed 23 February 2009).

Bellamy, A. J. (2002) *Kosovo and International Society*, London: Palgrave.

Caplan, R. (2005) *International Governance of War-torn Territories: Rule and Reconstruction*, Oxford: Oxford University Press.

Cunha, R. (2008) 'Interview', Osservatorio Balcani [online], 23 April. Available: www.osservatoriobalcani.org/article/articleview/9463/1/216 (accessed December 2008).

Daalder, I. and O'Hanlon, M. (2000) *Winning Ugly: NATO's Kosovo War*, Washington, DC: Brooking's Institution.

Fowler, M. R. and Bunck, J. M. (1995) *Law, Power and the Sovereign State: The Evolution and the Application of Sovereignty*, University Park, PA: University of Pennsylvania Press.

Gow, J. (2003) *The Serbian Project and its Adversaries: A Strategy of War Crimes*, London: Hurst and Co.

Gow, J. (2005) *Defending the West*, Cambridge: Polity.

Gow, J. (2007) 'Europe and the Muslim World: European Union Enlargement and the Western Balkans', *Journal of Southeast European and Black Sea Studies*, 7/3: 467–482.

Heathershaw, J. and Lambach, D. (2008) 'Introduction: Post-conflict Spaces and Approaches to Statebuilding', *Journal of Intervention and Statebuilding*, 2/3: 269–289.

Henkin, L. (1999) 'Kosovo and the Law of 'Humanitarian Intervention'', *American Journal of International Law*, 93/4: 824–828.

House of Commons Foreign Affairs Committee (2000) Fourth Report on Kosovo [online], London: HMSO, 7 June. Available: www.publications.parliament.uk/pa/cm199900/cmselect/cmfaff/28/2802.htm (accessed 17 February 2009).

Ischinger, W. (2008) 'Foreign and Security Policy: Focus on Kosovo', Paper presented at King's College London, 31 January.

Jackson, R. (ed.) (1999) *Sovereignty at the Millennium*, Oxford: Blackwell.

Judah, T. (2000) *Kosovo: War and Revenge*, New Haven, CT: Yale University Press.

Ker-Lindsay, J. (2009) *Kosovo: The Path to Contested Statehood in the Balkans*, London: I. B. Tauris.

King, C. (2008) 'The Kosovo Precedent', Newsnet, May.

Krasner, S. D. (1999) *Sovereignty: Organised Hypocrisy*, Princeton, NJ: Princeton University Press.

Lowe, V. (2000) 'International Legal Issues Arising in the Kosovo Crisis', *International and Comparative Law Quarterly*, 49/4: 934–943.

Lynch, D. (2004) *Engaging Eurasia's Separatist States: Unresolved Conflicts and de facto States*, Washington, DC: US Institute of Peace.

Mappes-Niediek, N. (2007) 'Kosovo Plan Nearing Defeat – UN Delegation Returns to New York Sceptically', *Frankfurter Rundschau*, 3 May.

Matheson, M. J. (2001) 'United Nations Governance of Postconflict Societies', *American Journal of International Law*, 95/1: 76–85.

Reuters (2007) 'Russia May Veto UN Kosovo Resolution: Churkin', May 12. Available: www.reuters.com/article/worldNews/idUSL1227625520070512 (accessed 14 February 2009).

Roberts, A. (2006) 'Transformative Military Occupation: Applying the Laws of War and Human Rights', *American Journal of International Law*, 100/3: 580–622.

Ruffert, M. (2001) 'The Administration of Kosovo and East-Timor by the International Community', *International and Comparative Law Quarterly*, 50/3: 613–631.

The European Commission (2007) 'Kosovo under UNSCR 1244 2007 Progress Report. Commission staff working document accompanying the communication from the commission to the European Parliament and the Council, enlargement strategy and main challenges 2007–2008', Com(2007) 663 Final, Brussels, 6 November. Available: ec.europa.eu/enlargement/pdf/key_documents/2007/nov/kosovo_progress_reports_en.pdf (accessed 12 February 2009).

UNMIK (2008) 'Kosovo in February 2008: Fact Sheet', Pristina: UNMIK.

UN Security Council (2007a) 'Comprehensive Proposal for the Kosovo Status Settlement', UN doc. S/2007/168/Add.1, 26 March. Available: www.un.org/Docs/journal/asp/ws.asp?m_S/2007/168/Add.1 (accessed 12 February 2009).

UN Security Council (2007b) 'Report of the UN Security Council Mission on the Kosovo Issue', S/2007/256 [online], 4 May. Available: www.realinstitutoelcano.org/especiales/misionespaz/Kosovo/SecurityCouncil_4May_Kosovo.pdf (accessed February 2009).

Wilde, R. (2001) 'From Danzig to East Timor and Beyond: The Role of International Territorial Administration', *American Journal of International Law*, 95/3: 583–606.

9 Kosovo, sovereignty and the subversion of UN authority

James Ker-Lindsay

Introduction

To suggest that Kosovo is one of the most important issues to have emerged in modern international politics might at first appear to be an unduly bold claim, if not a sweeping overstatement. In an era when terrorism and the threat of the proliferation of weapons of mass destruction pose a threat to many millions of people, or when gauged against global poverty and the dangers of pandemic disease, its importance may seem rather marginal; all the more since few believe that there will be any return to the bloody regional conflicts that blighted South-East Europe throughout the 1990s. Instead, Kosovo is a crucial issue because it raises profound questions about the future of the contemporary system of international politics that was first formulated at the end of the Second World War, over sixty years ago.

NATO's decision, in March 1999, to intervene in order to bring to an end fighting in Kosovo marked a watershed moment in contemporary international affairs. Acting without the authorisation of the Security Council, Western leaders decided that the protection of human rights outweighed the traditional importance attached to notions of sovereignty. Delivering a landmark speech at the time, and building on comments made the previous year by Kofi Annan, the UN Secretary General (Annan 1998), Tony Blair argued that non-interference, a bedrock principle of international affairs, could no longer be accepted without qualification. Under the right conditions, there was a duty to act in those cases where the behaviour of states against their own citizens was unacceptable – even if the UN could not, or would not, agree to sanction such actions (Blair 1999). Elucidating a new doctrine of 'humanitarian intervention', the British Prime Minister appeared to have radically shifted the boundaries of international politics. As one legal scholar noted at the time, the handling of the Kosovo situation reflected 'a far broader process of change in the international constitutional system as a whole' (Weller 1999: 211).

Six years later, in 2005, those boundaries would be challenged yet again as the logical consequences of the decision to intervene in Kosovo became apparent. Against a backdrop of growing frustration, the Kosovo Albanian population, who made up the vast majority of the province's inhabitants, demanded independence. However, Belgrade, which retained sovereignty over the internationally administered province, refused to accept any move towards statehood, countering with an offer of extensive autonomy. Once again, the established principles of post-war international politics were thus in the spotlight. This time, though, the significance of the decision went well beyond that of 1999. On this occasion, the international community had to decide whether a new sovereign country could be forcibly carved out of the territory of another state. In this sense, if the decision taken by NATO in 1999 to act over Kosovo without Security Council authorisation was one of the most momentous decisions of the end of the twentieth century, the debate over the future status of Kosovo became one of the most momentous choices facing the international community at the start of the twenty-first century. It was without exaggeration that Vitaly Churkin, the Russian permanent representative at the United Nations, noted in early 2007 that Kosovo might well be the most important issue to come before the Security Council in a decade (*International Herald Tribune* 2007).

In the end, however, the discussions in the Security Council failed to produce an outcome. Despite repeated attempts by the countries that supported independence to persuade Moscow to accept the inevitability of Kosovo's statehood, the Russian government remained adamantly opposed to any attempt to impose a settlement without the agreement of both the Serbian government and the Kosovo Albanians. As a result, on 17 February 2008 Kosovo unilaterally declared independence, with the support of a number of major states, including the United States, Britain, France, Italy and Germany. But hopes that most of the international community would follow suit were soon dashed. A year after the declaration of independence, less than a third of the world's states had recognised Kosovo.

This chapter analyses why Kosovo failed to achieve wider legitimacy. It contends that while efforts have been made to argue that there was no other alternative to bypassing the United Nations, given Russia's position, this argument has failed to win over the majority of the world's states for two principle reasons. First of all, even if Russia may have been acting for its own reasons, as has been suggested, its stand in favour of sovereignty and against separatism finds widespread appeal. At the same time, many other states, although perhaps sceptical about Russia's underlying reasons for acting in the way that it did, nevertheless respect the fact that its veto right is a legitimate tool of international law and cannot be ignored at will. To do so would be to subvert UN authority.

Sovereignty versus self-determination

While the Kosovo Albanians and the Serbian government draw on a wide range of political, legal, historical and functional arguments to support their respective cases (Security Council 2007: para 8), in essence their positions can be reduced to an apparent contradiction in international law between the fundamental right of self-determination and the principle of the territorial integrity of states. To the Kosovo Albanians, the arguments in favour of statehood are clear-cut.[1] Comprising over

90 per cent of the population of Kosovo, they argue that they should have the right to determine their own future and form their own state if they so wish. In order to lend further weight to their position, they draw on two key arguments. First of all, Kosovo should also be seen within the broader context of the break up of Yugoslavia. Just as Slovenia, Croatia, Bosnia and Herzegovina, Macedonia and, more recently, Montenegro had all been allowed to go their own way with international blessing, so the same right should be extended to Kosovo. After all, it too had been a distinct and autonomous entity within the former Yugoslavia. Secondly, the case for self-determination has a moral dimension. Given a long history of Serb repression in Kosovo, which culminated in the conflict of 1998–1999, Serbia has forfeited its right to exercise sovereign authority over the Kosovo Albanians (Ashdown 2007).[2] As one Kosovo Albanian explained, independence would be 'moral compensation' for past suffering (Jordan 2004).

Serbia's position is equally straightforward.[3] Even though Kosovo may be under international administration it still remains sovereign territory of the Republic of Serbia and, in line with the UN Charter and the 1975 Helsinki Final Act (Helsinki Declaration 1975), the Republic of Serbia has the right to have its territorial integrity recognised and respected. It rejects the argument that Kosovo should be seen as a part of the break up of Yugoslavia. While Kosovo may have enjoyed many of the rights of a republic, the fact nevertheless remains that it was not formally recognised as a republic and so did not enjoy the right of secession. Instead, it was always a constituent part of Serbia, even if it was granted certain rights at a federal level. Nor does it dispute the fact that the Kosovo Albanians represent a majority in Kosovo, or that they suffered under the Milošević regime. However, whatever the moral and political case for independence, there is simply no precedent, or justification, for the creation of a new state by outside states against the will of the sovereign power currently governing that territory (Philip 2007). Belgrade's view is that under international law its right to retain sovereignty over Kosovo – a land that is given immense cultural and religious significance in the Serbian mindset – is beyond doubt.

The international reaction to Kosovo

Under usual circumstances, Serbia's position would have been secure. In contemporary terms, the territorial integrity of states has been given far greater weight than the principle of self-determination. Indeed, self-determination as a concept has been subject to considerable limitations. Although, in theory, under Articles 1.2 and 55 the UN Charter extends a right of self-determination to all peoples, in reality it has been recognised as a right pertaining solely to cases to colonisation, and to be exercised at the point of decolonisation (Pellet 1992; Weller 1999). For obvious reasons, given the innate and understandable wish of states to maintain the principle of territorial integrity, the right of self-determination has not been viewed as the right to secession by a numerical minority within an established state (Heraclides 1998: 400). Instead, where claims by minority groups within states have resulted in separatist conflicts, efforts to broker a settlement have centred on solutions that do not require a redrawing of borders, but still offer communities a way to manage their own affairs. These have included confederation, federation, or varying degrees and types of autonomy.

And so it was with Kosovo. While advocates of independence argue that Kosovo cannot be compared to other conflicts, the truth of the matter is that, at least until 1999, and despite the events in Yugoslavia, Kosovo was seen as little different from the wide range of ethnic and separatist conflicts elsewhere in the world. The Badinter Arbitration Committee – a commission formed in 1991 by the European Union under the chairmanship of Robert Badinter, the president of the French Constitutional Court, to consider the legal implications of the break up of Yugoslavia – clearly stated that while the right of secession was open to the republics, it was not applicable to minority communities within the republics. In the case of Kosovo, the report made no recommendation for recognition alongside the republics (Brown 2005: 239). Thus, by default, the position of the Kosovo Albanians was regarded as analogous to that of the Serbs of Croatia and Bosnia, and by extension that of other minority communities throughout the republics. In these cases, the Committee ruled that right of self-determination was not conceived as a right to statehood; 'instead, self-determination in this context was reduced in content to human and minority rights, and to autonomous structures of governance in areas where Serb constituted a local majority' (Weller 1999: 214).[4] As a result of these decisions, when Kosovo came to prominence at the end of the 1990s the UN Security Council therefore resolved that any settlement must recognise Yugoslavia's territorial integrity, in accordance with the UN Charter and the Helsinki Final Act, and should therefore, according to Security Council Resolution 1160 passed in March 1998, be focused on some form of 'enhanced status', 'which would include a substantially greater degree of autonomy and meaningful self-administration'.

However, the decision to intervene in Kosovo, and subsequently establish an international administration, necessarily changed the parameters of a settlement – in reality, if not in principle. As far as the Kosovo Albanians were concerned, the NATO intervention had taken place for their benefit and represented a further step towards independence. While they were willing to accept a limited period of international rule, there was no question but that this would be a transitory phase leading to statehood sooner rather than later. Given rising frustrations in the province, and the danger that this could lead to violence directed towards international administrators and peacekeepers, it was seen as imperative to resolve the status issue, and do so in a manner acceptable to the majority. Thus, despite the recognition of Serbia's sovereignty over Kosovo, and the previous efforts to find a solution based on autonomy, a case for independence now had to be constructed, and justified in a manner that would not serve as a precedent for other ethnic conflicts in the world. To this extent, US officials, and officials from the other states that accepted the need for independence, argued that the Kosovo situation was certainly not a case of self-determination.[5] Instead, Kosovo must be seen in light of a unique set of circumstances emerging from the dissolution of Yugoslavia, including the brutal and bloody conflicts. Rather than a new precedent for the new century, it should be viewed as the final chapter in the Balkan conflicts of the 1990s.[6]

The status process

Despite the obvious complexity of the issue, and the fact that Kosovo appeared to run against prevailing norms of international politics, few envisaged the complications that would eventually emerge when, in the autumn of 2005, the United Nations Security Council authorised the start of final status negotiations for Kosovo. Most observers confidently predicted a fairly rapid decision to be made to draw to a close six years of international administration and grant the province some form of independence (Reuters 2005). Although Belgrade remained adamantly opposed to the idea, and was pushing its own ideas for some form of enhanced autonomy, the United States and a number of key European states that had led the 1999 intervention favoured statehood.[7] Moreover, even the agnostics and sceptics, who rejected the idea of independence in principle, were prepared to concede that the reality on the ground was that this was the only option that would be accepted by the Kosovo Albanian majority. To deny them statehood would almost certainly lead to further conflict, this time directed at the UN administration and the NATO peacekeeping mission in the province.

Even more importantly, Russia appeared to have accepted that a formal split from Serbia was the only viable option for the province. Its assent to the start of status talks, even though the previously required standards for the process to begin had not been met, was widely read to mean that it had also accepted that the status quo was untenable. Likewise, its decision to agree to a Contact Group statement that any final status decision must be acceptable to the people of Kosovo was seen as further evidence that it too was willing to accept independence (Ahtisaari 2008). And once again, practical political calculations entered the equation. Given Russia's decline in world politics since the end of the Cold War, few expected that Moscow would be willing or able to put up much of a fight even if it did oppose statehood – especially as this could disrupt relations with the United States and the European Union (Kupchan 2005: 20). Thus, the general optimism at the time of the start of talks seemed to be more than justified. As Janez Drnovšek, the Slovenian president, noted, it was not just the entire international community that knew that Kosovo would become independent; Serbia's politicians did too (STA 2005). This in turn gave rise to the belief that it would also be a relatively quick process. As one leading Balkan observer noted at the time, 'preliminary conclusions' could come as early as the spring of 2006 (Judah 2005).

Despite this apparent consensus, things did not go as planned. Notwithstanding numerous rounds of talks between the two sides – a process that was overseen by Martti Ahtisaari, the former president of Finland and the UN Secretary-General's Envoy for the Kosovo status talks – no effort was made to try to bridge the gaps over status (Weller 2008). Instead, the talks were focused on trying to reach an agreement that would protect the position of the Serbian population in Kosovo following independence.[8] At the same time, political developments in Serbia served to set back the timetable. Initial hopes that a status decision could be made by the end of 2006 were dashed by the passing of a new constitution in Serbia, which in turn led to elections and forced the status process into 2007. Thereafter, the question became caught up in international politics. While the United States and key members of the European Union accepted a set of proposals for supervised independence, unveiled by Ahtisaari in March 2007 (Ahtisaari 2007), the Russian government announced that it would block attempts to have the Security Council endorse the proposals on the grounds that the plan had not been agreed to by both sides (Reuters 2007a, 2007b).

After months of wrangling in the Security Council, it was clear that further talks would be needed. It was therefore decided that a new mediating process would take place under the auspices of the Contact Group and administered by a troika of senior officials representing Russia, the United States and the European Union. However, after just over four months of talks, this too failed to broker an agreement between the sides. Despite the fact that Serbia put forward a number of proposals for autonomy (Government of Serbia 2007b), the Kosovo Albanian leadership insisted that they would only accept independence (Associated Press 2007a), a position that had by now been openly supported by the US Government (Office of the Press Secretary 2007). In December 2007, over two years after the UN had first authorised the start of final status talks, the Troika delivered its final report, noting that the two sides had been unable to reach an agreement on the fundamental question of sovereignty (Security Council 2007). Despite strong opposition from Russia, the United States and the European Union now announced that the efforts to find a negotiated solution under UN auspices had failed. Leaving the Security Council, the representatives announced that:

> As today's discussions have once again shown, the Council is not in a position to agree on the way ahead. We regret this, but we are ready to take on our own responsibilities. We will work with the European Union and NATO in a careful and coordinated manner towards a settlement for Kosovo. We underline our shared view that resolving the status of Kosovo constitutes a sui generis case that does not set any precedent. We are convinced that its resolution is important, indeed necessary, for European and regional security and stability.
>
> (Permanent Representatives 2007)

Reactions to the declaration of independence

Instead of leading to international consensus, the two-year status process had ended in what could only be described as a 'mess' – as General Sir Mike Jackson, the former head of the NATO peacekeeping mission in the province

(KFOR), so memorably put it (Jackson 2007). Another observer described it as a 'diplomatic train wreck' eight years in the making (Sands 2007). The true consequence of this failure to reach an agreement was graphically highlighted when, just two months later, on 17 February 2008, Kosovo declared independence. Rather than leading to universal recognition by the other states of the world and a seat in the United Nations, the announcement instead led to a polarisation of global opinion. Within the Security Council, the permanent members were divided (Security Council 2008). While the United States, Britain and France quickly decided to recognise the new 'Republic of Kosovo', Russia and China rejected the declaration, arguing that, in the absence of a UN resolution on the matter, the declaration was against international law. Likewise, divisions opened up across the world. While most countries aligned to the West – including Australia, Canada, South Korea, Japan and the majority of the European Union – chose to recognise Kosovo, many others condemned the unilateral decision of the Kosovo Albanians, or avoided taking a position.

Despite initial claims by Hashim Thaçi, the Prime Minister of Kosovo, that 100 states would quickly recognise Kosovo (Reuters 2008a), in the two months following independence just thirty-six of the 192 UN members (19 per cent) had done so. Indeed, it soon became clear that the initial aim of securing the support of half the members of the UN by the time of the annual meeting of the UN General Assembly in the autumn, as had been originally hoped, was an overly ambitious target. Such pessimism was soon confirmed, as the number of recognitions diminished significantly following the flurry of recognition in the first six weeks or so. By the time Kosovo marked the first anniversary of the declaration of independence, only eighteen more countries had followed suit, taking the total to fifty-four states, or 28 per cent of UN members. On 19 May, Bahrain's recognition took the figure to sixty.[9]

As a result of this limited recognition, it soon became clear that Kosovo would not be able to join many of the key international organisations. Most importantly, membership of the United Nations was ruled out. Even if the required amount of support could be mustered in the General Assembly, Russia made it clear that it would block any move by the Security Council to recommend membership, a necessary prerequisite for an Assembly vote.[10] Likewise, membership of regional groups, such as the Council of Europe and the Organisations for Security and Cooperation in Europe (OSCE), both of which relied on consensus decisions on new members, appeared to be impossible given opposition from Serbia, Russia and others. Even membership of the Organisation of the Islamic Conference appeared unlikely due to concerns amongst a number of members about the wider effects of recognising Kosovo.[11] But most seriously, membership of the European Union and NATO, where support for Kosovo's statehood was strongest, appeared to be out of the question given the small but nevertheless significant opposition to independence within both groups as Greece, Romania, Slovakia, Spain and Cyprus (which was the only one that was not a NATO member as well) refused to accept the declaration. As a result, the European Union issued a statement noting that it had been agreed that members would decide individually on their relations with Kosovo, 'in accordance with national practice and international law' (EU 2008). In this sense, and despite the initial hopes and expectations that the status process would result in a clear and unambiguous result, Kosovo has become, 'a new frozen conflict' (Bolton *et al.* 2008).

The Russian position

In order to understand why Kosovo failed to achieve wider recognition, it is first necessary to analyse the Russian position. At the start of the process, almost all observers seemed to accept that when the process started there was little reason to suspect that Moscow would stand in the way of a settlement. As observers noted later on, the expectation had been that even if it did raise some objections, it would soon fall into line (Bugajski and Joseph 2007). To be fair, such views appeared to be justified. Quite apart from the fact that it had stood aside in 1999, there were numerous other signals that it was willing to accept an independent Kosovo. For instance, it signed up to the Contact group statement noting that any settlement must be acceptable to the people of Kosovo. Similarly, it also appeared to have accepted that Ahtisaari should be allowed to draw up a status process, despite the fact that it must have known full well what his eventual suggestions would entail. Certainly, these two factors could have been taken as signs that Moscow was willing to acquiesce to an independent Kosovo.

However, if one examines Russian statements more carefully, they should never have been read as an automatic endorsement of independence. Russian officials consistently noted in their pronouncements that any settlement must be based on two key principles. In the first instance, it must be acceptable to both sides. To this extent, Russia would be willing to accept independence, but only if Belgrade did. As several senior ministers pointed out at various points in the process, Russia would not be more Serbian than the Serbs (*New York Times* 2007; Dejevsky 2008). Second, the talks should not be managed according to timetables. There should be no rush. Likewise, Moscow had made it clear that while the UN Envoy was authorised to draw up proposals as a basis for a settlement, he was never given carte blanche to present a comprehensive plan that would then be subject to minor tweaking, as eventually happened. And yet, despite these frequently stated provisos, Western decision-makers consistently misread the Russian position (Abramowitz 2008). Even after Putin's tough warning over Kosovo – and a number of other issues – in Munich in early 2007, there was still a sense amongst western policymakers that he was bluffing. Consequently, or so at least one observer has argued, no real planning took place in case the Russian president was serious about his threat (Holbrooke 2007).

A number of theories have been put forward to explain Russia's reaction. Many observers have naturally assumed that Moscow's decision was based on power politics and malice (*Washington Post* 2006; Abramowitz 2008). Certainly, one cannot discount the argument that the desire to provoke a confrontation with Washington may have played a part in the process. Under Vladimir Putin Russia has sought to reassert its regional and international authority, and the discussions over Kosovo took place against a backdrop of growing tension between Russia and the West. However, it should also be borne in mind that Western policy over Kosovo was also criticised by many Russians who were known to be more liberal, or to take a generally more pro-Western approach towards international affairs. For example, in an article published in the Russian press, Mikhail Gorbachev called Kosovo a 'dangerous precedent' that would be capable of 'detonating' conflicts elsewhere in the world. He was also scathing of the decision by the EU and NATO to pursue a settlement outside of the UN Security Council (Gorbachev 2007). Neither can one dismiss the view that Moscow may also have been trying to exact some sort of revenge on the United States and NATO for the events of 1999 (Gwertzman 2008). However, Russian intentions may not have been as destructive and negative as this. Others have suggested that it may well have been the case that the Russian government, having been so obviously sidelined in 1999, had little inclination to help NATO out of its self-made predicament (International Crisis Group 2007).

Another argument that has been put forward is that Russia was acting out of some form of Slavic solidarity, or was attempting to exploit its support for Serbia's position in order to gain commercial and economic advantage in the Balkans, especially in the energy field; indeed, Serbia and Russia signed a major energy agreement in January 2008 (Dempsey 2008). In addition, one should also consider the importance of Russian public opinion. Kosovo was a far more important issue for Russians than many outsiders realised. For a start, it touched on notions of Slavic solidarity. There was no doubt that many ordinary Russians sided with Serbia. But, more to the point, it touched on Russian attitudes towards other regions in the former Soviet Union. If the Russian government was seen to allow Kosovo to become independent due to pressure from the United States, how could it not then respond by recognising the independence of South Ossetia, Abkhazia or Transdniestra? This appeared to be overlooked, wilfully or otherwise, with serious consequences. Indeed, just months later, Russia used the case of Kosovo to question Georgia's territorial integrity.[12]

However, one must also accept that Russia was acting out of concern for the international legal implications of imposing independence. Notwithstanding later developments in the Caucasus, it should be recognised that Russia harboured serious and legitimate concerns about the consequences of recognising an independent Kosovo against the will of the Serbian government – a move that would be unprecedented in modern international affairs. Having been recognised as Serbian territory under Resolution 1244, any attempt to end Belgrade's rule over the territory without Serbian consent would necessarily undermine international law and have an effect on a range of conflicts elsewhere. While this may not have been a convenient line for Russia to take, if one takes a step back and analyses the position adopted by Moscow, it is clear that its stance was actually far more in line with long-standing principles of international relations and international law than that of those who were pushing for independence for purely practical reasons. In the debate between the 'constitutionalists' and the 'pragmatists'

(*The Independent* 2007), Russia was the champion of the former position, whereas the United States led the latter camp (*The Economist* 2007a; Bugajski and Joseph 2007). As one observer noted, many in the West did not understand that when it comes to matters of international law and the authority of the UN, Moscow is not in fact a rogue actor. If anything, it is an arch-conservative.[13]

The views of other actors

Russia's stance is instrumental in terms of explaining why so many other countries decided not to recognise Kosovo. However, the way in which Russia shaped opinion is not as straightforward as it might first appear. Upon closer analysis, four very different strands of opinion emerged on the question of independence. The first category included the states that opposed independence because they were afraid that it could affect their own domestic political circumstances. Although Moscow proved to be the most outspoken opponent of any move to grant Kosovo independence without Belgrade's consent, Russia was certainly not alone in this position. Amongst the permanent members of the Security Council, such fears were also shared, though less openly stated, by China. Indeed, it was telling that relatively soon after the declaration of independence Tibet once again emerged as an issue on the world stage, a fact that some attributed to the Kosovo precedent – although the forthcoming Olympic Games could be seen as an equally valid, if not more plausible, explanation. Likewise, despite the repeated assurances that Kosovo could not be seen as a precedent (Associated Press 2008a), many other governments were fearful about the consequences that a decision on Kosovo might have on their own territorial integrity (Maddox 2007). As already noted, a number of members of the European Union chose to reject the declaration for this reason. However, many others also cited concerns about creating a precedent in justifying their own opposition. Such concerns were no doubt heightened by the fact that Kosovo was quickly seized upon by a number of separatist groups and secessionist entities to justify their own claims to statehood.[14] Certainly, the argument appeared to carry little weight on the wider international stage. As one leading commentator noted, 'Kosovo is unique, and there will be more Kosovos' (Ash 2008).

However, the states that opposed independence on the grounds of the implications that this could have on separatist activity in their own territory or region represented just one side of the argument. For a number of other states, the concerns about independence were less focused on the danger of separatism, and more on the legal implications of supporting independence without a clear UN Security Council authorisation. As already noted, Kosovo did not represent a straightforward case in international law. It was not, after all, created from an act of decolonisation, nor was it regarded as having a right to independence in the way that the other republics of the former Yugoslavia had. In this instance, therefore, it became especially important in the view of a number of countries for the Security Council to take a decision on the applicability of independence that could then be accepted by the wider international community. This was the position that was taken by a number of countries, such as Jordan and Thailand, both of which noted that they were waiting for a UN Security Council decision (Associated Press 2008b). Meanwhile, other states took a slightly different view, noting that they did not believe that independence was in accordance with the terms of Resolution 1244. In this context, it is presumably the case that if another resolution were to be passed, superseding the previous resolution, this would guide their position, so the argument could be put forward that they would have been willing to recognise Kosovo if a new resolution was put in place superseding this resolution. Others were less open in their position, but implied that UN approval would be necessary before they would be willing to act. This ambiguous position was taken by New Zealand, which noted that its policy was not to offer recognition under such circumstances. Conversely, others were more outspoken, arguing that the declaration of independence weakened international organisations, a line taken by Iran (*Moscow News* 2008).

Of course, it would be wrong to view this second category as mutually exclusive from the first. In fact, almost every state that feared secession naturally sought to uphold UN authority. However, this was not always the case. Israel, for instance, appeared to be inclined to follow the lead of the United States on recognition, but did not do so for fear of a unilateral declaration of independence by the Palestinians (Mizroch 2008).[15] Georgia also appeared willing to recognise Kosovo, at least at first.[16] At the same time, it must be recognised that many states simply decided to 'sit on the fence' – the third category. Relatively unconcerned about the prospects of secession, and unsure of the legal situation, they decided to wait to see how wider international opinion developed – and not to be seen to simply be following the West – before taking a firm decision (Associated Press 2008b). This camp can be identified by those states that simply took note of the declaration of independence, or announced that they were studying the declaration but did not produce any further official comment. Examples of this group include a number of African and South American states, such as Zambia, Uganda and Paraguay (Xinhau 2008; ZNBC 2008; Ministry of External Affairs 2008). Fourth, and finally, there was also a small group of Balkan states – Bosnia-Herzegovina, FYR Macedonia and Montenegro – that withheld recognition out of concern about the effects on domestic politics. In the cases of Macedonia and Montenegro, they eventually chose to coordinate their recognition of Kosovo, on 9 October 2009, in order to align themselves with the United States and the larger states of the European Union (Associated Press 2009). In contrast, Bosnia, which remains 'deeply divided' over the question (Somum 2008), is unlikely to recognise Kosovo for the foreseeable future.

Conclusion

There can be little doubt that Kosovo has emerged as one of the most significant issues on the world stage. By declaring independence without the approval of the United Nations, albeit with the support of the United States and most of the European Union, Kosovo has failed to achieve the widespread legitimacy that many hoped it would receive. While there is no doubt that it is accorded a far greater degree of legitimacy than many other disputed territories vying for international recognition, such as the Turkish Republic of Northern Cyprus or Transdniestra, its legality has been fundamentally questioned, to a greater or lesser degree, by most of the world. More to the point, even though further recognitions can be expected, it appears as though Kosovo's status will remain contested for many years to come (Eyal 2008). To this extent, rather than assume a universally recognised place in the international community, Kosovo has instead entered a grey zone of international politics.

In explaining why this is the declaration of independence failed to gain widespread legitimacy, Russia's opposition was indeed vital. However, as has been shown, Moscow's response to the issue is far more complex than many observers realise. While there may be an element of mischief making, there is no doubt that Russia harboured a range of deeper concerns over Kosovo, including the consequences that this would have on domestic public opinion. However, it also held legitimate concerns over the implications that recognising Kosovo would have on a range of other separatist conflicts elsewhere. Russia simply refused to accept that Kosovo could be regarded as a unique case, outside of the existing parameters of international law, as many Western policymakers repeatedly insisted. However, it was by no means alone in this view. In this regard, Russia reflected wider international opinion, and provided a voice for this worldview. It was certainly not, therefore, the lone entity opposing statehood that many of the supporters of independence appeared to suggest.

However, it must also be recognised that there are many countries that harbour deep-seated concerns about recognising Kosovo independence without UN approval. Yet again, even if the argument that Russia acted as a lone agent and stood against an international consensus is accepted, the fact nevertheless remains that the right of veto is a right enshrined under Article 27 of the UN Charter. This states the following:

> Decisions of the Security Council on all other matters shall be made by an affirmative vote of nine members including the concurring votes of the permanent members; provided that, in decisions under Chapter VI, and under paragraph 3 of Article 52, a party to a dispute shall abstain from voting.

To this extent, Moscow's decision to cast a veto against a resolution opening the way for statehood was in accordance with its prerogative under the UN Charter. As many countries saw it, to make an exception in this case, however justified this may have been under the circumstances and no matter how much Kosovo could be seen as a special case, would undermine the UN system as a whole, as it would create a precedent whereby members could pick and choose when to recognise UN authority, and under what conditions, which in turn would have opened the way for a further violations of the UN Charter.

For all these reasons, the argument that Russia is responsible for obstructing Kosovo's quest for recognition is broadly correct. Had Moscow accepted independence, it seems likely that China would have at least abstained and the Security Council would have supported a resolution opening the way for statehood. However, to argue that under these circumstances the Security Council should have been bypassed when Russia blocked a resolution is quite clearly wrong. For a start, it is obvious that Moscow's position was not at odds with wider international opinion. It found a far greater resonance than supporters of independence have been willing to concede. Rather than stand against international consensus, Russia in effect reflected deep-seated concerns about separatism and the erosion of sovereignty and territorial integrity. At the same time, many other states saw the dangers of trying to bypass the United Nations, recognising that this would set a dangerous precedent, no matter how worthy the cause, and thus resisted the pressure to do so. This groundswell against recognition in turn provided a catalyst for others to hold off recognition until some further clarity emerged on the issue. In this sense, Western states may have felt that they had little choice but to act in support of independence without UN approval, given the implications that this would have for security in the region. However, any expectation that the majority of the world would follow suit in such a groundbreaking venture was always rather over-optimistic.

Notes

1 For a sample of Kosovo Albanian arguments in favour of independence, see *Newsweek* (2006); Çeku (2006); Surroi (1998).
2 Martti Ahtisaari also agreed with this view in comments to the author in September 2008.
3 For a sample of Serbian arguments against independence, see Koštunica (2006); Jeremić (2007); Tadić (2006); Government of Serbia (2007a); Samardžić (2000).
4 The full second opinion of the Committee can be found as an appendix to Pellet (1992).
5 As one British official told the author, the word 'self-determination' was being avoided at all costs. Kosovo was not a case of self-determination; it was a unique case devolving from the dissolution of Yugoslavia in the 1990s. However, speaking on the margins of a UN Security Council debate in December 2007, Sir John Sawers, the British permanent representative at the UN, stated the following: 'You have the principle of territorial integrity. You also have the principle of self-determination. There are times when those principles are in tension with one another, and the principle of territorial integrity is qualified by the principle of self-determination' (Maximsnews 2007).
6 See *International Herald Tribune* (2007). This editorial was signed by ten former foreign ministers: Madeleine Albright (United States), Lloyd Axworthy (Canada), Jan Eliasson (Sweden), Gareth Evans (Australia), Joschka Fischer (Germany), Bronislaw Geremek (Poland), Niels Helveg Petersen (Denmark), Lydie Polfer (Luxembourg), Jozias van Artsen (Netherlands) and Hubert Vedrine (France).
7 During a trip to Pristina in February 2006, just weeks after the talks had started, John Sawers, the Political Director of the Foreign Office, stated that independence was the likely outcome of the status talks (Reuters 2006).
8 The fact that independence was effectively decided at the very start of the status process has been confirmed by Ahtisaari (see Ahtisaari 2008).
9 In date order of recognition, the states recognising Kosovo from 17 February 2008 until 1 July 2009 were: Costa Rica, Afghanistan, Albania, France, Turkey, the United

States, United Kingdom, Australia, Senegal, Latvia, Germany, Estonia, Italy, Denmark, Luxembourg, Peru, Belgium, Poland, Switzerland, Austria, Ireland, Sweden, Netherlands, Iceland, Slovenia, Finland, Japan, Canada, Monaco, Croatia, Hungary, Bulgaria, Liechtenstein, South Korea, Norway, Marshall Islands, Nauru, Burkina Faso, Lithuania, San Marino, Czech Republic, Liberia, Sierra Leone, Colombia, Belize, Malta, Samoa, Portugal, Montenegro, FYR Macedonia, United Arab Emirates, Malaysia, Federated States of Micronesia, Panama, Maldives, Palau, Gambia, Saudi Arabia, Comoros, Bahrain.

10 See, Charter of the United Nations, Chapter II, Article 4, paragraph 2.
11 Although the Secretary-General of the fifty-seven-member Organisation of the Islamic Conference (OIC) issued a statement supporting the declaration of independence (OIC 2008), in the month after independence just five Islamic states recognised Kosovo. While there was sympathy for the Kosovo Albanians across the Islamic world, many Muslim countries – such as Azerbaijan, Indonesia and Sudan – expressed serious concern about endorsing independence, and prevented a joint statement endorsing statehood.
12 As Dmitry Medvedev, the Russian President, stated during a press conference with President Sarkozy: 'You were right in asking if the Ossetians and Abkhazians can and want to live within Georgia. This is a question for them to ask of themselves and it is they who will give their own clear answer. It is not for Russia or any other country to answer this question for them. This is something that must take place in strict accordance with international law. Though, over these last years international law has given us numerous very complicated cases of peoples exercising their right to self-determination and the emergence of new states on the map. Just look at the example of Kosovo' (Medvedev 2008).
13 Retired senior diplomat from an EU member state, comments to the author, November 2006.
14 See, for example, Associated Press (2007b); *The Economist* (2007b); Almond, (2007). To gain a sense of how the situation was viewed in other regions vying for independence, see *Tiraspol Times* (2007); Sathananthan (2007); *Turkish Daily News* (2007); Reuters (2008b).
15 In the days after the declaration of independence, a close aide to the Palestinian president noted that Kosovo's unilateral declaration of independence might be an avenue for the Palestinians to take (Reuters 2008c)
16 In an interview, Lado Gurganidze, the Prime Minister, suggested that Tblisi was willing to recognise Kosovo, as it had been recognised by the United States and the European Union. This was later refuted by President Saakashvili (B92 2008).

References

Abramowitz, M. (2008) 'Putin's Balkan mischief', *Guardian Unlimited*, 29 January.

Ahtisaari, M. (2007) 'Report of the Special Envoy of the Secretary-General on Kosovo's Future Status', *UN Security Council Document*, S/2007/168, 26 March.

Ahtisaari, M. (2008) 'Kosovan Questions: National, Regional, International', Roundtable held at the School of Slavonic and East European Studies, University College London, 9 September.

Almond, M. (2007) 'Unrecognized States', *International Herald Tribune*, 6 December.

Annan, K. (1998) 'Intervention', *Ditchley Foundation Lecture XXXV*, 26 June.

Ash, T. G. (2008) 'The Kosovo Precedent', *Los Angeles Times*, 21 February.

Ashdown, P. (2007) 'Interview with Sky News', 9 December.

Associated Press (2007a) 'Kosovo Albanians reject Serbs' Latest Autonomy Offer in Status Talks', *Associated Press*, 19 November.

Associated Press (2007b) 'Push at U.N. for Kosovo Independence could Bolster Secessionist Demands around the World', *Associated Press*, 17 May 2007.

Associated Press (2008a) 'Bush Administration Tells Congress Recognizing Kosovo was an Exception', *Associated Press*, 12 March.

Associated Press (2008b) 'The Kosovo Conundrum: Nations around the World Ponder whether to Recognize Kosovo', *Associated Press*, 22 February.

Associated Press (2009) 'Montenegro, Macedonia Recognize Kosovo Statehood', *Associated Press*, 9 October.

B92 (2008) 'Georgia Will Not Recognise Kosovo', *B92*, 9 May.

Blair, T. (1999) 'Doctrine of the International Community at the Economic Club', Chicago, 24 April. Available: www.number10.gov.uk/Page1297 (accessed 24 June 2009).

Bolton, J., Eagleburger, L. and Rodman, P. (2008) 'Warning Light on Kosovo', *The Washington Times*, 31 January.

Brown, B. S. (2005) 'Human Rights, Sovereignty, and the Final Status of Kosovo', *Chicago-Kent Law Review*, 80: 235–272.

Bugajski, J. and Joseph, E. P. (2007) 'Seize the Opportunity with Russia on Kosovo', *Washington Post*, 24 October.

Çeku, A. (2006) 'Meeting: The Future Of Kosovo', *Chatham House*, London, 12 October.

Dejevsky M. (2008) 'The Russian Speech We didn't Hear About', *The Independent*, 12 February.

Dempsey, J. (2008) 'Serbia Deal Tightens Russia's Grip on European Energy', *International Herald Tribune*, 22 January.

EU (2008) 'Council Conclusions on Kosovo', 2851st External Relations Council meeting, Brussels, 18 February.

Eyal, J. (2008) 'Is Kosovo Really Independent?', *RUSI Commentary*, 18 February.

Gwertzman, B. (2008) 'Wisner: Russian Opposition to Kosovo Independence "Unbelievably Regrettable"', *Council on Foreign Relations*, February 12. Available: www.cfr.org/publication/15483 (accessed 23 June 2009).

Gorbachev, M. (2007) 'Gorbachev: Kosovo Unrelated to EU, NATO', *UPI*, 29 December.

Government of Serbia (2007a) 'Politically, Historically and Legally Kosovo-Metohija Is and Will Remain Part of Serbia', *Press Release, Government of Serbia*, 6 January.

Government of Serbia (2007b) 'Comparative Autonomy Model Analysis', 20 November. Available: www.osce.mfa.gov.yu/index.php?option=content&task=view&id=347&Itemid= (accessed 24 June 2009).

Helsinki Declaration (1975) 'The Final Act of the Conference on Security and Cooperation in Europe', 1 August, 14 I.L.M. 1292.

Heraclides, A. (1998) 'Ethnonational and Separatist Conflict Settelment', in T. Vermis and E. Kofos (eds) *Kosovo: Avoiding Another Balkan War*, Athens: Hellenic.

Holbrooke, R. (2007) 'Back to the Brink in the Balkans', *Washington Post*, 25 November.

International Crisis Group (2007) 'Kosovo: No Good Alternatives to the Ahtisaari Plan', Europe Report No. 182, 12 May.

International Herald Tribune (2007a) 'Russia Urges Security Council to Visit Kosovo and Belgrade Before Deciding on Status', *International Herald Tribune*, 27 March.

Jackson, M. (2007) 'There's a Minefield Just Ahead in Kosovo', *Sunday Telegraph*, 9 December.

Jeremić, V. (2007) 'Serbia's Path to Europe through Regional Peace and Reconciliation', *Chatham House*, London, 19 September.

Jordan, M. (2004) 'Even in Eager Kosovo, Nation-Building Stalls', *Christian Science Monitor*, 22 September. Available: www.csmonitor.com/2004/0922/p01s04-woeu.html (accessed 12 June 2009).

Judah, T. (2005) 'Defining Kosovo', *ISN Security Watch*, 10 October.

Kupchan, C. A. (2005) 'Independence for Kosovo: Yielding to Balkan Reality', *Foreign Affairs*, 84/6: 14–20.

Koštunica, V. (2006) 'Serbia's European Integration', *Royal United Services Institute*, 27 June.

Maddox, B. (2007) 'Kosovo Signals the Age of the Micro-state', *The Times*, 6 December.

Maximsnews (2007) 'Media Stakeout: Informal Comments to the Media by the Permanent Representative of the United Kingdom, Ambassador Sir John Sawers KCMG, on the Situation in Kosovo and Other Matters', Webcast, 19 December 2007. Available: www.maximsnews.com/people108mnun00002.htm (accessed 24 June 2009).

Medvedev, D. (2008) 'Press Statement following Negotiations with French President Nicolas Sarkozy', The Kremlin, Moscow, 12 August.

Ministry of External Relations (2008) 'Comunicado de Prensa sobre la Declaración de Independencia de Kosovo', Ministry of External Relations, Republic of Paraguay, 25 February.

Mizroch, A. (2008) 'Israel Won't Recognise Kosovo, For Now', *Jerusalem Post*, 19 February.

Moscow News (2008) 'Golamreza Ansari, Iran's Ambassador to Russia: 'We don't have such missiles' ', *Moscow News*, 13 March.

New York Times (2007) 'Russia Seeks New Mediator in Kosovo Talks', New York Times.com, 18 March. Available: 2007www.nytimes.com/2007/03/18/world/europe/18kosovo.html?pagewanted=print (accessed 21 June 2009).

Newsweek (2006) '"Respect and Rights" Newsweek Interview with the Kosovo Prime Minister Agim Çeku', *Newsweek*, 3 May.

Office of the Press Secretary (2007) 'President Bush Participates in Joint Press Availability with Prime Minister of Albania, Dr. Sali Berisha', Courtyard Council of Ministers, Tirana, Albania, June 10, Available: georgewbush-whitehouse.archives.gov/news/releases/2007/06/20070610-1.html (accessed 25 June 2009).

OIC (2008) 'OIC Declares Solidarity with Kosovo', *OIC Newsletter*, 8, 20 February.

Pellet, A. (1992) 'The Opinions of the Badinter Arbitration Committee: A Second Breath for the Self-Determination of Peoples', *European Journal of International Law*, 3/1: 178–181.

Permanent Representatives (2007) 'Informal comments to the Media by the Permanent Representative of Belgium, Ambassador Johan C. Verbeke, the Permanent Representative of France, Ambassador Jean-Maurice Ripert, the Permanent Representative of Italy, Ambassador Marcello Spatafora, the Permanent Representative of the United Kingdom, Ambassador Sir John Sawers KCMG, the Permanent Representative of the United States of America, Ambassador Zalmay Khalilzad, the Permanent Representative of Slovakia, Ambassador Peter Burian and the Permanent Representative of Germany, Ambassador Thomas Matussek on the situation in Kosovo.', *UN Website*, 19 December.

Philip, C. (2007) 'Kosovo Deadlock puts Balkans on the Brink', *The Times*, 29 November.

Reuters (2005) 'UN Council Endorses Start of Kosovo Status Talks', 24 October.

Reuters (2006) 'Kosovo Can Win Independence, says British Diplomat', 6 February.

Reuters (2007a) 'Russia Rejects West's U.N. plan on Kosovo's Future', *Reuters*, 17 July.

Reuters (2007b) 'EU–US Debate Whether to Call Vote on Kosovo at U.N.', *Reuters*, 18 July.

Reuters (2008a) 'Kosovo Expects Quick Recognition by "100 countries"', *Reuters*, 8 February.

Reuters (2008b) 'Kosovo "will boost Karabakh recognition drive"', *Reuters*, 16 February.

Reuters (2008c) 'Palestinians could Declare Independence: Abbas Aide', *Reuters*, 20 February.

Samardžić, S. (2000) 'Should Kosovo-Metohija Remain a Part of Serbia/Yugoslavia? A Plea for a Just Solution', in W. J. Buckley (ed.) *Kosovo: Contending Voices on Balkan Interventions*, Grand Rapids, MI: William B. Eerdmand Publishing.

Sands, D. (2007) 'Negotiations Fail to Settle Kosovo's Fate', *Washington Times*, 8 December.

Sathananthan, S. (2007) 'What Lessons could Tamils draw from the Kosovo Experience?', *NorthEastern Monthly*, May–June.

Security Council (2007) 'Report of the European Union/United States/Russian Federation Troika on Kosovo', *UN Security Council Document*, S/2007/723, 10 December.

Security Council (2008) '5839th Meeting of the Security Council', UN Security Council Document, S/PV5839, 18 February.

Somum, H. (2008) 'Doubtful Kosovo Passports', *Today's Zaman*, 27 August.

STA (2005) 'International Community Knows "Kosovo Will Become Independent" – Slovene leader', *STA News Agency*, 27 October.

Surroi, V. (1998) 'Kosova and the Constitutional Solutions', in Thanos Veremis and Evangelos Kofos (eds), *Kosovo: Avoiding Another Balkan War*, Athens: ELIAMEP and the University of Athens.

Tadić, B. (2006) 'Opportunity in the Balkans', *Washington Post*, 7 June.

The Economist (2007a) 'Enter, Pursued by the Bear', *The Economist*, 13 September.

The Economist (2007b) 'The Independence Precedent: If Kosovo goes Free', *The Economist*, 29 November.

The Independent (2007) Leading article: 'Local Passions and the Desire to Divorce', *The Independent*, 5 December.

Tiraspol Times (2007) 'Kosovo Report linked to Transnistria Independence', *The Tiraspol Times*, 27 March.

Turkish Daily News (2007) 'Turkish Cypriots Eye Kosovo for Own Future', *Turkish Daily News*, 27 December.

Washington Post (2006) 'Here Comes Kosovo', Editorial, *Washington Post*, 10 November.

Weller, M. (1999) 'The Rambouillet Conference on Kosovo', *International Affairs*, 75/2: 211–251.

Weller, M. (2008) 'The Vienna Negotiations on the Final Status for Kosovo', *International Affairs*, 84/4: 659–681.

Xinhua (2008) 'Kosovo's Proclamation of Independence Triggers More Mixed Responses', *Xinhua*, 18 February.

ZNBC (2008) 'Zambia to Decide on Kosovo', *ZNBC*, 2 March.

10 Microcosm, guinea pig or *sui generis*?

Assessing international engagement with Kosovo

Aidan Hehir

Introduction

In Chapter 9, James Ker-Lindsay wrote: 'Kosovo is a crucial issue because it raises profound questions about the future of the contemporary system of international politics that was first formulated at the end of the Second World War' (p. 168). This is undeniably the case, and the chapters in this book have each attempted to draw out and answer these 'profound questions' so that we may be better able to discern future trends in international relations.

NATO's intervention in Kosovo in 1999 constitutes one of the defining moments in post-Cold War international relations, and its importance is described by Nicholas Wheeler as 'immense' (2002: 242). The fusion of many major international relations themes generated great interest in the intervention and its possible repercussions, and led to a plethora of academic investigations. Likewise, the international administration of Kosovo is of major international significance. UNMIK described its own mission as 'a sweeping undertaking ... unprecedented in both its scope and structural complexity' (UNMIK 1999). UNMIK's administration of Kosovo certainly broke new ground, and the new phase of international administration by the EU constitutes a work in progress of major significance. Kosovo's declaration of independence in 2008 added a new dimension to Kosovo's importance, and precipitated myriad speculations on the broader implications of the 'Kosovo precedent'.

These three phases in Kosovo's recent history – intervention, statebuilding and independence – have thus attracted extensive international attention. It is striking, however, that much of this interest in Kosovo has not been born from a concern with the people of Kosovo. Rather, interest stems from the fact that this small corner of Europe has served as something of a microcosm of broader international trends and also, in many respects, a guinea pig upon which new ideas and policies have been tested.

The chapters in this book have addressed different aspects of the international engagement with Kosovo over the past twenty years, with a particular emphasis on 1999–2009. As is to be expected, these chapters outline differing perspectives on the international engagement. Nonetheless, reflecting on these chapters it is possible to identify certain generic themes and salient trends. This is the aim of this final chapter.

Kosovo and the international community

In 1994, James Gow summarised the international community's response to the disintegration of the Socialist Federal Republic of Yugoslavia as follows:

> At virtually every stage the international community reacted to rather than anticipated events. The consequence was that at every stage action which could have made all the difference three to six months earlier came too late and usually, with too little commitment.
>
> (1994: 22)

This critical appraisal – widely endorsed – could easily have been repeated verbatim in 1999 with reference to the response to the crisis in Kosovo. As has been highlighted by many of the preceding chapters, international policy towards Kosovo was predominantly reactive from 1989–1998. Alex J. Bellamy has suggested three reasons why Kosovo was so marginalised during the various international diplomatic initiates on the Balkans during this period (2002: 24–26). First, prior to 1998 there was not an alarming level of violence in Kosovo. While allegations of oppression were made by NGOs such as Amnesty, Save the Children and Oxfam, and also Tadeusz Mazowiecki, the UN's Special Rapporteur on human rights in the former Yugoslavia, it seems that the only statistics that would prompt an international response were those relating to deaths, and these did not become significant until 1998. The second reason was that it was felt that to engage with the secessionists in Kosovo would have sparked a similar cry for secession from the Serbs in Croatia and Bosnia and further destabilize the region. The final reason is that those seeking independence for Kosovo were not in control of the territory. Had the Kosovo Albanians been in positions of political, judicial and military power in Kosovo, as the Croats and Slovenes were in 1991, then the international community may have countenanced the separation. It is tragically ironic that the two scenarios the international community sought to avoid – an escalation of violence in Kosovo and a 'Kosovo precedent' destabilising the Balkans – have in fact materialised; international policy towards Kosovo served to contribute to the dramatic spike in violence in 1998 that led to NATO's intervention in 1999, which in turn led inexorably to Kosovo's declaration of independence and the opening of the Pandora's box that is secession.

The claim that the international community didn't do enough and should have adopted a more hands-on approach to the situation in Kosovo is not, however, applicable with respect to the period since 1998. During 1998, international mediation efforts (such as the ill-fated agreement brokered in October) and direct international intervention on the ground (through the Kosovo Verification Mission which comprised 2,000 OSCE observers) failed to arrest the escalation of tension. In fact, a strong case can be made that the extensive international engagement in Kosovo from 1998 to the commencement of the bombing campaign contributed to the tension in Kosovo and made outright military confrontation more likely. Alan Kuperman claims that 'the undeniable effect' of NATO's

threats to use force against the FRY in 1998 was to 'embolden the rebels to esca-
late their offensive, which predictably triggered an even bigger crackdown by
Serb forces' (2003: 66).

NATO's intervention in 1999 stands in sharp contrast to the previous policy
of reactive and timid engagement. The desire to take military action appears to
have significantly impacted on the negotiations at Rambouillet prior to the initiation of the air campaign (see Chapter 1). Lord Gilbert, Minister of State in the
UK Ministry of Defence from 1997 to 1999, stated, while giving evidence to the
Defence Select Committee of the House of Commons:

> I think certain people were spoiling for a fight in NATO at that time.... If
> you ask my personal view, I think the terms put to Milošević at Rambouillet
> were absolutely intolerable; how could he possibly accept them; it was quite
> deliberate. That does not excuse an awful lot of other things, but we were at
> a point when some people felt that something had to be done, so you just
> provoked a fight.
>
> (Wintour 2000)

It seems clear that to some significant extent the intervention was prompted
by a desire to recover some of the credibility the West had lost as the situation in
Kosovo degenerated. According to General Wesley Clark, NATO's Supreme
Allied Commander at the time of Operation Allied Force,

> ... what Milošević never really understood was this wasn't a conflict strictly
> about Kosovo. It wasn't even a conflict ultimately about ethnic cleansing. It
> was a battle about the future of NATO, about the credibility of the United
> States as a force in world affairs. And the longer it went on the more clearly
> the nations of the West could see those issues.
>
> (quoted in Prokopijevic, 2004: 187)

In his televised address to the nation when the campaign began, President
Clinton warned that not acting 'would discredit NATO, the cornerstone on
which our security has rested for 50 years now' (Foreign Desk 1999: 15). The
events in Kosovo in the two years prior to the intervention had created the
impression in certain quarters that NATO was toothless and unable to act on its
threats. In September 1998 General Clark met with the Estonian President
Lennat Meri, who warned, 'NATO is failing in the Balkans. With every passing
day you lose credibility' (Clark 2001: 132). At this time NATO was negotiating
its Eastern expansion; clearly, maintaining credibility at this juncture was
important if prospective members were to maintain their interest in joining.

This is not to argue that NATO's humanitarian rhetoric was entirely cynical,
as some suggested (Chomsky 1999). Additionally, it would be unreasonably
onerous to require a 'humanitarian intervention' to be motivated solely by altruism (Brown 2001: 23). Yet this concern with credibility and the international
community's perception of NATO does help to explain both the manner in

which Operation Allied Force was prosecuted and the curious lack of fore-thought regarding what would happen after the military campaign. At the initiation of the air strikes, General Clark outlined three 'Measures of Merit' that would determine the prosecution of the campaign and the analysis of its success or failure. They were, first, 'not to lose aircraft'; second, to 'impact the Yugoslavian military and police activities on the ground as rapidly and as effectively as possible'; and third, to 'protect our ground forces' (Clark 2001: 185). Curiously, these guiding principles make no mention of the welfare of the Kosovar Albanians. The decision to fly at 15,000 feet had the effect of ensuring that no NATO troops were killed, but enabled the FRY military to initiate a campaign which resulted in the 'ethnic cleansing' which came to be the iconic image of the campaign. The ethnic cleansing in fact became the rationale for Operation Allied Force, despite the fact that the cleansing began *after* NATO started its bombing campaign. As Misha Glenny observed, 'Instead of preventing a humanitarian disaster NATO's decision contributed to a flood of biblical proportions' (1999: 658). The campaign against the ethnic Albanian community was hardly a surprise; in a meeting on 6 March 1999, US Secretary of State Madeline Albright asked General Clark, 'If we commence the strikes will the Serbs attack the population?' to which he replied, 'Almost certainly' (Clark 2001: 173). While UK Prime Minister Tony Blair said that the campaign's objective was 'to avert a humanitarian catastrophe' (Bellamy 2002: 157), General Clark admitted:

> [Operation Allied Force] was not designed as a means of blocking Serb ethnic cleansing. It was not designed as a means of waging war against the Serb and MUP forces in Kosovo. Not in any way. There was never any intent to do that. That was not the idea.
>
> (Chomsky 1999: 36)

As Alynna J. Lyon and Mary Fran T. Malone's chapter demonstrates, however, this strategy was not solely the product of a cold-hearted politico/military elite. In fact, the strategy reflected the desires of the general public – certainly within the US. Their analysis shows that while there was significant support amongst the US public for a 'humanitarian intervention', there was a marked unwillingness to put US soldiers' lives at risk.

Operation Allied Force had an enormous impact on international relations, and sparked a heated debate about much more than the merits of the campaign in Kosovo. As Bellamy demonstrates, this international furore led to the convening of the International Commission on Intervention and State Sovereignty and its seminal report, *The Responsibility to Protect* (R2P). Anthony F. Lang, Jr notes that the controversy in Kosovo served to highlight the need for a 'constitutional revolution' (p. 75). He rightly characterises the debate about Operation Allied Force as the 'formulaic recitation of rules in response to conflict' (p. 61). Without some means by which these competing claims could be judged, he notes, there was no way to move beyond division. And yet, while both Bellamy and Lang correctly identify the extent to which Kosovo encapsulated a pervasive tension within the global constitutional order, it is not at all clear that the debate sparked by NATO's intervention has brought us any closer to resolving the tension between the rights of individuals and the rights of states, and the duty the international community has towards those suffering at the hands of their own government. The invasion of Iraq in 2003 and the non-intervention in the face of the crisis in Darfur from 2003 on has demonstrated that, post-Kosovo, the international community has still not resolved the dispute regarding the norms and laws governing the use of force. Since 1999 there has been no fundamental reform of international law or the architecture of the UN which could be identified as having clarified the status of humanitarian intervention (Hehir 2009a).

Little forethought appears to have been given to what would happen in Kosovo after Operation Allied Force. As noted in a number of the preceding chapters, the provisions of Security Council Resolution 1244 recognised the territorial integrity of FRY. Of course, the Russian and Chinese veto precluded the SC from taking the logical step – given the intervention and expulsion of the FRY military and police from Kosovo – of recognising Kosovo as an independent state-in-waiting under UN supervision. But given that NATO had acted without UN support in invading Kosovo, it would not have been out of character at this juncture to have rebuilt Kosovo without explicit UN support. It could not have been a surprise that Russia and China would insist on recognising the territorial integrity of FRY before sanctioning any post-conflict recovery operation, so, given the inevitability of the Russian and Chinese positions, what did NATO expect would happen after its military campaign? The Kosovar Albanians obviously had their preference, and one can understand their confusion and anger at the manner in which the rout of the FRY military was followed by an endorsement of the FRY's jurisdiction over Kosovo. As Ker-Lindsay notes, 'As far as the Kosovo Albanians were concerned, the NATO intervention had taken place for their benefit and represented a further step towards independence' (p. 171). Michael Mandelbaum points to the paradoxical outcome of NATO's intervention: 'NATO intervened in a civil war and defeated one side, but embraced the position of the party it had defeated on the issue over which the war was fought' (1999: 2). The subsequent tension in Kosovo between the ethnic Albanians and the international administration was a function of this bizarre turn of events. This is all the more peculiar given that the declaration of independence in 2008 – supported by the major NATO powers – was undertaken without Russian and Chinese (and Serbian) assent. Therefore, the outcome we now have – contested statehood – is that which the post-intervention agreement sought to avoid, and thus the long fudge from 1999 to 2008 – which proved decidedly counterproductive – was clearly of no utility. Ker-Lindsay's characterisation of the process of determining Kosovo's final status – namely, 'a 'diplomatic train wreck eight years in the making' – is therefore quite apposite (p. 174).

The record of statebuilding in Kosovo since 1999 evidences a manifest disjuncture between external expectations of the Kosovar Albanians and the actual nature and agenda of this community. NATO arguably intervened in 1999 to defend not only the Kosovar Albanians but also the very the idea of human rights as conceived in the West. Routing the Serbs – portrayed as villainous human rights violators – was conceived as enabling the progressive human rights ideal – embodied in the normative vision of the stoic Kosovar Albanians – to emerge and take root. In fact, the 'victims' – the Kosovar Albanians – whose human rights were ostensibly being defended turned out to have goals which in principle were not unlike those of the vanquished villains, and were certainly inimical to the creation of a multi-ethnic society. The initial round of counter-ethnic cleansing in June 1999 and the mass violence in March 2004 demonstrated that the Kosovar Albanian community was not predisposed to tolerance and pacifism, and did not share the vision of a multi-ethnic society advocated by UNMIK. It is therefore ironic that the West found itself supporting a community which has been accused by reputable international human rights organisations of systematic ethnic cleaning in 1999 and 2004, and of demonstrating an active hostility to multi-ethnicity. Attempts to finesse the image of the Kosovo Albanians as passive victims peacefully pursuing a noble cause became increasingly untenable. Ironically, as noted in Chapter 1, when this caricature of the Kosovo Albanians was arguably accurate – from 1989 to 1995 – the international community ignored the situation in Kosovo. The International Crisis Group (ICG) described post-intervention Kosovo Albanian society as 'damaged' and 'slow, and even reluctant, to face up to its own visage' (ICG 2004: 32). It noted the influence of 'semi-literate extremists' who have been free to 'dictate their terms with threats to prominent Albanian intellectuals who have spoken out against attacks on minorities' (ibid.: 33) According to the ICG, the ethnic Albanians aimed to 'cleanse the entire territory of foreign bodies' (ibid.: 33). As the interview with the President of Kosovo (see Appendix) attests, even now, and at the highest level, there is unwillingness within the Kosovo Albanian society to accept culpability for wrongs committed since 1999. President Sejdiu's answer to a question about crimes committed against Serbs – 'your assertion that there has been attacks on Serbs is not true' – stands in sharp contrast to many reports by reputable international human rights organisations (p. 200).

During an informal conversation I had in June 2009 with legal advisors to the President of Kosovo, it was suggested that to expect the Kosovo Albanians to welcome the presence of Serbs in Kosovo was totally unrealistic given the scale of the atrocities perpetrated against the Kosovar Albanian community in 1999. Such logic, it was claimed, was akin to asking Jews to work with perpetrators of the Holocaust in forging a new Germany in 1945. While this may be an exaggerated comparison, it is hard to disagree with the basic principle. Kosovar Albanians have very strong moral grounds for resisting any forced accommodation with Serbia, and understandably cannot forget the hardships and terror endured at the hands of Milošević's regime. Yet this was seemingly what UNMIK sought through its attempt to forge a multi-ethnic society and political system. The conflict in Kosovo, as Lang notes in Chapter 4, was not simply about human rights; rather, the key contention was control over Kosovo, and hence this was a civil war. The attempt to create a multi-ethnic society without addressing the fundamentals of the conflict – namely who controls Kosovo – can therefore be seen as an ahistorical and ultimately impossible goal. In different historical contexts such pluralist projects were not undertaken, as was especially evident in post-Second World War Eastern Europe; the idea of creating multi-ethnic states in the wake of that particular conflagration was not entertained, as is particularly evident in the demographics of post-war Poland. In the post-Cold War era, however, such realism was abandoned in Kosovo in favour of a policy built on hubris and hope.

Perhaps the greatest folly has been the attempt to contrive ethnic pluralism. The police, judiciary and political systems, including even the parliament, have been manipulated to ensure that there is a particular ratio of Albanians, Serbs and 'others'. How such a policy of formally embedding ethnicity in the new system was meant to diminish the importance of ethnicity and foment pluralism is difficult to fathom – especially so in the context of the ethnic conflict which had claimed so many lives. Indicatively, Barry J. Ryan's chapter demonstrates how 'community policing' certainly constituted a theoretically sound solution to the divisions within Kosovo, but was in practice unworkable regardless of the extent to which the ethnic composition of the force was manipulated. The new police force was thus asked to 'enforce a liberal democratic multi-ethnic constitutional order that does not exist' (p. 115). He notes, 'the vast majority of ethnic Albanians do not want a multi-ethnic final status', and yet this obvious desire amongst the majority population was essentially ignored by UNMIK in favour of an externally conceived notion of peaceful pluralism which did not reflect the reality in Kosovo (p. 125).

UNMIK established ethnicity as the defining social characteristic in Kosovo, and the administration embedded ethnic identity in the new political system, making it a crucial factor in the apportioning of power (Hehir 2006). This policy has been a consistent feature of UNMIK's administration, and has manifestly failed to diminish the division between Serbs and Albanians. Such a policy has reinforced difference by making ethnicity a basis for administrative and political delegation, and therefore societal divisions were formally incorporated into the new polity. It has failed to encourage the development of a new shared identity, as simply forcing the new political structures to superficially appear multi-ethnic has not encouraged genuine cross-community cooperation. Ensuring that there is a particular ratio of Albanians to Serbs within the various organs of the new system did not, and arguably could not, address the underlying divisions, particularly with respect to the issue of Kosovo's final status.

In response to the inability of Albanians and Serbs to abandon their mutually antagonistic ethnic identities – which were arguably heightened by NATO's intervention and the nature of the system created by UNMIK – the international community came to return again to the 'ancient ethnic hatreds shibboleth' described in Chapter 1. The currency of this perspective on Kosovar society, which suggested that the people within Kosovo were too blinded by hate to run their own society, resulted in the gradual expansion of UNMIK's power. In particular, the powers of the Special Representative to the Secretary General (SRSG), which were already extensive in 1999, grew. By 2003, the SRSG had 'powers far beyond the necessary means to support the institutions of self-government' (Sobjerg 2006: 67). And yet, while the international administration of Kosovo accumulated ever greater power and embedded itself ever deeper in the day-to-day running of Kosovo, there was little tangible progress on the central issue of status.

This inability to create the conditions for a permanent settlement of the underlying conflict was exacerbated by UNMIK and KFOR's many failings in the security sector. The International Commission on the Balkans stated, in 2005,

> the international community has clearly failed in its attempts to provide security and development to [Kosovo] ... the demand for sovereignty has not diminished; on the contrary is has increased in the past year. UNMIK is perceived by the local population as corrupt and indecisive.
>
> (2005: 19–20)

This was obviously clear in March 2004, but could be identified in less explosive ways through the general polarisation and anger evident throughout Kosovo during UNMIK's tenure.

The abandonment of the 'Standards before Status' policy led finally to a focus on Kosovo's status. It became clear that during the interim between the end of Operation Allied Force and the start of the Vienna negotiations on Kosovo's status the positions of the parties had altered little, and they remained 'diametrically opposed' (Weller 2008: 659). During the negotiations the Kosovo Albanians 'would not settle for anything other than independence', and this position remained immutable (ibid.: 659). The Serbian negotiators, by contrast, advanced a number of scenarios which, though all formally include Kosovo as a part of Serbia, comprised a range of arguably innovative scenarios which constituted a significant diminution of the official position in 1999. Thus, as Giovanna Bono notes in Chapter 7, the Kosovar Albanians quite successfully tailored their stance to exercise the maximum leverage on the Western states involved in the negotiations, who were forced to accept the ultimate logic of their intervention in 1999. The 'intransigence' of the Kosovar Albanians, therefore, worked in their favour despite the fact that such inflexibility is routinely unrewarded in other diplomatic contexts. This is not to criticise the Kosovo Albanians; they are, of course, perfectly entitled to advance an inflexible position, and can certainly make a strong moral claim for the necessity of such a strategy. But, given the extensive international engagement with Kosovo from 1998 on, the inability to temper the position of the community most directly embraced and guided by the international community can only been seen as a failure.

The negotiating strategy of the Kosovar Albanians corresponds well with the general theme of Rick Fawn and Oliver P. Richmond's chapter. They argue that the nature of international engagement with Kosovo has meant that 'vertical relationships with internationals are more significant than horizontal relationships among local actors' (p. 81). This can be seen to have impacted on the negotiations on Kosovo's final status; from the Kosovo Albanians' perspective, reaching an agreement with Serbia was of far less importance than maintaining good relations with powerful Western states in the hope and expectation that a breakdown in the negotiations would lead to a Western-supported unilateral declaration of independence. The declaration of independence has created a scenario whereby Serbs and Albanians in Kosovo are once again divided, the West and Russia are at odds, and even within the EU there is division over the issue. While the Kosovar Albanian community is quite understandably pleased with the events of February 2008, this episode has profoundly negative implications for the international community, and the West in particular.

In 2005, the ICG described Pristina as 'culturally and educationally underpowered' and expressed concerns about the influx of hard-line rural Albanians who brought criminality and extremist views on to the capital's streets (2004: 33). This image of Pristina certainly didn't correspond to the vibrant, relaxed city I visited in June 2009. The city has a thriving café culture, is clean and safe, and all around there are construction sites, indicative of Kosovo's broader reconstruction. The declaration of independence appears to have bolstered confidence within Kosovo Albanian society, and there was a palpable sense of excitement amongst those involved in establishing and running the various new government departments scattered throughout the city. The idea that Kosovo could ever again become formally part of Serbia is almost unimaginable, although this does not mean that partition north of the River Ibar is out of the question – though this too appears unlikely. The division within the international community over recognising Kosovo is bound to gradually lessen. As former NATO Secretary General Lord Robertson noted:

> I said to a number of Serbs that I've met 'Do you actually seriously imagine that the US, the UK, France and all the other countries that have recognized Kosovo will de-recognize Kosovo?' Nobody realistically expects that to happen at all.
>
> (Hehir 2009b: 265–266)

While, as Ker-Lindsay notes in his chapter, and the President of Kosovo admits in the Appendix, the number of states that have recognised Kosovo has not been as great as many Kosovar Albanians expected, the status of many of those states that have recognised Kosovo essentially ensures that Kosovo will, over time, become a fully-fledged state. It is additionally not beyond the bounds of possibility that Serbia, and Kosovo's Serbs, will gradually come to some unofficial accommodation with Kosovo which could lead to the normalisation of relations. This would certainly be a *sine qua non* for membership of the EU, which all Balkan states seek to achieve. Indeed, within Serbia the issue of Kosovo may well be a boon to the major political parties, much like Northern Ireland served as such for parties in the Republic of Ireland for decades; difficult domestic situations can be periodically sidelined by deflecting attention to the issue of Kosovo, and 'Kosovo' could additionally serve as a ready-made source of all the ills within Serbian society. Provided Serbian historical sites and Serbs themselves, within Kosovo, are protected – which certainly hasn't been the case since 1999 – then it is quite possible that the issue of Kosovo's independence will lose its importance, though resentment will doubtless linger for many years.

President Sedjiu's claim that 'Kosovo is a *sui generis* case and as such cannot be a precedent' reflects the understandable desire amongst Kosovo's political hierarchy to deny that Kosovo could have a deleterious effect on other contested territories (p. 201). In Chapter 8, however, James Gow argues that while the declaration of independence in Kosovo was 'an exception founded on an exception', this cannot mean that Kosovo can be deemed to have no precedential qualities (p. 149). He notes that 'despite the wishful protestations of Western diplomats that Kosovo was "unique", it was not and never could be, in any politically meaningful sense' (p. 163). It is perhaps too early to identify what exactly the 'Kosovo precedent' might entail, though Russia's recognition of South Ossetia and Abkhazia in 2008 gives some indication. What is clear is that the nature of Kosovo's declaration of independence has done little to clarify the rules governing secession and recognition, and has merely highlighted the lack of unity on this fundamentally important issue which will inevitably arise again in the future.

Conclusion: three lessons of the international engagement with Kosovo

In summarising the international community's engagement with Kosovo, and drawing on the chapters in this book, three lessons of the international engagement, particularly the West's engagement, can be discerned which have implications for future international responses to intra-state crises.

1   *Policies towards Kosovo have consistently been shaped with the interests of external actors to the fore.* The decision to use force to 'preserve NATO credibility', the strategy employed during the bombing campaign, UNMIK's attempt to create a 'multi-ethnic' Kosovo, and the delay in focusing on Kosovo's final status each reflected the prioritisation of the interests of external actors over the welfare and wishes of people in Kosovo.

2.   *External intervention – both military and diplomatic – does not guarantee that intra-state conflicts will be resolved peacefully or quickly.* Inevitably when an intra-state crisis erupts there are calls for the international community to 'do something'. The escalation of crises is additionally routinely blamed on the lack of international engagement. The events in Kosovo since 1999, however, cast significant doubt on the assumption underlying these claims that international engagement is a good thing, and should happen more often and be more direct. The recent crisis in Kosovo occurred in tandem with extensive direct international engagement, and does not, therefore, cohere with the notion that either early or direct intervention leads to peace.

3.   *Tangible evidence of the need for reform of international law and the international political system does not necessarily lead to actual reform.* What is striking about Kosovo's recent history is that for all the analysis it has

provoked, international commissions it has catalysed and introspection it has precipitated, it is not at all clear that we are any closer today to a resolution of the major controversies highlighted by Kosovo in the past twenty years. It is dispiriting that the shortcomings so graphically highlighted by Kosovo relating to the laws governing the use of force, the practice of international administration, and international recognition, have not led to consensus on reform but rather served to highlight the depth of the existing divisions.

Regardless of one's perspective on the merits of Kosovo's independence, one can only hope that the future will be peaceful for all its inhabitants. Even if outright violence is avoided, however, there seems little doubt but that Kosovo will continue to generate controversy and contestation within the Balkans and indeed the wider world. International engagement with Kosovo since 1989 tells us much about the changing nature of the international system, and the future trajectory of Kosovo will doubtless continue to reflect broader trends in international relations. Interest in Kosovo will therefore surely be maintained for the foreseeable future. Citizens of Kosovo have long known the meaning of the Chinese proverb (or indeed curse) 'may you live in interesting times'. Kosovo's future is bound, at the very least, to be 'interesting'.

Bibliography

Bellamy, A. J. (2002) *Kosovo and International Society*, Hampshire: Palgrave Macmillan.

Brown, C. (2001) 'Ethics, Interests, and Foreign Policy', in K. E. Smith and M. Light (eds) *Ethics and Foreign Policy*, Cambridge: Cambridge University Press.

Chomsky, N. (1999) *The New Military Humanism: Lessons from Kosovo*, London: Pluto.

Clark, W. (2001) *Waging Modern War*, Oxford: Public Affairs.

Foreign Desk (1999) 'Conflict in the Balkans', *New York Times*, 25 March, Section A: 15.

Glenny, M. (1999) *The Balkans, 1804–1999*, London: Granta Books.

Gow, J. (1994) 'Nervous Bunnies: The International Community and the Yugoslav War of Dissolution, the Politics of Military Intervention in a Time of Change', in L. D. Freedman (ed.) *Military Intervention in European Conflicts*, Oxford: The Political Quarterly.

Hehir, A. (2006) ' "Autonomous Province Building": Identification Theory and the Failure of UNMIK', *International Peacekeeping*, 13/2: 200–213.

Hehir, A. (2009a) 'NATO's Humanitarian Intervention in Kosovo: Precedent or Aberration?' *Journal of Human Rights*, 8/3: 1–20.

Hehir, A. (2009b) 'Interview with Lord Robertson of Port Ellen', *Journal of Intervention and Statebuliding*, 3/2: 259–275.

International Commission on the Balkans (2005) *The Balkans in Europe's Future*. Available: www.balkan-commission.org/activities/Report.pdf (accessed June 2008).

International Crisis Group (2004) 'Collapse in Kosovo', Balkans Report no. 155, 22 April. Available: www.crisisgroup.org/home/index.cfm?id=2627&l=1 (accessed 30 July 2009).

Kuperman, A. (2003) 'Transnational Causes of Genocide', in R. Thomas (ed.) *Yugoslavia Unraveled: Sovereignty, Self Determination, Intervention*, Oxford: Lexington Books.

Mandelbaum, M. (1999) 'A Perfect Failure', *Foreign Affairs*, 78/5: 2–8.

Prokopijevic, M. (2004) 'Humanitarian Intervention' in G. Meggle (ed.) *Ethics of Humanitarian Intervention*, Frankfurt: Ontas.

Sobjerg, L. M. (2006) 'The Kosovo Experiment', in T. B. Knudsen and C. B. Laustsen (eds) *Kosovo Between War and Peace*, London: Routledge.

UNMIK (1999) 'UNMIK at a Glance', UNMIKonloine, Available: www.unmikonline.org/intro.htm (accessed April 2006).

Weller, M. (2008) 'The Vienna Negotiations on the Final Status for Kosovo', *International Affairs*, 84/4: 659–681.

Wheeler, N. (2002) *Saving Strangers: Humanitarian Intervention in International Society*, Oxford: Oxford University Press.

Wintour, P. (2000) 'Ex-Minister Attacks Kosovo War Tactics', *Guardian*, 21 July: 1.

Appendix

Interview with Dr Fatmir Sejdiu, President of the Republic of Kosovo

Dr Aidan Hehir interviewed President Sejdiu, at the office of the President, Pristina, Kosovo, on 17 June 2009.

AIDAN HEHIR (AH): How would you assess the period since Kosovo's declaration of independence on the 18th February 2008?

PRESIDENT SEJDIU (PS): This has been an important period for Kosovo during which it has had to prove that it is ready to be an independent and sovereign state. Kosovo has been able to prove itself first by virtue of the stability that has existed here since the declaration, and secondly through all the major decisions made in the parliament of the Republic of Kosovo by both the government and opposition parties. This has also been proven by the fact that Kosovo has been able to build up the institutions like the Kosovo Security Force, the constitutional court, the Kosovo Security Council and the intelligence agency. We have built up a very good diplomatic network including the opening of eighteen embassies around the globe and we have been recognized by sixty countries. We have promoted a friendly policy with our neighbors. We have made significant steps regarding membership of international organizations, including financial institutions such as recently the IMF and the World Bank. We have continued to cooperate well with the international mechanisms operating here in Kosovo, including EULEX and the ICO. We provide good guarantees for all the communities living in Kosovo, which have been accepted by these communities with the exception of a small number of the Serb community. There are still parallel structures existing in certain areas which continue to cause problems for Kosovo, but we will continue with our approach and we will continue treating them as equal citizens of Kosovo, and we continue to believe in our common, inclusive vision for the future.

AH: Regarding recognition; are you happy with the fact that sixty states have recognized Kosovo, or disappointed that the figure is not higher?

PS: It would be better if the number was greater, however, we are satisfied that sixty countries have recognized Kosovo. This number includes some of the most important countries in the world, and this process continues and will not stop. We are making serious efforts to gain further recognition, as are our friends. In the near future we expect that a greater number of countries will make the decision to recognize Kosovo. The fact that many of the countries who have not recognized Kosovo voted in favor of Kosovo's membership of the IMF and the World Bank is a strong, positive signal in the right direction. We will continue to wait for, and continue to work towards, further recognition.

AH: Can Kosovo exist as an independent state outside of the EU?

PS: Realistically, we are part of Europe. We are continually working on a number of projects with the EU. Everything we've done here, including the building of institutions and the drafting of the legislative corpus, has been in accordance with EU directives. We are not yet in the EU; however, we are working steadily to make the road to membership as short as possible. If I may use a colloquialism, in spirit we are already in Europe, now we just have to do the leg work to get there. Also, it is the responsibility of the EU to ensure that no part of Europe remains isolated from its policies. It is not in the interest of the EU to have a particular country left out of the EU. So we will continue to work in that direction, and we believe and hope that other countries in our region will do the same to work towards common membership, as it's in the interests of the entire region.

AH: Many people find it strange, however, that all EU member states were independent prior to EU membership and voluntarily chose to join the EU, whereas it appears Kosovo can only be fully independent *after* it has joined the EU and cannot choose not to join.

PS: Kosovo now has some degree of international supervision, and the supervision is primarily European but it has an American component. I must state, however, that every country that has recognized Kosovo has recognized it as an independent and sovereign country. So that means that Kosovo is independent, and we cannot think any differently. So the international presence that is here is in a supportive role as opposed to imposing some kind of limitation on independence. Our path to independence has been unique or *sui generis*, as President Ahtisaari has stated, but it is good that this long process has been concluded with the eventual declaration of independence which was a common decision.

AH: Within the EU, and especially amongst the general population, there appears to be a lot of opposition to enlargement, and the process has therefore lost momentum. Additionally, given that there are a number of states ahead of Kosovo in the queue to join the EU, do you fear that this means that Kosovo will not be able to join the EU for a very long time?

PS: Membership depends on both sides – on the EU's readiness to accept new members, but also our work towards meeting the EU's criteria. I cannot imagine a scenario where Albania, Serbia and Macedonia join the EU and Kosovo is left out. Kosovo is in the heart of this region, and it is the wish of the people here that Kosovo join the EU. And it must be taken into account that these people have suffered immensely in recent times. We have continuously stated that we are willing to leave our suffering as a chapter of history and move forward. So Kosovo has had opportunities in recent times to become a sustainable state, of course in cooperation with other regional countries, with good values.

AH: What would you say to those people within the EU who see countries in the Balkans, and especially Kosovo, as constituting a source of great problems and likely only to drain money from the EU? What positive contribution can Kosovo make to the EU?

PS: This is a process that has occurred with respect to all the other candidates, so Kosovo must go through it as well. It is the process that was followed by other countries in the region, including Romania and Bulgaria. The important thing to note is that Kosovo is not lagging that far behind the standards that the EU asks members to fulfill. You have to understand that Kosovo is a country that was totally destroyed by war, and yet it has managed to move forward very quickly in a short period of time. We continually get praised for the huge steps forward we are taking in developing. Kosovo is not a foreign object in Europe; it's in Europe geographically, it's part of European history, it shares European values and it will be a part of the European future. This is our desire and our wish, though this is not only a desire to capitalize on the benefits available from the EU but at the same time to be integrated into all the decision-making processes and to contribute to these processes. We want to be a serious partner.

AH: Do you believe there is any possibility of finding an accommodation with Serbia on the issue of Kosovo?

PS: We have always expressed our desire and readiness to work together as two sovereign countries. I mentioned before that we can never forget the tragedies that were committed against to our people here, and the main cause of those tragedies has been Serbia. Serbia has also been the cause of wars in other countries, such as Croatia and Bosnia. Our vision is to have good cooperation with all our neighbors, including Serbia. Irrespective of the fact that Serbia refuses to apologize for the crimes it committed in Kosovo, we nevertheless continue to push forward and look towards the future. So this is a paradox. We are very aware that the region needs countries to cooperate, and we are aware of the need for the youth of Kosovo to travel freely. Why not have the youth of Pristina work and use their talents in Berlin or Vienna, or Paris or London and vice versa? We are eager to ensure that the citizens of Kosovo and Serbia communicate and travel freely, to have good economic and cultural cooperation and, of course, those who have committed crimes have to be brought to justice. Serbia owes a debt to international law, to the international community and everyone else to hand over war criminals. I've stated many times that every Serbian government has known the exact whereabouts of every single war criminal. So it is the duty of [the Serbian] President [Boris] Tadić and his government to show the true value of cooperation and to demonstrate Western values. We are always ready to cooperate with them, but only as two independent states. Serbia cannot behave like a dictator or hegemon towards any other state, including Kosovo.

AH: How can you appeal to the Serbs living in Kosovo, particularly those living north of the River Ibar, who reject your government?

PS: We continue telling them they are citizens of Kosovo. They have full guarantees under the constitution of the country, we continually call on them to join us and become part of the institutions and society in Kosovo and to take full advantage of the preferential treatment that we give them through the constitution and the laws. One portion of the Serb community has already integrated in the central and local government and the society in general, but I also call on the rest of the Serb community that is lagging behind on integration to take their position and join us. The Albanian community in Kosovo, which is in the majority here, never toys with the idea of revenge, but rather has taken the higher ground and offered its willingness to cooperate and coexist in this society. Serbs have guarantees that they can return to their homes; nobody will touch them. Local community leaders often go and visit those who have returned. Albanians too should return to their homes in the northern part of Kosovo. Kosovo is everybody's; it's a country of all its citizens, including Albanians, Serbs, Turks, Bosniaks, the Roma. The Serbs have guarantees that make them equal if not better off than the Albanians. The Serbian population makes up about 5–6 percent of the population, and the Serbian language has been recognized as one of the two official languages in Kosovo, which makes it equal to Albanian which is spoken by over 90 percent of the population. There are many other guarantees provided to the Serb community by the constitution and Kosovo laws.

AH: Accepting that, since 1999, there have been a number of incidents where Serbs have been attacked by Kosovo Albanians and there hasn't seemed to have been a particularly good level of protection afforded to Serbian religious sites, and thus many Serbs fear that, for all the guarantees, actual security is lacking.

PS: First of all, your assertion that there has been attacks on Serbs is not true. There are many issues that were not fully explained. As a lawyer, I never jump to a conclusion without first of all having all the facts. I apologize for saying this, but this is part of the Serbian propaganda that they continuously promote abroad. There has been evidence that in fact there were Serb families attacking Albanian families to provoke a reaction from them so that they can then claim to have been attacked by the Albanians. Serbs have killed a Ukrainian policeman and an African policeman both working for UNMIK. We have to be really careful about the kinds of assertions we make in respect of these issues. So, especially in the last three to four years there is no evidence of inter-ethnic conflict, with the exception of those incidents which are general in nature and that can occur anywhere in the world.

AH: How do you reconcile that view with the riots which took place in March 2004?

PS: The events of March 2004 are a dark part of Kosovo's history. We need to fully investigate all the actors involved in those events. But it's important to say that the Kosovo institutions have been fully committed and have invested significantly in resorting anything that was destroyed to its prior state. As far as religious sites go – they are fully guaranteed, nobody touches them. In fact, Albanians consider those sites their own, as well as the assets of Kosovo. So any of the Serbs that wish to do so can freely come to Kosovo, to the Grand Hotel or any of the cafés in Pristina or any other city in Kosovo, and they will be welcomed. The problem is a few members of the Serb community want to make a spectacle of it and they come to some areas of Kosovo to show that apparently there is some kind of insecurity. It's a bad message that they send. I go out and I visit all parts of Kosovo, and literally I cannot see any person from any other community that touches the Serbs anywhere I go. The Serb community has to realize that Kosovo is independent and Kosovo laws have to be respected. How can you excuse the fact that there is some €100 million that the Serbs owe in electricity bills? Is it excusable for a person to use electricity to entertain guests, to cook, to maintain a household, and yet not pay for that electricity? This has nothing to do with politics; it is just a practical issue. All the people living in Kosovo have to pay for their electricity. There are many Serbs that have taken advantage of the rights that have been given to them and the security they enjoy in Kosovo, and have become part of the Kosovo institutions and Kosovo society. However, they suffer a lot of pressure from the Serb government; over 200 policemen have withdrawn from the Kosovo police. There were about 800 altogether. Those 200 who withdrew have been receiving salaries for two years, yet they stay at home. Their colleagues work rain or shine, and are always in the line of duty, yet these people who have withdrawn receive the same salary for just staying at home. This is not OK. We have tolerated this for two years; however, at the end of June the period of grace is over, and if they do not return to their positions their salaries will be stopped. Of the original 200 about forty have returned, which is a good sign. If the others do not return, there are many interested candidates willing to take their positions. So this is an issue of perception; what kind of perception do you have of the environment here? There are people who know in their conscience that they have debts to Kosovo society. Let us not forget that there were occasions here in Kosovo where our Serbian neighbor killed his neighbor, raped his neighbor's daughter and committed other atrocities against his neighbors. So we have to be careful.

AH: Do you accept that Russia's policies towards Georgia have been shaped by the West's support for Kosovo?

PS: I cannot really do those kinds of comparisons and comment on what leads Russia's policies. I know that Georgia is an independent country and is considered so by the EU and the United States and many other countries. There are absolutely no similarities between South Ossetia, Abkhazia and Kosovo. As I stated earlier, Kosovo is a *sui generis* case, and as such cannot be a precedent. As far as the processes that led to Kosovo's independence, Russia has always been a part of the process, including the Troika and the negotiations team and the Contact Group, so when the decision was made in the

Contact Group to respect the wishes of the majority Russia was present. Russia has always stated that it is interested in stability; the resolution of the final status of Kosovo as independent is actually the best possible solution for stability in the region. We know that Russia's exchanges with the West are not related to Kosovo, and the West knows this as well.

AH: Do you feel that UNMIK assumed too much power during its tenure?

PS: UNMIK of course had a lot of responsibilities. It was an international mechanism put in place in Kosovo with the consensus of the international community. There were a lot of good developments and progress made in Kosovo; we never thought it would last this long but, irrespective of this, UNMIK is a success story. We are fully supportive of UNMIK's quick reconfiguration. We are not in favor of returning responsibilities to UNMIK. It's important to say that the Kosovo institutions have proven themselves to be able to govern Kosovo, of course with the support of EULEX.

AH: Do you feel that the powers currently vested in the International Civilian Representative undermine Kosovo's independence?

PS: The mandate of the ICR is very clear and it's part of the Joint Action Plan, was part of the Ahtisaari package and now it's part of the constitution. We will continue to cooperate within those parameters. The ICR cannot have additional powers. The civil presence here in Kosovo is simply to oversee the implementation of the project. I cannot really talk about whether someone has a vision of returning competencies to UNMIK. In their role as a supporter and in their monitoring role they are fully supported.

AH: What do you consider to be the key challenges facing Kosovo?

PS: First the economy; we have a lot of natural resources here in Kosovo and we just have to figure out how to use them most effectively. We are almost done with the privatization process, and we have to continue working on the projects on the big industries here. There are three main issues here; energy, agriculture and mining. Of course, some of the top priorities for the government here are the rule of law, education and health. Going back to the economy; our economy shows about a 5 percent growth of GDP. So if we have a strong economy moving forward, it will make it easier for us to move the other aspects forward. We are not currently in an ideal situation, but we believe in our perspective and in a good future ahead. We see challenges for what they are; we don't try to make them look prettier, and then make problems later on.

AH: Looking into the future, how long do you imagine the international oversight is going to last?

PS: Of course, our wish is to have it as short as possible! I cannot give you an exact prognosis; however, I think within two years we need to re-examine the arrangements. It is important that the initial results have shown improvement, and we will see how we can cooperate in the future. We never look at it as our need to isolate ourselves and keep the international community out. So all the international policies of the EU are international policies based on cooperation.

Index

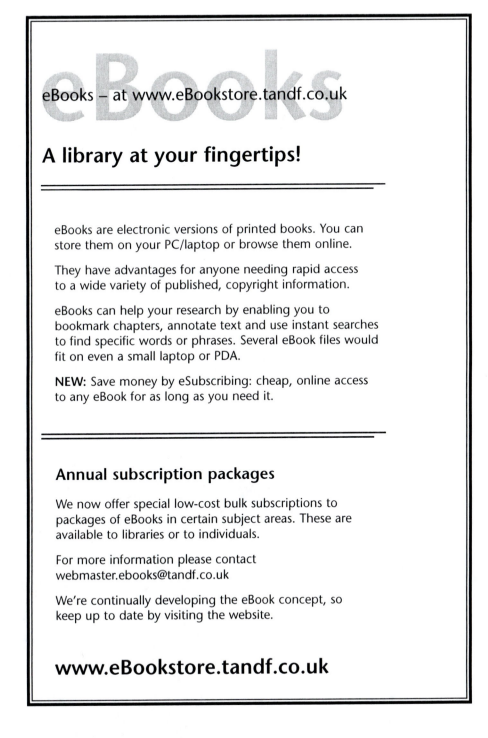